SPANISH SYNTAX LIST

Publications of
the Committee on Modern Languages
American Council on Education

Analytical Bibliography of Modern Language Teaching, 1927–1932
Compiled by ALGERNON COLEMAN
with assistance of Agnes Jacques
University of Chicago Press

Experiments and Studies in Modern Language Teaching
Compiled by ALGERNON COLEMAN
University of Chicago Press

*Spanish Syntax List, A Statistical Study of Usage in
Contemporary Prose*
By HAYWARD KENISTON

SPANISH SYNTAX LIST

A STATISTICAL STUDY OF GRAMMATICAL USAGE
IN CONTEMPORARY SPANISH PROSE ON THE
BASIS OF RANGE AND FREQUENCY

BY

HAYWARD KENISTON

PROFESSOR OF THE SPANISH LANGUAGE
IN THE UNIVERSITY OF CHICAGO

NEW YORK
HENRY HOLT AND COMPANY

X764059172

FOREWORD

The present work is the fulfillment of a project which has been under way for a number of years. During the progress of the investigation of modern language teaching carried on by the American and Canadian Committees on Modern Languages, 1924–28, plans were made for a series of quantitative studies of the materials of instruction. As a result, investigations of word and idiom frequency were organized and carried through, resulting in the publication of word and idiom lists in French, German and Spanish. These have found wide acceptance and use by teachers and text-book makers. The investigation of the syntactical phenomena on a similar basis of frequency of use was taken into consideration at the same time and a beginning was made. However, as Professor Keniston points out below, the difficulties inherent in syntax study were too great to be overcome within the period of the Committee's activity.

The Committee on Modern Language Teaching, which was organized in 1929 to carry on work of research and experimentation initiated during the previous investigation, gave support to Professor Keniston's study of Spanish syntax frequency so far as it related to contemporary Spanish. The successor of that committee, the present Committee on Modern Languages, also working under the sponsorship of the American Council on Education, was organized in 1935 with a somewhat expanded program. As one of its early tasks it undertook the publication of Professor Keniston's results. It is likewise furthering similar studies in French and German syntax, which it hopes may follow the present work without too long delay.

Professor Keniston's study is the first work of its kind that has appeared. Its general purpose is to determine the relative frequency of use of the syntactical phenomena of the Spanish language of the present day; in other words, to furnish criteria for measuring the relative usefulness of these phenomena to the learner. As is pointed out by the author, the validity of such a study has its limits. Obviously the sources which could be investigated are limited and the establishment of a frequency series for syntactical uses can therefore make no claim to absolute accuracy. The reliability of any numerical placement of individual usage diminishes rapidly as these forms become less frequent in the field of investigation. On the other hand, the validity of the principle that the usefulness of any syntactical form depends on the frequency of use by those who employ Spanish can hardly be attacked successfully any more than in the case of words and idioms. The high importance of the more frequent elements in the syntax list cannot be denied.

The importance of these results as a measuring tool for those who make up Spanish books of instruction and reading texts is unquestionable. It need scarcely be pointed out to those teachers who are familiar with Buchanan's *Graded Spanish Word Book* and Keniston's *Spanish Idiom List* that the present work brings material that must be studied and adapted by the teacher before it is usable for the learner. In the hands of the teacher it is a reliable instrument for the establishment of the relative usefulness of a Spanish syntactical expression for purposes of instruction as well as for the measurement of the rationality and difficulty of texts and grammars.

Acknowledgment is hereby made to the Carnegie Foundation for the Advancement of Teaching and the Carnegie Corporation of New York for support of the Committee and its program.

COMMITTEE ON MODERN LANGUAGES

515 West 116 Street,
New York City

ACKNOWLEDGMENTS

The chief financial support for the Spanish syntax count has come from the Modern Foreign Language Study and its successor, the Committee on Modern Language Teaching. The former defrayed the costs of mimeographing the first two versions of the Check-List; the latter has provided most of the funds to engage expert assistance in the actual checking. I should also acknowledge with gratitude the support of the American Council of Learned Societies, which provided the funds for mimeographing the third version of the Check-List, and of the Research Committee of the Division of the Humanities of the University of Chicago, whose grants to the larger project in Spanish syntax made possible the compilation and printing of the fourth version of the Check-List and also paid for a considerable part of the actual checking.

I have been fortunate in the perseverance and enthusiasm of my co-workers on the project: Robert Ashburn of the University of West Virginia, H. B. Winchell of the U. S. Naval Academy, Frederick Steinhauser, and the late Hal W. Arden. I should also include in the group Gordon W. Harrison, whose work on the medieval period of the study has so often cast light on the present, and Lawrence Poston, II, who has given signal aid in the preparation of the materials for this manuscript. Finally, and above all, I would express my appreciation to the Chairman of the Modern Foreign Language Study and its successors, Robert H. Fife, not merely for his financial support of the project, but even more for his faith in the method under which it was undertaken and carried to a conclusion.

H. K.

TABLE OF CONTENTS

SPANISH SYNTAX LIST

INTRODUCTION

The publication of the present volume marks the completion of a study which began ten years ago. At the meeting of the Committee of the Modern Foreign Language Study, held in Chicago in January, 1926, the Chairman of the Committee appointed a special committee, consisting of J. P. W. Crawford, E. C. Hills, and Hayward Keniston (chairman), to undertake a Spanish syntax frequency count. This count was to be the third of the basic frequency studies in vocabulary, idiom, and syntax.

In the following months, the chairman of that committee, who had also been encharged with the task of organizing the Spanish idiom count, undertook to draw up check-lists in the two fields. It soon became apparent that the organization of the idiom count would be relatively easy, for here it was possible to compile an alphabetized check-list, based upon simple, even if arbitrary rules of entry. This count was therefore carried on diligently, largely by volunteer workers drawn from the ranks of Spanish teachers, and was completed, with some help from trained assistants, late in 1927.[1]

The task of organizing the syntax count proved more difficult, for it was necessary to devise a check-list based upon some kind of logical classification. The study began with an examination of a number of contemporary prose texts. The first problem which arose was that of limitation of the field; definite decisions had to be made concerning the boundaries which separate syntax from morphology, lexicography, idiom, stylistics, and the other branches of linguistic study. In general, therefore, syntax was defined as concerned with the functional patterns established by usage for the expression of a thought or an emotion. In practice, however, it was still necessary to make many arbitrary decisions concerning the inclusion or exclusion of given phenomena. Thus, form and function are so interrelated in the use of personal and other pronouns that pronominal forms were included as forms. In the discussion of prepositions, meaning and function are almost synonymous, but an attempt to include all of the meanings of each preposition could result only in a lexicographical study, like that of Cuervo, and prepositional

---

[1] *Spanish Idiom List, Selected on the Basis of Range and Frequency of Occurrence.* Compiled and edited by Hayward Keniston. New York, 1929. (Publications of the American and Canadian Committees on Modern Language, Vol. XI.)

meanings were therefore excluded. The order of words in the sentence, including the position of adjectives and adverbs, might properly be considered a part of syntax, but the attempt to gather material made it clear that for Spanish, at least, statistical materials would have little value, except in the case of the position of personal object pronouns, and this aspect of the language was therefore consigned to stylistics.[1]

The second problem which required a solution was that of the type of classification. There are two natural approaches to the study of expression: the formal and the functional. The latter approach has certain advantages over the former as an instrument of analysis. But the present study was intended for teachers and had to be carried out by workers who were familiar with the conventional formal approach. It therefore seemed advisable to attempt a compromise: the basic classifications adopted should be formal, that is to say, the various phenomena should be classified under the traditional " parts of speech " — nouns, verbs, etc., — but the ultimate subclassifications should be functional. Thus, in the classification of the verb, all uses of the preterite indicative are brought together in a formal classification of tense, but the detailed analysis of the uses of the preterite is on a functional basis.

With these general principles established, a tentative Check-List was drawn up early in 1927, based in part upon materials drawn from the study of contemporary texts and in part on the currently familiar Spanish grammars, such as Bello-Cuervo and Ramsey. This Check-List was tried out on additional texts; many lacunæ were discovered and filled; classifications which proved unworkable were revised. In June, 1927 the corrected version was mimeographed in three parts of about equal length, containing: I. Verbs, II. Pronouns, III. Other Phenomena (Adjectives, Adverbs, Articles, Conjunctions, Negatives, Nouns, Numerals, and Prepositions). This Check-List was tried out during the summer of 1927 in a seminar in Spanish at the University of Chicago. While the results were in one respect discouraging, in that they revealed how imperfect were the classifications and how numerous the omissions, they were also heartening, because they seemed to prove that other workers besides the compiler could learn to use the List and that it might therefore serve as an instrument for investigation.

By this time it had become clear that the difficulties involved were so great as to make impossible the completion of even a cursory study of Spanish usage during the life of the Modern Foreign Language Study, and the original project was therefore abandoned. But the possibilities in the use of the technique in a wider field of linguistic investigation tempted the writer into continuing the study. For if it could only be developed, to establish what usage was in each succeeding century of

---

[1] Studies are now being carried on at the University of Chicago in the effort to develop a technique for investigating problems in word order.

Spanish speech, it would make available the materials on which a history
of Spanish syntax could be based. And so began the second phase of
the project.

In the autumn of 1927, a seminar on the syntax of *Lazarillo de Tormes*
added materials on the sixteenth century; another on the *Setenario* of
Alfonso el Sabio tapped some of the problems of medieval Spanish. In
1928 a revised version of the Check-List was mimeographed, and during
1929 the author made a study of a unit of 10,000 running words from
each of ten prose texts of the sixteenth century. The results of this
more extended use of the Check-List were altogether disappointing. It
was clear that the List, in its existing form, was not an adequate device
for analyzing the more complicated phases of usage. The next six
months were therefore spent in a detailed study of the whole bibliography
of Spanish syntax and the establishment of classifications with far more
minute subdivisions.

On the basis of this work, a third version of the Check-List was compiled and mimeographed in 1930. The next three years were devoted to
a detailed study of the syntax of Castilian prose in the sixteenth century.
The manuscript of that study, completed in 1933, is now in press.
Work on the other volumes is already well advanced. When completed,
it will comprise a complete chronological survey of Castilian syntax from
the Middle Ages to the present day.

In the meantime, the Committee on Modern Language Teaching had been
formed to carry on the work initiated by the Modern Foreign Language
Study, and in April, 1932 the Committee invited the author to consider
the possibility of taking up again the task of organizing a frequency
count of contemporary Spanish syntax. Since several trained assistants
were available, the task was undertaken at once.

The general plan of the project was similar to that which had already
been followed in the study of the sixteenth century. Since the method
is new, it will be well to describe it in some detail. It is, in principle,
a sampling technique, which aims by a wide choice of samples to set up
statistics concerning the range and frequency of usage for each construction, which, for the higher ranges and frequencies, would be valid with
any other sampling.

Units. The sample unit studied from each text was one of 10,000
running words, equivalent to about 35 pages of 300 words each, chosen
from three different sections of the text, at the beginning, the middle,
and the end. There is no objective test for determining the best size of
a sample unit, but the experience of the Spanish idiom count and the
French word count had made it clear that a unit of 10,000 words was
sufficiently large to furnish an adequate sample, provided the number
of units was sufficiently large. In general it seems apparent that in
covering a given amount of material, it is preferable to use a large num-

ber of small units, rather than a small number of large units, in order that the significance of individual vagaries may be minimized.

Entry in the Check-Lists. For each unit studied, a separate copy of the Check-List was used, and in that copy each appearance of each construction was entered with a page and line reference. When three such references had been entered for a single construction, subsequent occurrences of the construction in that unit were entered with a mark, to provide information concerning the total frequency. In practice it was found expedient to check each unit three times, once for verbs, once for pronouns, and once for other phenomena, corresponding with the three parts into which the Check-List is divided. Whenever a construction was found for which no provision had been made in the List, a new category was inserted in the proper place by the checker, and further, all examples which offered some special interest were quoted in full. On the completion of the checking of each unit, the total frequency of each construction was entered in the margin of the List.

Elimination of items. The preliminary checking had made it clear that there are a number of constructions, such as the simple agreement of adjectives with nouns, the use of *no* to negate a finite verb, or the use of the indicative in main clauses to express a fact, which are of such high frequency as to make it unprofitable to attempt to establish their approximate frequency. Some of these were counted for a single unit, as for example the use of the present indicative as a regular tense, which occurred 531 times in one unit; others were estimated by sampling 100 running words out of each thousand. There are approximately seventy such constructions. All constructions thus eliminated from the actual count are indicated in the Check-List and in the present study by an *. Furthermore, at the completion of the count of the first ten units, a master list was drawn up and at that time all constructions which occurred in each of the ten units and whose total frequency was fifty or more, were eliminated from further counting. Similarly at the completion of the count of the second ten units, another master list was compiled and combined with the first master list, and at this point, all constructions which occurred in fifteen or more of the first twenty units were eliminated. Finally at the conclusion of the third group of ten units, there was an elimination of all constructions which had occurred in twenty or more of the first thirty units. All remaining constructions were counted in the last thirty of the sixty units studied.

Equation of the range and frequency of eliminated items. These eliminations made it possible to progress with far greater rapidity in the remainder of the work. In fact, if they had not been made, it is doubtful whether the task could have been finished within a decade. From a practical standpoint, therefore, the method followed was justified. But it involved a number of difficulties. In the first place, it was necessary to use some device to equate the range and frequency of the eliminated constructions with those of the constructions which had been counted in all sixty units. The simplest method seemed to be to assume that the eliminated constructions would have continued to appear with approximately the same range and frequency, if they had been counted throughout. The range and frequency of constructions which were eliminated after the count of the first ten units were therefore multiplied by six, so that (10–80) became (60–480). Thus the use of an adjective with the definite article as a substantive occurred in each of the first ten units counted, with a total frequency of 176 examples in these ten units; to equate its total range and frequency, these figures are multiplied by six, so that it is recorded with a range and frequency of (60–1056); see 25.431. In the same way, the range and frequency of constructions eliminated after the count of twenty units were multiplied by three, and of constructions eliminated after the count of thirty units, were multiplied by two. A second difficulty, of a quite different sort, was the fact that the elimination of a given construction tended to eliminate related constructions, just as the elimination of *antes* from the Spanish word count seems to have carried with it *ante*. Thus the elimination of the normal use of the pluperfect indicative tended to make workers overlook its use in backshifted clauses in indirect discourse.

Accuracy of the checking. It will be well to discuss at this point the fundamental question of the accuracy of the checking. It goes without saying that the work is far from perfect. No worker can be sure of catching every example, even when he is hunting for a single phenomenon. The present work, which was done by five different workers and which involved thousands of constructions, is inevitably full of omissions and of incorrect identifications. The inaccuracy varies in different sections of the study. Where the phenomena are concrete and objective, the accuracy is high. This is particularly true where it is a question of checking individual Spanish words: verbs, adverbs, prepositions, etc. But where the constructions are subjective, there is inevitably a certain variation in the assignment of examples to a given section. On successive days the same worker will assign the same construction to different categories. Some of the topics which have offered the greatest difficulty in this respect are the uses of the modal auxiliaries, the functions of the preterite of verbs of state, the use and omission of the definite article, the use and omission of personal *a*. The author has been conscious of this weakness from the beginning and has attempted to control it, as far as possible, by constant conferences of the whole staff, by the establishment of standard practices of entry, and finally, as a last resort, by rechecking the fifty units which were checked by his assistants. But there still remains the inevitable margin of error.

Relative value of the statistics. It is important to remember that, as in any statistical study, the figures given for range and frequency have no absolute value. At best they can only be relative. Even if the range of error be as high as 10%, and in most cases it is probably less than 5%, a construction with a high range and frequency will still be more important than one with a low range and frequency. For the rechecking makes it clear that workers are fairly catholic in their omissions, though occasionally they may develop a blind spot. One worker overlooks *cerca de* in one unit, but it is *delante de* which escapes his notice in the next unit. So it is that over a wide variety of texts and workers, the omissions are leveled out and the final figures still retain their relative value.

Number of units studied. As with the size of the sample unit, so with the number of samples, the decision made was perforce arbitrary. But the study of the six master lists which had been compiled at the end of the count of sixty units made it clear that for practical purposes the count had covered sufficient ground to establish the validity of the higher ranges and frequencies. The relatively slight validity of words beyond the first fifteen hundred or two thousand words in the French and Spanish word counts, which covered a million or more running words, makes it obvious that a count of millions of words is necessary, if we hope to secure valid results outside of the relatively few frequent phenomena. It is almost certain that a count of another sixty units would not change greatly the relative range and frequency of constructions which occur in a third or more of the units counted.

Choice of texts. The texts studied are all in prose of the period between 1900 and 1933. The aim was to test as varied a cross-section as possible of contemporary prose usage. To that end a number of requirements were kept in mind:

(1) The texts are distributed chronologically: 1900–1909, 20 texts; 1910–1919, 21 texts; 1920–1933, 19 texts.

(2) The texts are distributed geographically: from Spain, 40 texts; from Spanish America, 20 texts. Within Spain, the authors are distributed by region as follows: Andalusia, 6; Aragon, 1; Asturias, 4; Canary Islands, 1; Castile, 12; Catalonia, 2; Galicia, 5; Extremadura, 1; Murcia, 1, Valencia, 5, Vizcaya, 2. In Spanish America, the distribution by authors is as follows: Argentina, 4; Colombia, 1; Cuba, 2, Chile, 2; Ecuador, 1; Mexico, 2; Nicaragua, 1; Peru, 1; Puerto Rico, 1, República Dominicana, 1; Uruguay, 2; Venezuela, 2.

(3) The texts are distributed by literary types, as follows: Fiction (novel and short story), 21; Drama (comedy, drama, sainete, and dialogued novel), 20; Critical essays, 7; Journals and reviews, 4; Humorous essays, 3; Autobiography (fictional), 3; History, 2. Including the dialogue which occurs in non-dramatic types, over half of the materials studied represents a literary version of conversational style.

(4) The texts are distributed by styles of composition. Eight are in a learned or formal style (Altamira, Balseiro, Darío, Henríquez Ureña, Menéndez Pidal, Menéndez y Pelayo, Ortega y Gasset, Rodó). Seven are wholly or in part in colloquial style (Arniches, Álvarez Quintero, Campa, Campos, López Pinillos, Muñoz Seca, Florencio Sánchez). Five are in a more or less mannered style, (Azorín [*Las confesiones*], Gómez de la Serna, Jiménez, Nervo, Valle-Inclán). The remaining forty texts are written in everyday Spanish prose.

This brief outline will give some idea of the extent to which the material studied may stand as representative of the whole range of Spanish usage to-day. It should perhaps be remarked that no example of so-called scientific prose was included because most scientific works use such a narrow range of constructions as to make them unprofitable material for study.

The present *List*. The *List* as here printed is a descriptive presentation of the commonest syntactic phenomena in contemporary Spanish prose. It does not aim to offer a historical picture nor to interpret usage as a reflection of psychological or social motivations. Its purpose is the identification and description of the function which each construction performs. It contains only those constructions which were recorded in three or more of the sixty units studied. A single example of each construction is cited, with a page reference to the text from which it is drawn. The illustrative examples have been abbreviated, where necessary, and even at times unessential words have been changed, to bring the citation into reasonable length, but in no case has the construction which is exemplified in a given illustration been altered. Constructions which are followed by (*) were those of such assured high frequency that they were not counted (see p. 4). The figures given in parenthesis after each construction indicate the range and frequency: thus (7–12) indicates that the construction was found in seven units with a total frequency of twelve cases.

Normal ranges and frequencies. In a number of constructions the usage was recorded only as it appeared with specific words. Thus the figures for the use of the infinitive as subject of *ser* with a predicate adjective (*es fácil hacerlo*, etc.; see 37.241) were recorded only under the individual adjectives. While it is possible in this case to give the exact total frequency of the construction, the range cannot be determined from the materials as gathered. To meet this situation a study of the relation of range and frequency was necessary. From the materials gathered it was possible to draw up a table of the median frequency corresponding to each range. This relationship was plotted as a graph and then reduced to a standard curve of hyperbolic type. The results of this study gave the following results.

Range	Actual Median Frequency	Normalized Frequency	Range	Actual Median Frequency	Normalized Frequency
60	684	590	31	65	67
59	—	520	30	59	63
58	468	463	29	58	59
57	498	415	28	60	56
56	304	372	27	60	53
55	—	337	26	50	50
54	345	307	25	43	47
53	333	282	24	45	44
52	190	260	23	41	41
51	203	240	22	40	38
50	218	222	21	37	35
49	—	206	20	34	33
48	198	192	19	33	31
47	—	179	18	30	29
46	134	167	17	26	27
45	127	156	16	23	25
44	133	146	15	22	23
43	139	137	14	20	21
42	122	129	13	17	19
41	118	122	12	16	17
40	108	115	11	15	15
39	—	108	10	14	13
38	95	101	9	13	12
37	90	95	8	10	11
36	84	89	7	9	9
35	83	84	6	8	7
34	70	79	5	7	6
33	80	75	4	4	5
32	77	71	3	4	4

On the basis of this table of normalized frequencies corresponding to each range it is possible to indicate the approximate range of a given known frequency. This range is indicated by the use of square brackets: thus ([28]–56) means that the actual frequency of the construction is 56, and that the approximate range which corresponds to that frequency is 28; see 28.211.

Spanish words used in a given construction. To make the study more specific and more useful for teachers and textbook-makers, the actual words which occur in many constructions were listed separately. Thus the *List* gives concrete data on the frequency of individual indefinite adjectives and pronouns, adverbs, negative expressions, prepositions, conjunctions, etc. It lists, for example, the specific verbs most frequently followed by the infinitive, the verbs which are used with an indirect object expressing separation, the phrases formed with an indefinite feminine adjective, etc. The teacher may profitably use these lists as a guide in choosing materials to illustrate and practice a given construction. Thus, in teaching the use of the subjunctive in object clauses of desire, he will prefer to stress the use of *querer, decir, dejar,* and *hacer* and will leave *aconsejar, consentir, mandar, suplicar,* and the like in the background (see 29.341). To print the complete list of these individual words would make too great a demand on space, and the lists are therefore usually limited to those words (or phrases) which occur in five or more units. In a few cases, only words which occur in ten or more units are listed.

Number of constructions and Spanish forms. The total number of constructions included in the present volume is slightly less than 2200. Of these, about 70 proved, in the preliminary survey, to be of such assured high frequency that they were eliminated from the count; these items are indicated by an asterisk: (*). In addition, there are recorded the figures for the range and frequency of use of over 1600 individual Spanish forms, words, and phrases.

How to find a given construction. It would have been most desirable to provide a complete index of constructions and Spanish forms. But the cost of compiling such an index was prohibitive. To compensate in some measure for this lack, the " Table of Contents " has been made relatively detailed. In seeking for a given construction, the reader should first familiarize himself with the opening chapter on " The Sentence ", in order to understand the basic classification. He will then be able to determine the main heading under which the construction is entered and from the " Table of Contents " he will be able to find the section in which the construction is discussed. If, for example, he wishes to find what the *List* has to offer on the use of *lo* as an adverb, he must first identify *lo* as a form of the definite article (18.). Turning to the " Table of Contents " he will find the uses of *lo* under 18.9. Finally turning to the text, he will find the detailed discussion under 18.97. Or, if he wishes to know whether *es necesario* or *es preciso* is more frequently used with an infinitive complement, he will find the Infinitive studied under verbs (37.) The " Table of Contents " shows that the complementary infinitive, without a preposition, used as subject is treated in 37.21. Under 37.241 he will find that the range and frequency of *es necesario* is (8–10) and of *es preciso* is (18–23). Cross-references have been used in abundance. Thus, a reader seeking the section on the use of reflexives under personal object pronouns (7.49), will there find a cross-reference to the detailed discussion under Verbs, under Types of Verb, 27.3.

Comparison with the *Spanish Idiom List*. In a number of cases, the same words which had been counted in the Spanish idiom count were also counted in the syntax count. It should be remembered that the idiom count covered approximately 1,000,000 running words, as compared with the 600,000 words covered by the syntax count. But the materials offered by the two studies have a value because they are based on different texts and because they show such close relationship in the determination of the higher frequencies. There follow the lists of the commonest reflexive verbs and the commonest compound prepositions, as presented by the two counts.

The commonest reflexive verbs:

Idiom Count	Frequency	Syntax Count	Frequency
irse	351	irse	312
acercarse	229	ponerse	212
levantarse	203	quedarse	196
sentarse	201	casarse	185
ponerse	198	marcharse	127
casarse	189	acercarse	126
quedarse	168	sentarse	125
hallarse	163	figurarse	114
dirigirse	154	morirse	113
volverse	149	hacerse	112
llamarse	144	atreverse	104
acordarse	134	levantarse	104
marcharse	129	llamarse	98
tratarse	117	acordarse	94
atreverse	111	volverse	94
reírse	110	encontrarse	92
detenerse	87	reírse	87
encontrarse	72	sentirse	83
hacerse	72	hallarse	80
fijarse	71	fijarse	76
morirse	70	tratarse	76
figurarse	65	detenerse	75
llevarse	65	llevarse	72
sentirse	65	dirigirse	67

It will be noted that although the actual order is not identical, the lists as presented show a high correlation and that their content is identical for these 24 commonest verbs.

The commonest compound prepositions:

Idiom Count	Frequency	Syntax Count	Frequency
después de	456	después de	280
antes de	226	dentro de	148
a pesar de	175	antes de	130
dentro de	158	junto a	113

Idiom Count	Frequency	Syntax Count	Frequency
cerca de	117	fuera de	100
en cuanto a	102	a pesar de	90
junto a	102	cerca de	67
en medio de	95	delante de	66
en vez de	94	frente a	59
detrás de	91	al lado de	53
delante de	89	en medio de	51
por medio de	85	detrás de	44
además de	79	lejos de	43
fuera de	78	en vez de	37
frente a	76	en casa de	36
al lado de	73	gracias a	36
a través de [1]	66	a través de	34
lejos de	56	en cuanto a	31
a fin de	45	a fin de	25
acerca de	44	además de	23

Again there is the same general relationship, even though the actual order and actual content is different. In other words, the two counts present valid evidence, not that a given word in either of these lists is more or less common than another word in the list, but that any word which appears in these lists is actually one of the commonest words of its type in Spanish.

Significance of the figures given for range and frequency. The figures given for the range and frequency of each construction deserve some interpretation, if they are to be useful to the teacher of Spanish. Perhaps the easiest approach will be through some comparison of the present materials with those offered by Buchanan's *Graded Spanish Word Book*, the first of the frequency studies conducted under the auspices of the Modern Foreign Language Study. The word count covered 1,200,000 running words, exactly twice the ground covered by the syntax count. It should therefore follow that any word which was counted in both counts should show one-half the frequency in the syntax count which it showed in the word count. Thus *contra*, which had a frequency of 324 in the word count, should show a frequency of 162 in the syntax count; in actual fact, it has a frequency of 168. This principle would apply in general to all frequencies. And it is therefore possible to determine what range and frequency in the syntax count will correspond with any particular rank in the *Word Book*. For example, the word which is numbered 1,000 in the *Word Book* has a mean frequency of 90, as determined by the average frequency of words 991–1010. The mean frequency corresponding to this in the syntax list is 45, the approximate

[1] In compiling the figures for the *Idiom List*, the frequencies of *a través de* and *al través de* were reversed through error.

range is [24]. In other words, a construction with range and frequency of (24–45) is of approximately the same frequency as the 1,000th word in the *Word Book*.

Let us try to translate these figures into some relationship with an actual text. A word which occurs with a frequency of 90 in the *Word Book* or with a frequency of 45 in the *Syntax List*, will occur on the average once every 46 pages (of 300 words each) in a running text. We may extend this picture to other points in the *Word Book* and the *Syntax List*.

Rank of word in *Word Book*	Frequency in *Word Book*	Frequency in *Syntax List*	Range in *Syntax List*	Occurs once (pp.)	Number of occurrences in 100 pp.
375	226	113	40	17	6.0
650	128	64	30	31	3.2
1,000	90	45	24	46	2.2
1,200	70	35	21	57	1.8
1,300	64	32	20	60	1.7
1,500	55	27	17	73	1.4
2,000	43	21	14	93	1.1
3,000	23	11	8	175	.6
5,000	13	6	5	333	.3

From this table we may see more clearly the meaning of range and frequency in the *Syntax List*. Constructions which occur in 30 or more texts, that is, in one half the units, are comparable in importance to the first 650 words in the *Word Book*. Constructions which occur in 20 or more units are comparable to the first 1,300 words; constructions which occur in a quarter of the units are approximately comparable to the first 2,000 words in the *Word Book*.

It is, of course, impossible to make any concrete statement as to the amount of vocabulary, idiom, and syntax which a person must know in order to be able to understand a language. But certain things are clear. It is idle to attempt to learn linguistic phenomena, if the probability of their occurrence is so slight that one may read hundreds of pages without ever meeting an example of a given phenomenon. If we look at the table above, it appears that words beyond the rank of 2,000 and constructions with a range of less than 14 are not likely to occur more than once in every 100 pages of text. Surely it can profit little to attempt to learn materials beyond that range. And it is questionable if there is sufficient profit in learning constructions or words which occur less frequently than once every 50 pages. Opinions differ greatly in this matter. The writer's personal opinion is that for a normal two-year high school course, the required basic materials should not attempt to include more than a vocabulary of 1,300 to 1,400 words, which would correspond to a range and frequency of (20–33) in the *Syntax List*.[1] With such an equipment the student should be able to understand from 85% to 90% of the average prose text.[2]

Comparison of *Syntax List* with current Spanish grammars. In general, the *Syntax List* may be said to demonstrate that the current Spanish grammars intended for school use do include the most common constructions. That is almost inevitable. It was not necessary to make the present count to prove that the preterite indicative enjoys frequent use in Spanish. But the *List* does show that there are a number of constructions of relatively high frequency (that is to say, with a range of 20 or more) which are not usually included in elementary grammars and which, if the testimony of the count be valid, should certainly find a place there; that there are also a considerable number of constructions which seem to have found a consecrated place in elementary books for whose inclusion there is no justification on the basis of usage; and above all, on almost every page the *List* casts light on the relative frequency of variant forms of the same construction.

Frequent constructions. It is not necessary here to list all of the constructions whose frequency would justify their inclusion in even an elementary grammar. But the following will serve as illustrations: personal *a* with nouns referring to things after verbs which personify the object (2.351); the " independent subject " (2.95); the plural of abstract nouns to express concretes (3.233); a pronominal subject expressed with the imperative (5.13); *la* and *las* as indirect object forms (7.324); *lo* as a subjective complement (7.34); object pronouns placed before an auxiliary verb (10.731); placed after an auxiliary infinitive (10.831); *éste* used alone to indicate " the latter " (11.325); *los suyos*, etc. as a noun (12.7); the definite article used with a subjective complement (18.711); with a noun in apposition (18.731); *un* before *alma*, etc. (20.11); the indefinite article with a subjective complement (20.431); appositive uses of adjectives (25.34); a possessive adjective used to form the superlative (26.691); an adjective agrees with the first of two co-ordinated nouns (26.831); *uno* as an indefinite subject (27.545); the imperative and the present indicative in future conditions (31.213–14); incomplete conditional sentences (31.6); the imperfect indicative in indirect discourse (32.331); the future perfect indicative of inference (33.43); *debía* as a present of obligation (34.3); *debo* (rather than *debo de*) to express inference (34.372); present participles in absolute constructions (38.31); past participles with active force (38.62); adverbs used with an indirect object pronoun as the equivalent of a preposition (39.551).

[1] My *Basic List of Spanish Words and Idioms* (University of Chicago Press, 1933) is built on a vocabulary of 1,421 words.
[2] See A. Coleman, *Experiments and Studies in Modern Language Teaching*, 1934, pp. 231–43.

Infrequent constructions. Among the constructions of low frequency for which traditional textbook-makers show an undue favoritism may be listed the following as examples: personal *a* with proper names of place (2.251); *ello es que* (5.162; cf. *es que* (46–203), 28.273); *éste* and *aquél* as a pair (11.321); possessive pronouns as subjective complement (12.22); neuter possessive pronouns (12.8); *lo* (*fácil*) *que* (14.881); *¡ qué* (*torre*) *más* (*alta*)! (22.325); *de quién* for *cúyo* (22.4); *del que* after a comparative (under 26.42); proportionate comparison (26.73); complex agreement of adjectives (26.845 ff.); devices for reinforcing a reciprocal (27.73); *ojalá* with the subjunctive (29.153); subjunctive after interrogative verbs of believing (29.528); in generalizing relative clauses (29.645); with *cual si*, for *como si* (29.74); *quedaos* for *quedad-os* (30.53); various forms for past contrary-to-fact conditions (31.43); past subjunctive in *–ra* as a pluperfect indicative (32.89); future subjunctive (32.9); preterite perfect (33.31); temporal use of the future perfect indicative (33.42); *debiera* for *debo* (34.3); present participle introduced by *en* (38.27); perfect active participle (38.41).

Relative frequency of variant forms. In cases where usage varies and where grammars are usually content to note that there is variation, the *List* brings positive evidence of actual usage. Illustrations may be found on almost every page of the text. But it will be well to cite a few specific examples. In less vivid future and present contrary-to-fact conditions, it becomes clear that the only types in frequent use are *si tuviese, daría* and *si tuviera, daría* (*si tuviese, diera* does not occur at all). Similarly it appears that the clarification of the antecedent of a possessive adjective of the third person is more often effected by replacing the possessive with the definite article (19.32). As attributive adjective, *qué* is far more common than *cuál*. After *dejar, hacer,* and *mandar* the use of the infinitive predominates over the subjunctive; after *impedir* and *permitir* usage is about equally divided; after *aconsejar* and *consentir* only the subjunctive is found (37.341). To express " as soon as ", the only commonly used conjunction is *en cuanto* (28.49 and 29.82), not *así que* or *luego que.*

Terminology and definitions. I have been conservative in the matter of terminology, preferring always the commonly accepted term, if it could be used consistently. But I have tried to define anew the particular meaning in which the term is used in the present study. In general the definitions are functional, rather than logical. Thus I would say that a word which is used to modify a substantive is called an adjective. As a result of this approach, many words which are normally considered adverbs will be found in the present *List* as coordinating conjunctions, since their function is often to connect, rather than to modify a verb. But I have not succeeded in being rigorously consistent; adjectives which are used as nouns will be found discussed under adjectives.

Description of functions. In the attempt to describe the functions, I have tried to state each usage as accurately and as clearly as possible, indicating the limits by analysis rather than by the use of an English equivalent. But English translations are sometimes added to make the category more readily recognizable. In a number of cases, " type sentences " have been used to express in a kind of short-hand a complicated combination of forms. So, under Conditional Sentences, the different forms are represented by " type sentences ", as: *si tuviera, daría,* which may be translated: " The conditional sentence consists of a condition, expressed by the imperfect subjunctive in *–ra,* and a conclusion, expressed by the conditional."

Paragraph numbers. The paragraphs are numbered in a loose decimal system, in which sub-sections under each section are indicated by the addition of another decimal place. Thus, under **Substantives (2.),** " Independent Uses " are numbered 2.9; under " Independent Uses ", " Uses in Conversation " are numbered 2.91; and under " Uses in Conversation ", " Individual Uses " are numbered 2.911, 2.913, etc. It should be noted that the numbers do not follow each other in unbroken sequence, because a large number of constructions for which place was provided in the study as a whole are not included in the present volume. It should be added that the numbering is not rigorously systematic; the only purpose was to insure flexibility, in order that new constructions might be introduced into the system without disturbing the basic numbering. In arrangement, numbers with two decimal places follow numbers with one decimal place (2.91 after 2.9), and numbers with three decimal places follow numbers with two decimal places (2.911 after 2.91).

The present volume is far from perfection. It is little more than a skeleton, containing less than half of the constructions and forms already gathered, perhaps a quarter of those which will be presented in the extensive study of contemporary syntax which is now in preparation. But even with all of its faults, it contains so much that is assuredly of value for the teacher and student of Spanish that it is offered without apology. For it is the first attempt in the field of language to present a complete statistical statement of actual syntactic usage.

ALPHABETICAL LIST OF AUTHORS AND TITLES

(With indication of the date of the text, author's origin,
and abbreviation used)

A B C. Madrid, 15 July, 1933.　　　　　　　　　　　　　　　　**ABC**
　　1933 — Spain

Alfau de Solalinde, Jesusa — *Los débiles; novela.* New York, 1930. **DEB**
　　1912 — Vigo (Galicia) and República Dominicana

Altamira y Crevea, Rafael — *Historia de España y de la civilización
　　española.* 3a ed. Madrid, 1913. Tomo II.　　　　　　　　**ALT**
　　1912 — Albacete (Murcia)

Álvarez Quintero, Serafín and Joaquín — *Drama, comedia y sainete.*
　　Madrid, 1912.　　　　　　　　　　　　　　　　　　　　　**SJQ**
　　1908 — Sevilla (Andalusia)

Arniches, Carlos — *Del Madrid castizo; sainetes.* Madrid, 1919.　**ARN**
　　1919 — Alicante (Valencia)　　　　　　　　　．

Azorín (José Martínez Ruiz) — *Brandy, mucho brandy; sainete sen-*
　　timental. Madrid, 1927.　　　　　　　　　　　　　　　　**BRA**
　　1927 — Mondovar (Valencia)

Azorín (José Martínez Ruiz) — *Las confesiones de un pequeño filósofo.*
　　Madrid, 1920.　　　　　　　　　　　　　　　　　　　　　**PEQ**
　　1904 — Mondovar (Valencia)

Balseiro, José A. — *El vigía; ensayos.* Madrid, [1928]. Tomo II. **VIG**
　　1928 — Puerto Rico

Baroja, Pío — *Paradox, rey.* Madrid, 1917.　　　　　　　　　**REY**
　　1906 — San Sebastián (Vizcaya)

Benavente, Jacinto — *Los malhechores del bien.* 2a ed. Madrid,
　　1912.　　　　　　　　　　　　　　　　　　　　　　　　　**BEN**
　　1905 — Madrid

Blanco-Fombona, Rufino — *El hombre de hierro; novela.* Madrid,
　　n.d.　　　　　　　　　　　　　　　　　　　　　　　　　　**FOM**
　　1905 — Venezuela

Blanco y negro. Madrid, 18 August, 1929.　　　　　　　　　　**BYN**
　　1929 — Spain

Blasco Ibáñez, Vicente — *La horda.* Valencia, n.d.　　　　　　**IBA**
　　1905 — Valencia

Camba, Julio — *La rana viajera.* Madrid-Barcelona, 1920.　　　**RAN**
　　1920 — Pontevedra (Galicia)

Campa, Joaquín — *Teatro breve.* Buenos Aires, 1931.   JOA
    1931 — Argentina

Campos, José Antonio — *Rayos catódicos y fuegos fátuos.* 2a ed.
    Guayaquil, 1911.   CAT
    1911 — Ecuador

Castellanos, Jesús — *La conjura (novela).* Madrid, n.d.   JES
    1908 — Cuba

Darío, Rubén — *Los raros.* 2a ed. Barcelona, 1905.   RUB
    1905 — Nicaragua

Díaz Rodríguez, Manuel — *Ídolos rotos; novela.* París, 1901.   IDO
    1900 — Venezuela

Dicenta, Joaquín — *Amor de artistas; comedia.* Madrid, 1906.   ART
    1906 — Calatayud (Aragon)

Duayen, César (Emma de la Barra) — *Stella (novela de costumbres
    argentinas).* Barcelona, 1909.   STE
    1905 — Argentina

Espina, Concha — *Altar mayor.* New York, 1930.   MAY
    1926 — Santander (Asturias)

Espinosa, Januario — *La vida humilde; novela.* Santiago de Chile,
    1914.   JAN
    1914 — Chile

Gómez de la Serna, Ramón — *6 falsas novelas.* Madrid, [1927].   FAL
    1927 — Madrid

Grau, Jacinto — *Entre llamas; tragedia.* Madrid. 1915.   LLA
    1915 — Barcelona (Catalonia)

Henríquez Ureña, Max — *El retorno de los galeones (bocetos hispáni-
    cos).* Madrid, [1930].   RET
    1930 — República Dominicana

Hoyos, Julio de — *Tigre Juan; síntesis teatral de la novela de Ramón
    Pérez de Ayala.* Madrid, 1928.   TIG
    1928 — Valencia

Jiménez, Juan Ramón — *Platero y yo.* 2a ed. Madrid, 1917.   JIM
    1916 — Moguer (Andalusia)

León, Ricardo — *Casta de hidalgos.* Madrid, [1923].   RIC
    1908 — Málaga (Andalusia)

Linares Rivas, Manuel — *El abolengo.* In his *Teatro,* Madrid,
    1914, II.   LIN
    1904 — Santiago (Galicia)

López de Haro, Rafael — *La imposible; novela.* Madrid, n.d.   **IMP**
   1912 — Cuenca (Castile)

López Pinillos, J. — *La tierra; tragedia.* Madrid, 1921.   **PIN**
   1921 — Sevilla (Andalusia)

Luca de Tena, Juan Ignacio — *El dinero del duque; comedia.*
   Madrid, 1924.   **IGN**
   1924 — Sevilla (?) (Andalusia)

Marquina, Eduardo — *Una mujer; comedia.* Madrid, 1915.   **MUJ**
   1915 — Barcelona (Catalonia)

Marroquín, Lorenzo — *Pax; novela de costumbres latinoamericanas.*   **PAX**
   3a ed. París, n.d.
   1919 (?) — Colombia

Martínez Sierra, Gregorio — *Mamá; comedia.* Madrid, 1925.   **SIE**
   1912 — Madrid

Menéndez Pidal, Ramón — *El romancero.* Madrid, n.d.   **ROM**
   1928 — La Coruña (Galicia)

Menéndez y Pelayo, Marcelino — *Juan Boscán.* Madrid, 1908.   **PEL**
   1908 — Santander (Asturias)

Mundo gráfico. Madrid, 2 August, 1933.   **MGR**
   1933 — Spain

Muñoz Seca, Pedro and Juan López Núñez — *El rayo; juguete có-*
   mico. Madrid, [1917].   **SEC**
   1917 — Cádiz (Andalusia)

Nervo, Amado — *Ellos.* Madrid, 1920.   **NER**
   1919 — Mexico

Orrego Luco, Luis — *Al través de la tempestad; novela.* Santiago de
   Chile, 1914. 2 vols.   **ORR**
   1914 — Chile

Ortega y Gasset, José — *El espectador.* 2a ed. Madrid, 1921.
   Tomo I.   **ORT**
   1916 — Madrid

Palacio Valdés, Armando — *La novela de un novelista.* Madrid,
   1922.   **PAL**
   1921 — Entralgo (Asturias)

Pani, Alberto J. — *Cuestiones diversas.* México, 1922.   **DIV**
   1919 — Mexico

Pérez de Ayala, Ramón — *La pata de la raposa.* Madrid, 1923.   **PAT**
   1912 — Oviedo (Asturias)

Pérez Galdós, Benito — *El abuelo*. Madrid, 1912.   **ABU**
1904 — Canary Islands

Pérez Lugín, Alejandro — *La casa de la Troya*. Madrid, 1924.   **LUG**
1915 — Madrid

Pérez Zúñiga, Juan — ¡ *El disloque!* Madrid, [1923].   **ZUN**
1923 — Madrid

Revista de Occidente. Año II, N°. VIII. Madrid, 1924.   **OCC**
1924 — Spain

Rodó, José Enrique — *Motivos de Proteo*. Madrid, 1920.   **ROD**
1909 — Uruguay

Rusiñol, Santiago — *Buena gente; versión de G. Martínez Sierra*.
París, n.d.   **RUS**
1907 — (Martínez Sierra — Madrid)

Sánchez, Florencio — *M'hijo el dotor*. In his *Teatro*, 2a ed. Valencia, 1919.   **URU**
1903 — Uruguay

Sassone, Felipe — *El miedo de los felices; drama*. 2a ed. Madrid,
n.d.   **SAS**
1913 — Peru

Trigo, Felipe — *Así paga el diablo*. 2a ed. Madrid, 1912.   **TRI**
1912 (?) — Villanueva de la Serena (Extremadura)

Ugarte, Manuel — *Cuentos argentinos*. París, n.d.   **UGA**
1910 — Argentina

Unamuno, Miguel de — *Tres novelas ejemplares y un prólogo*.   **UNA**
Madrid-Barcelona, 1920.
1920 — Bilbao (Vizcaya)

Valle-Inclán, Ramón del — *Sonata de primavera*. [Madrid, 1922]   **SON**
1904 — Pontevedra (Galicia)

Wast, Hugo (Martínez Zuviría) — *Desierto de piedra*. Boston,
[1930]   **WAS**
1925 (?) — Argentina

Zamacois, Eduardo — *Teatro galante*. Madrid, 1910.   **ZAM**
1909 — Cuba

LIST OF ABBREVIATIONS

ABC — *A B C*
ABU — Pérez Galdós — *El abuelo.*
ALT — Altamira — *Historia.*
ARN — Arniches — *Del Madrid castizo.*
ART — Dicenta — *Amor de artistas.*
BEN — Benavente — *Los malhechores del bien.*
BRA — Azorín — *Brandy, mucho brandy.*
BYN — *Blanco y negro.*
CAT — Campos — *Rayos catódicos.*
DEB — Alfau — *Los débiles.*
DIV — Pani — *Cuestiones diversas.*
FAL — Gómez de la Serna — *6 falsas novelas.*
FOM — Blanco-Fombona — *El hombre de hierro.*
IBA — Blasco Ibáñez — *La horda.*
IDO — Díaz Rodríguez — *Ídolos rotos.*
IGN — Luca de Tena — *El dinero del duque.*
IMP — López de Haro — *La imposible.*
JAN — Espinosa — *La vida humilde.*
JES — Castellanos — *La conjura.*
JIM — Jiménez — *Platero y yo.*
JOA — Campa — *Teatro breve.*
LIN — Linares Rivas — *El abolengo.*
LLA — Grau — *Entre llamas.*
LUG — Pérez Lugín — *La casa de la Troya.*
MAY — Espina — *Altar mayor.*
MGR — *Mundo gráfico.*
MUJ — Marquina — *Una mujer.*
NER — Nervo — *Ellos.*
OCC — *Revista de Occidente.*
ORR — Orrego Luco — *Al través de la tempestad.*
ORT — Ortega — *El espectador.*
PAL — Palacio Valdés — *La novela.*
PAT — Pérez de Ayala — *La pata de la raposa.*
PAX — Marroquín — *Pax.*
PEL — Menéndez y Pelayo — *Juan Boscán.*
PEQ — Azorín — *Las confesiones.*
PIN — López Pinillos — *La tierra.*
RAN — Camba — *La rana viajera.*
RET — Henríquez Ureña — *El retorno de los galeones.*
REY — Baroja — *Paradox, rey.*
RIC — León — *Casta de hidalgos.*
ROD — Rodó — *Motivos de Proteo.*

ROM — Menéndez Pidal — *El romancero.*
RUB — Darío — *Los raros.*
RUS — Rusiñol — *Buena gente.*
SAS — Sassone — *El miedo de los felices.*
SEC — Muñoz Seca — *El rayo.*
SIE — Martínez Sierra — *Mamá.*
SJQ — Álvarez Quintero — *Drama, comedia y sainete.*
SON — Valle-Inclán — *Sonata de primavera.*
STE — Duayen — *Stella.*
TIG — Hoyos — *Tigre Juan.*
TRI — Trigo — *Así paga el diablo.*
UGA — Ugarte — *Cuentos argentinos.*
UNA — Unamuno — *Tres novelas.*
URU — Sánchez — *M'hijo el dotor.*
VIG — Balseiro — *El vigía.*
WAS — Wast — *Desierto de piedra.*
ZAM — Zamacois — *Teatro galante.*
ZUN — Pérez Zúñiga — *¡ El disloque!*

SPANISH SYNTAX LIST

SPANISH SYNTAX LIST

I. THE SENTENCE

1. Any complete expression of a thought or an emotion is a sentence. It may consist of a single sound; it may present a complicated structure of central and subordinate notions. If it be complete in itself, it is a sentence. The sentence is the basic unit of speech. Syntax is the study of sentence patterns; it seeks to describe the functions which each of the elements in the sentence performs in relation to the other elements of the sentence in the expression of a given notion. Syntax is concerned with the forms of words only in so far as the forms serve to indicate the function.

1.1 Forms of the sentence. Sentences are expressed in three forms: declarative, interrogative, and exclamatory. The declarative sentence makes a statement. The interrogative sentence asks for a statement or implies a wish. The exclamatory sentence expresses an emotion — fear, hope, surprise, and the like — or conveys a command or wish.

1.2 Elements of the sentence. In its simplest, most primitive form the sentence may consist of a single sound, used as an exclamation. Or in conversation, individual words, used without relationships of any kind, may serve as a wholly adequate means of communication. But in normal discourse, even in conversation, there are two essential elements in every sentence: a subject, which indicates the person, thing, or theme that is the matter of discourse, and a predicate which states the action or state in which the subject is involved. Since syntax is concerned with the patterns of speech, it cannot derive data from the formless, patternless types of the exclamatory sentence. It must devote itself to the normal type of sentence which contains the essential elements necessary to form a pattern.

1.21 The Subject. The subject is normally expressed in Spanish. But since the personal endings of the verb indicate the subject of the sentence, the actual pronoun may be left unexpressed. Thus *hablo* as clearly indicates the subject in Spanish as does " I speak " in English.

1.22 The Predicate. In its simplest form the predicate consists merely of a verb: *Juan canta*. But the verb may require a complement to achieve complete predication. This complement may be a direct object, used with transitive verbs; an indirect object, used with both transitive and intransitive verbs; a subjective complement, used with copulative verbs; or an objective complement, used with transitive verbs.

1.23 Modifiers. In addition to the essential elements of the sentence there are other elements which are used to modify the essential elements. A modifier which is used to qualify the subject or object or complement is an adjectival modifier. A modifier which is used to modify the verb is an adverbial modifier. Adverbial modifiers are also used to qualify other modifiers, adjectival or adverbial.

1.24 Relaters. There are, finally, two elements in the sentence which serve to indicate the relationships between the other elements: the prepositions and the conjunctions.

1.3 Terms used to indicate the elements of the sentence. It is convenient to have specific terms to indicate the different elements of the sentence. In the present study the terms used are based upon the function of the several elements.

1.31 Substantive. An expression which is used as subject, object, or complement of a verb, or as object of a preposition is called a substantive. The words most commonly used as substantives are nouns, pronouns, and infinitives.

1.311 Noun. A word which is used to indicate the name of a person, a thing, or an abstraction is called a noun.

1.313 Pronoun. A word which is used to take the place of a noun is a pronoun.

1.315 Infinitive. The infinitive is that form of the verb, ending in –*r*, which is used to present the action or state expressed by the verb as a substantive.

1.32 Verb. A word which is used to predicate an action or a state is called a verb. Verbs may be transitive, intransitive, reflexive, reciprocal, copulative, or auxiliary. They may also express an action actively or passively.

1.33 Adjective. A word which is used to modify a substantive is an adjective. Simple adjectives are either limiting or qualifying. The limiting adjectives are determinative (definite article, demonstrative, possessive), or indeterminate (indefinite article, indefinite adjective, interrogative, relative, negative, numeral). The qualifying adjectives are distinguishing or descriptive. The different situations in which an adjective is found are: attributive, predicate (either as subjective or as objective complement), and appositive.

1.34 Adverb. A word which is used to modify a verb, adjective, or another adverb is an adverb. Adverbs modifying verbs express such notions as cause, degree, manner, place, time, etc. Adverbs modifying other modifiers express only degree.

1.35 Preposition. An expression which connects a substantive with another element of the sentence (substantive, verb, adjective, adverb) is called a preposition. The combination of preposition and substantive forms a phrase which is either adjectival or adverbial.

1.36 Conjunction. There are two types of word which are called conjunctions.

1.361 Coordinating conjunction. A word or expression which is used to connect two sentences, or two elements of the sentence which are of equal rank (substantives, verbs, adjectives, etc.) is called a coordinating conjunction. When a sentence contains two or more independent propositions connected by a coordinating conjunction it is called a compound sentence.

1.363 Subordinating conjunction. An expression which is used to connect a clause containing a finite verb with the main verb of the sentence in such a way as to subordinate the proposition of that clause to the main proposition is called a subordinating conjunction. Since such a clause modifies the verb, it is an adverbial clause and expresses the same types of modification as other adverbs. A sentence which contains both a main clause and a subordinate adverbial clause is called a complex sentence.

1.4 Independent elements. Not all the elements of connected discourse are integrally related to the structure of the sentence.

1.41 Interjections. A word which is used alone to express an emotion on the part of the speaker or to imitate a sound is called an interjection. Some interjections are words which are limited to such an exclamatory utterance. But other words, verbs, nouns, adjectives, etc. may be used as interjections. An interjection never forms an integral part of the sentence.

1.42 Absolute constructions. A substantive and an adjective, particularly a participle, are often used together without any indication of their relation to the rest of the sentence. Such a construction is called an absolute construction. They are of two types: in the first, the noun and the adjective or participle form an expression which is the equivalent of a subordinate clause; in the second, the noun and the adjective form the equivalent of a descriptive prepositional phrase introduced by *con*. The second type may be called the descriptive absolute construction.

1.43 Independent elements in conversational and emotional utterance. In the rapid exchange of conversation, any element of the sentence may be used alone, without relationship to any other element, and still convey a complete thought or emotion.

1.5 Elliptical expressions. In the flow of all ordinary discourse, both conversational and literary, there are a large number of situations in which it is not necessary to repeat an element which has already been used in a preceding sentence. The simplest cases are those in which an identical subject or verbal element is not repeated. But the practice is extended to a variety of other situations. The commonest are those which are found after expressions of comparison (involving *que* and *como*) and after expressions of exception. These incomplete or abridged constructions are called elliptical.

1.6 Order of the elements in the sentence. The order of the elements in the sentence is a problem for syntax only if that order is of value in determining the function of the elements. While it is true that, in general, Spanish had developed a normal pattern of word-order of Subject-Verb-Complement, there is no fixity in this pattern and other devices are used to indicate which word is object of the verb. Questions of emotional stress are therefore likely to be the determining factor in establishing the order of any given sentence. An attempt to reduce the problem to some objective basis having proved futile, the matter has been omitted from the present study. This applies as well to the question of the position of attributive adjectives and of adverbs which modify a verb.

1.7 Stylistic phenomena. Outside of the realm of syntax lies a wide range of expression which is primarily individual and which gives to each utterance or each composition its peculiar style. There are two aspects of any individual style. On the one hand it is marked by the particular choices of the speaker in cases where there is more than one possible device for expression; on the other hand it is marked by the expressions which are peculiar to the individual and fall outside the normal syntactic pattern. It should also be remarked that groups of individuals have a style peculiar to the group. In rare cases such a style is the result of conscious effort to secure specific effects. More often the style is the subconscious reflection of the individual speaker's *milieu*. The scholar has his jargon of style as clearly as the *pícaro*. Diplomatic correspondence falls into its own special patterns, just as does the language of the *barrios bajos*. But within all these varying styles there lies a common core of speech, used by all those who speak the Spanish tongue. The patterns of that common core are the subject of Spanish syntax.

II. SUBSTANTIVES

2. In the present chapter are treated all of the functions of substantives which are common alike to nouns, pronouns, infinitives, clauses, etc. The detailed discussion of the use of particular pronouns, of infinitives, clauses, adjectives, and adverbs in each of these functions will be found under the several elements.

2.1 As subject.

2.11 With a finite verb. IBA 33 *A mí siempre me ha gustado vestir bien. ¿ Ven ustedes esta prenda, que ni el rey la lleva ?* (*)

2.111 The subject may be restricted by an indefinite pronoun. ORT 112 *Tiziano y Poussin son, cada cual a su modo, temperamentos religiosos.* (5–6)

2.113 The subject may be introduced by *entre.* MUJ 13 *Entre los dos dejan sobre la mesa el montón de flores.* (9–11)

2.12 With an infinitive. PEL 468 *Sin ser muy severo el gusto de Vall-fogona, escribía con relativa sencillez.* (*)

2.15 As direct object.

2.16 Referring to a thing. IGN 36 *¿ Pero tú crees que yo robo el dinero ?* (*)

2.17 Referring to a person. One of the devices which Spanish has developed to identify the direct object is the use of *a* as a sign of the accusative case. For the most part this use is restricted to the identification of persons and of proper names, for persons and proper names are the categories which are most frequently found as subject of the sentence and which therefore require some special indication when they are used as object. But the use of *a* has spread in two directions. On the one hand it may be used with any noun to insure its identification as object; on the other hand, because certain verbs are usually followed by nouns which refer to a person, these verbs may be said to personify the object and so make natural the use of *a* even with nouns referring to things. The difficulty of establishing any general principles is greatly increased by the identity of form for direct and indirect objects, not only in the case of nouns, but also in the case of the personal pronouns. For it is certain that some verbs are intransitive and therefore followed by an indirect object, yet the form of this indirect object will be identical with that of the direct object, if it is a person.

2.18 It is, however, possible to establish certain generalizations concern-

29

ing the use of *a* before the direct object in contemporary Spanish. It is, in effect, a "personal *a*", that is to say, it is normally used with words referring to persons, whether they be definite, indefinite, or collective. With the stressed forms of the personal pronoun and with proper names referring to persons it is almost never omitted; with unmodified nouns (indefinite or negative) and with nouns modified by a numeral it is more often omitted than employed. In cases where usage varies, it may be said that the more specific the person, the greater the likelihood that *a* will be used. At the same time, the character of the verb involved will also exercise an influence. If the verb be one which is normally used with a thing as object (e.g. *llevar, tener*), it may "depersonalize" the object and hence *a* will be omitted. But if the verb be one which is normally used with a person as object, it will make the use of *a* natural, even when a thing is the object. In the following presentation of materials, cases of the use of *a* are followed immediately by cases of the omission of *a*.

2.21 With stressed personal pronouns. LLA 30 *Me tienes a mí siempre.* (*)

2.22 With other pronouns referring to persons.

2.221 Demonstratives. ZUN 56 *Lo primero que se le ocurrió después de bendecir a éstos fué llamar a la criada.* (18–43)

2.223 Interrogatives. ZAM 141 *¿ A quién llamas?* (14–15)

2.225 Negatives. JOA 27 *El tiempo no espera a nadie.* (5–6)

2.227 Possessives. RIC 37 *Amaba a los suyos.* (3–4)

2.231 Indefinites. With *a*. SJQ 124 *Llama a otro.* **(48–135)**

2.232 Without *a*. RUS 78 *Otra mejor que yo podrían encontrar.* (12–16)

2.235 Relatives. With *a*. RAN 80 *Los primeros amigos a quienes vi prorrumpieron en ayes lastimeros.* **(45–119)**

2.236 Without *a*. ART 21 *No encontramos quien nos comprenda.* All cases noted are substantive *quien* in negative or indefinite constructions. (4–5)

2.237 Never before *que*. IGN 90 *Un amanuense que tenía mi tío.* (*)

2.24 Proper names of persons.

2.241 Used alone. ORR 95 *Tal respuesta desazonó a Elisa.* **(57–489)**

2.243 The name of an author is used to represent his work. DEB 53 *Paso las tardes leyéndole a Boccaccio.* (7–14)

2.245 An appellative is used as proper noun. RUS 25 *Ha sido que el padrino no puede ver a madre.* **(21–39)**

2.247 A proper noun is accompanied by a title. REY 89 *Un golpe de mar arrancó del puente al capitán Jenkins.* (17–24)

2.25 Other proper nouns.

2.251 Names of places. With *a*. DIV 169 *Han venido millones de hombres para salvar a Francia.* (13–17)

2.252 Without *a*. RAN 94 *Los gallegos están modernizando Galicia.* (6–6)

2.253 Names of animals. JIM 96 *Acaricié a Platero.* (3–6)

2.26 Nouns referring to definite persons, in the singular. The noun is modified by a determinative; the indefinite article identifies a particular person.

2.261 Modified by definite article. With *a*. FOM 98 *Apenas si recordaba al difunto amante.* (**60–308**)

2.262 Without *a*. IBA 363 *¡ Lo que ha llorao esa chica antes de que nos llevásemos el pequeño!* (A very small baby is hardly a person.) (9–10)

2.263 Modified by a demonstrative adjective. With *a*. PEQ 30 *Nosotros admirábamos profundamente a esta criada.* (**26–43**)

2.264 Without *a*. RUS 122 *¿ Ves este joven ?* (6–7)

2.265 Modified by a possessive adjective. With *a*. SIE 16 *Viene a arrinconar a su madre.* (**44–178**)

2.266 Without *a*. RET 36 *Las nuevas tendencias encontraron su intérprete en Rufino Blanco-Fombona.* (4–4)

2.267 Modified by an indefinite article. RUS 147 *¿ A quién van a prender ? — ¡ A ti, que robas a una mujer!* (**20–26**)

2.27 Nouns referring to definite persons in the plural.

2.271 Modified by the definite article. With *a*. ARN 18 *No recojan a los pobres que piden.* (**48–201**)

2.272 Without *a*. REY 134 *Me traen las mujeres más hermosas del reino.* (5–5)

2.273 Modified by a demonstrative adjective. ABU 196 *No puedo seguir a estas criaturas.* (11–12)

2.275 Modified by a possessive adjective. With *a*. ORR 171 *Todas engañan a sus maridos.* (**25–36**)

2.276 Without *a*. ABU 18 *¿ Apostamos a que doña Lucrecia viene a llevarse sus niñas ?* (4–4)

2.28 Nouns referring to indefinite persons, singular or plural.

2.281 Modified by the definite article, usually generic. With *a*. CAT 3 *El mérito del gallo consiste en descubrir a los embusteros.*   (**43–102**)

2.282 Without *a*. ALT 193 *Las Juntas eran también las que elegían los procuradores o diputados.*   (8–10)

2.287 Modified by an indefinite article. With *a*. RAN 95 *Cuando vea usted a un celta migratorio, ofrézcale una patata.*   (**33–57**)

2.288 Without *a*. PAT 217 *¿ Cómo no escogió usted un banquero de más confianza ?*   (**35–69**)

2.291 Modified by an indefinite adjective. With *a*. RIC 259 *¿ Has oído a algún « virtuoso » ?*   (**23–31**)

2.292 Without *a*. RUS 24 *Yo no quiero desollar más pobres.*   (8–10)

2.293 Modified by a numeral adjective. With *a*. ABC 41 *El Papa ha recibido a ocho oficiales y a 42 marineros ingleses.*   (4–7)

2.294 Without *a*. PEL 11 *La ciudad de Barcelona diputó doce notables.*   (11–14)

2.295 The noun is unmodified. With *a*. JOA 77 *Pero yo no quiero trabajar para mantener a vagos.*   (4–6)

2.296 Without *a*. MUJ 34 *Amigo mío, se hacen viajes para conocer mujeres.*   (**24–49**)

2.297 The noun is a collective. With *a*. MGR 31 *Era frecuente que después de dominar a la tripulación, se apoderaran de una embarcación.* (**30–64**)

2.298 Without *a*. DEB 50 *Le veía inclinarse hacia la tierra, contemplando la multitud.*   (8–8)

2.31 Nouns referring to animals. The use or omission of *a* depends upon the degree to which the animal is presented as a sentient person.

2.311 With *a*. JES 35 *De los emparrados del patio volaba una brisa juguetona, enardeciendo a los canarios.* (*Ardor* is a *personal* attribute). (**26–62**)

2.312 Without *a*. LLA 15 *He encontrado esta paloma.* (The bird is presented as a mere object.)   (19–41)

2.35 Nouns referring to inanimate things. The normal construction is of course without *a* (2.16). But *a* is found when the verb involved tends to personify the object and there are also a few cases which seem to reveal an "accusative *a*", employed as a sign of the direct object.

2.351 The verb is one which normally has a person as a direct object. UNA 9 *Eso de nívola, como bauticé a mi novela, fué una salida que encontré para mis . . . ¿ críticos ?*   (26–50)

2.355 If both subject and object are nouns of the same number referring to things, the use of *a* distinguishes object from subject. DIV 23 *Una distancia enorme separa a este proyecto de la idea original.*   (5–9)

2.356 Especially if the object precedes the verb. MUJ 30 *Y a la bondad y al corazón les parta un rayo.*   (4–8)

2.4 Special considerations which affect the use of "personal *a*".

2.41 The noun or pronoun is used in an elliptical construction. When a noun or pronoun is used without a verb after *como, que,* etc. the use of *a* makes it possible to distinguish whether the substantive in question is subject or object.

2.42 After *como.* In this situation *a* is sometimes used even with the names of things. On the other hand, the development of *como* as a particle of comparison makes it possible to consider the noun which follows as an objective complement.

2.421 With *a.* ABU 14 *El Conde quiere a su hija como a un dolor de muelas.*   (15–35)

2.422 Without *a.* ALT 11 *Maquiavelo le hubiera saludado como aventajadísimo precursor de sus máximas.*   (8–11)

2.43 After *que.* The use of *a* is the normal practice. URU 26 *¿ Por qué ha de tratar uno a su padre con menos confianza que a un extraño ?* (8–10)

2.44 When a noun or pronoun referring to a person is accompanied by an adjective objective complement, the use of *a* is regular. BEN 15 *Deseosa de poder hacer felices a los demás.*   (16–24)

2.46 After special verbs. As has already been remarked, certain verbs which normally are followed by an object referring to a thing tend to depersonalize an object referring to a person. Typical verbs are *encontrar, llevar(se),* and *tener.* It should be remarked that even with these verbs the preposition is regularly used when the object is a stressed form of the personal pronoun or a proper noun. Verbs which imply a negative, like *buscar,* will more frequently be followed by an indefinite than a definite object, but they too will be followed by the preposition if the object is a specific person. No attempt has been made to gather materials which would illustrate the use after each particular verb in Spanish (this would be an interesting study), but it may be well to illustrate the use with two typical verbs: *buscar* and *tener.*

2.461 *buscar* With *a*.   RUS 26 *Ahora se ha ido a buscar a la inclusera.*

2.462 Without *a*.   PEL 27 *Hay que buscar los poetas y novelistas de más mérito.*

2.465 *tener* With *a*.   RUB 15 *Tiene cerca a Jersey.*

2.466 Without *a*.   BEN 10 *Tendrás en ella la mujer que faltaba en tu casa.*

2.467 After *aquí (ahí) tiene usted*.   When *aquí tiene usted* is used in the sense of "here is", to point out a person, the person is regularly specific and hence preceded by *a*.   ART 45 *¡ Ahí tiene usted a su amiguito!*
(6–7)

2.47 The personal direct object is accompanied by another expression introduced by *a*.   If a sentence which has a personal direct object contains also another phrase introduced by the preposition *a*, either an adverbial phrase or an indirect object introduced by *a*, there is no evidence that the presence of the second phrase affects the use or omission of *a* with the direct object.

2.471 An adverbial phrase with *a*.   With *a*.   ARN 27 *Con obreros que no mandan a los chicos a la escuela . . . ¿ qué quieres que sea España?* (13–16)

2.472 Without *a*.   UNA 153 *Alejandro se llevó su mujer a su casa.*   The verb itself explains the omission of *a*.   (4–4)

2.475 An indirect object with *a*.   With *a*.   UGA 60 *Abandonando a su suerte a los caballos, se alejó.*   (7–7)

2.476 Without *a*.   BYN 69 *Tal vez el mayor acierto del autor haya sido confiar su heroína a la genial inspiración de la ilustre actriz argentina.*   The "heroine" is presented, not as a person, but as a fictional character.   (3–4)

2.5 Other uses of the substantive as direct object.

2.51 After normally intransitive verbs.   Certain verbs which are normally intransitive are occasionally used as transitives with a direct object.   SON 111 *¡ Hemos corrido toda Liguria!*   ([18]–20)

The only common verb is: *correr* (8–10).

2.52 A direct object referring to a person is sometimes used after verbs which normally are followed by a direct object referring to a thing and an indirect object referring to a person.   BEN 69 *Pregunte usted a don Heliodoro.*   (8–11)

2.53 A direct object is used after a verbal locution consisting of a verb and a noun object.   ARN 35 *Si no los separo, la hacen migas.*   (11–14)

2.6 Substantives used as indirect object. In general, the indirect object indicates the person who is in some way affected by the action or state of the verb. The relationship may be immediate and material, when the action is directed explicitly toward the person; it may be loose and merely psychological. In all cases, the indirect object with substantives is expressed by the preposition *a*. The indirect object is found with transitive verbs which also have a direct object, and with intransitive verbs, both those used impersonally or with inanimate subjects, and with intransitives which have a personal subject. The present section includes the use of all substantives except personal pronouns; the materials parallel those presented in 8.21.

2.61 After transitive verbs which have a direct object. RIC 19 *Jesús iba harto embebido en sus pensamientos para dar pábulo al temor.* ([60]–681)

The commonest verbs are: *avisar* (5–6), *ceder* (6–6), *comunicar* (9–9), *conceder* (7–12), *confiar* (6–7), *consagrar* (8–9), *dar* (**48–144**), *deber* (13–22), *decir* (**34–100**), *dedicar* (8–11), *dejar* (5–5), *dirigir* (11–16), *echar* (8–8), *entregar* (10–15), *escribir* (7–7), *hacer* (**25–42**), *indicar* (5–5), *llevar* (5–5), *mandar* (5–5), *mostrar* (5–5), *ofrecer* (18–28), *oponer* (6–8), *ordenar* (5–5), *poner* (9–15), *presentar* (10–17), *prestar* (9–12), *referir* (6–11), *rendir* (5–5), *tener* (6–6), *traer* (7–8).

2.621 After *llamar*. With *llamar*, what was originally an indirect object has become logically a direct object and the original direct object has become logically an objective complement. IMP 17 *Llamaban el* Roncón *a una caverna socabada en las rocas.* (26–62)

2.63 After intransitive verbs.

2.631 Impersonal verbs or verbs used only with an inanimate subject. RIC 28 *No hubiera faltado a don Pedro puesto decoroso en escuela o teatro.* ([40]–112)

The commonest verbs are: *corresponder* (7–10), *dar* (5–9), *faltar* (10–14), *ocurrir* (5–5), *tocar* (5–6).

2.633 Verbs with a personal subject. This group is one in which it is difficult to gather data, since the forms for direct and indirect object referring to persons are identical. Only cases in which the indirect object is a thing have been included, if the verb is one which may also be considered a transitive verb. FAL 17 *Siguió mirando al vacío luminoso.* ([55]–353)

The commonest verbs are: *aludir* (8–11), *aspirar* (5–5), *atender* (6–7), *ayudar* (6–8), *contestar* (10–14), *dar* (5–10), *escribir* (8–10), *faltar* (6–7), *hablar* (10–12), *mirar* (**24–38**), *obedecer* (9–12), *pertenecer* (18–37), *renunciar* (12–15), *resistir* (6–6), *responder* (11–12), *seguir* (7–10), *servir* (15–19), *suceder* (5–6).

2.635 Reflexive verbs. ORR 184 *Tenía que guardar secreto, salvo en cuanto se refería a su padre.* ([39]–106)

The commonest verbs are *dirigirse* (10–18), *entregarse* (7–8), *parecerse* (12–13), *referirse* (13–28)

2.64 The indirect object modifies the whole sentence rather than the verb. In a number of situations the indirect object indicates, not the person who is immediately affected by the action or state of the verb, but the person who is remotely concerned with that action or state. In this case, the indirect object may be said to modify the whole sentence rather than the verb. While all of the constructions are closely related, it is possible to distinguish special categories; see also 8.22.

2.641 The indirect object indicates the possessor.   ORR 174 *El corazón saltaba dentro del pecho al doctor.*   **(25–44)**

2.643 The indirect object indicates a place.   DIV 20 *La opinión unánime de los franceses no reconoce ningún carácter revolucionario al movimiento bolchevik.*   **(5–6)**

2.645 The indirect object indicates separation.   ORT 134 *En este ensayo se habla de un hombre que no quiere pedir a nadie nada.*   **([44]–150)**

  The commonest verbs are: *arrancar* (7–8), *oír* (6–6), *pedir* (**28–41**), *preguntar* (15–24), *quitar* (10–13), *rogar* (5–7), *sacar* (5–5).

2.647 The indirect object indicates the person to whom the action or state is of interest.   SIE 88 *Abra usted la puerta a este caballero.*   **(25–43)**

2.66 Direct or indirect object after verbs of causation and perception. When a verb of causation or perception is followed by an infinitive, it becomes a problem to determine what is the construction of the substantives involved. It should be said again that the problem is rendered difficult by the identity of forms of direct and indirect objects in both pronouns and nouns referring to persons. Only when a speaker habitually differentiates between *lo* as direct object and *le* as indirect object, or between *los* and *les*, or when the person is expressed by a feminine pronoun, or when the noun involved is one referring to a thing is it possible to draw any conclusions. The materials gathered seem to make clear that the substantive which is the logical subject of the dependent infinitive is usually considered as the direct object of the main verb.

2.67 The infinitive is transitive.

2.671 The personal subject of the infinitive is not expressed.   MUJ 7 *Deja ver el cielo.* In this case, although the subject of the infinitive was probably indefinite in origin, the infinitive is now felt to be passive.   **(41–87)**

2.673 The personal subject of the infinitive is expressed and normally has the form of a direct object of the main verb. RAN 95 *Al verlos correr el mundo se dice que tienen un espíritu muy aventurero.* **(47–184)**

2.68 The infinitive is intransitive.

2.681 The subject of the infinitive is indefinite. MGR 44 *Oí hablar de las asombrosas propiedades que posee.* (18–39)

2.683 The subject of the infinitive has the form of a direct object of the main verb. JAN 104 *Vió llegar con honda pena el día del regreso.* **(50–240)**

2.685 The subject of the infinitive has the form of an indirect object of the main verb. RIC 277 *¿ Qué le pasa a Rosuca ? — Estos versos le han hecho llorar.* The indirect form is more common with verbs of causation (*dejar, hacer*) than with verbs of perception (*oír, ver*). (19–24)

2.687 The form of the subject of the infinitive may be either direct or indirect. TIG 24 *En ella me veré vivir.* **(49–200)**

2.7 As complement.

2.71 Substantives are used as complements to the subject and to the object of the verb. In either case they may be specific or generic, that is to say, they may indicate an individual which is identified with the subject or object, or they may indicate the class to which the subject or object belongs. In the first case they are normally introduced by an article or other determinative; in the second, they are normally used without limiting modification. In either case, also, the complement may be introduced by a preposition. Since adjectives are found as complements in identical constructions with substantives, they will, for convenience, be included in the present section.

2.72 Subjective complement. A subjective complement is regularly used in the predicate after a copulative verb. If the subjective complement is identical with the subject, the normal copulative is *ser* and the complement is accompanied by a determinative. If the subjective complement indicates the class to which the subject belongs, the copulative is *ser* and the complement, either noun or adjective, is not modified by an article or other determinative; a noun used in this construction is adjectival rather than substantival in function. If the subjective complement indicates the state of the subject, the copulative is *estar* and the complement is regularly an adjective. Both *ser* and *estar* may be replaced by other verbs, see 35.39 and 35.56.

2.73 The subjective complement is not usually introduced by a preposition. But just as in English "as" or "for" may be used, so in Spanish the subjective complement is at times introduced by *de, en, por,* etc.

2.731 Without a preposition. Identified with the subject. IBA 157 *Yo*

soy un pazguato. Indicating the class to which the subject belongs.
LUG 1 *Eran los viajeros, en su mayoría, estudiantes.*   (*)

For examples of adjectives after *estar,* see 35.32.

2.733 The complement is introduced by *como.* ORR 94 *Cada una había sido recibida como acontecimiento importante.*   **(27–67)**

2.734 The complement is introduced by a preposition. The complement may be either specific or generic.

2.735 *de*. RET 31 *Más de una vez sirvió de tema a Altamirano.*   **([34]–81)**

The only common verb is *servir* (**27–51**).

2.736 *en*. ALT 464 *Las delegaciones se convirtieron en tribunales.*   **([19]–31)**
The only common verbs are: *convertirse* (17–20) and *trocarse* (3–3).

2.739 *por*. RAN 26 *La mujer que habla de política pasa por un marimacho.*   **([8]–11)**

The only common verb is *pasar* (7–9).

2.74 Objective complement. When a substantive is used as objective complement, it usually indicates the class of the object, less often it is specific. An adjective used as objective complement usually indicates the state of the object, less often the class.

2.741 Without a preposition. BEN 43 *Rompí todo freno al verme libre.*   **([60]–923)**

The commonest verbs are: *considerar* — With adj. (10–13), *creer* — With adj. (**30–46**), With noun (8–12), *declarar* — With adj. (6–8), *dejar* — With adj. (**40–84**), *encontrar* — With adj. (**22–24**), *hacer* — With adj. (**38–73**), With noun (**25–40**), *hallar* — With adj. (10–14), *juzgar* — With adj. (7–7), *llamar* — With adj. (10–11), With noun (**35–119**), *llevar* — With adj. (5–7), *mostrar* — With adj. (7–10), *poner* — With adj. (15–22), *sentir* — With adj. (12–19), *tener* — With adj. (**36–82**), With past participle (5–10), *tomar* — With adj. (6–7), *traer* — With adj. (5–6), *ver* — With adj. (**40–88**), with past part. (10–20), *volver* — With adj. (16–18).

2.743 Introduced by *como.* RAN 87 *Los vigueses debieran considerar a Pontevedra como un barrio del Vigo futuro.*   **([27]–52)**

The commonest verbs are: *considerar* — With noun (12–14), *reconocer* — With noun (6–6), *señalar* — With noun (4–8).

2.745 Introduced by a preposition. Nouns are somewhat more frequently introduced by a preposition than are adjectives.

2.746 *de*. LLA 31 *Me toma a mí de pretexto para seguir haciendo su voluntad.*   **([16]–26)**

2.747 *en.* OCC 130 *Para conservar esta evolución ha habido que convertirla de nuevo en fragmentos.* ([29]-58)

The only common verbs are: *convertir* — With noun (**20–37**), *dividir* — With noun (5–5).

2.749 *por.* PAT 21 *Me moriría de desconsuelo si no tuviera por sostén ciertas facultades poéticas.* ([33]-74)

The commonest verbs are: *dar* — With adj. (12–13), *tener* — With adj. (5–5), With noun (11–19), *tomar* — With noun (9–13).

2.75 Substantives in apposition with another substantive. All types of substantive may be used in apposition with another substantive. The identification of the two substantives may be complete, or the second substantive may indicate the class to which the first substantive belongs. IBA 28 *Ahora tenía otro perro, una verdadera alhaja.* (*)

For examples of the use of individual substantives, see 5.35; 25.55; 37.43.

2.76 Substantives as object of a preposition. Any substantive can be used as the object of a preposition to form an adjectival or an adverbial phrase. Only the personal pronouns of the first and second person singular and of the reflexive have special forms which are used after prepositions. With the preposition *a*, a substantive is used to express the indirect object and, with persons, the direct object as well. The usual preposition used to connect a substantive with another substantive or with an adjective is *de*. With other prepositions, are formed phrases expressing the various adverbial notions of cause, manner, place, time, etc.

2.761 Uses with *de*. The various relationships which were expressed in Latin by the genitive case are largely expressed in Spanish by the use of the preposition *de* before the substantive. The most important construction is the possessive. Other common uses of *de* are the appositive, the objective, and the partitive. IGN 61 *El* auto *del duque.* (*)

2.8 Substantives in elliptical constructions without a verb. Substantives are frequently found in expressions in which a verb is not repeated or in which a verb is implied.

2.81 In coordinated expressions.

2.811 Copulative. PAX 338 *En aquel instante resuena una descarga y con ella un grito salvaje.* (19–37)

2.813 Adversative. PEL 227 *Los versos son de varia acentuación, pero todos de once sílabas.* (6–8)

2.817 Asyndetic. IMP 206 *Otro gustaría la cálida ventura; para otro el nido de plumas de golondrina, el collar de rubíes para otro.* (11–18)

2.82 In subordinated expressions.

2.83 Of comparison.

2.831 After *como.* TIG 3 *Hay que tener un puesto como el tuyo.* **(60–1104)**

2.835 After *cual.* JIM 22 *Canta entonadamente cual una princesa.* (4–15)

2.837 After *que.* IBA 28 *Era de menos mérito que el otro.* **(60–348)**

2.85 After a subordinating conjunction.

2.851 *aunque.* TIG 7 *Aunque viuda, paréceme mujer que nunca probara varón.* (3–3)

2.853 *cuando.* NER 35 *Cuando niño, vivía yo en un caserón desgarbado.* (4–4)

2.9 Independent uses of substantives. In conversation, the normal, complete sentence is often replaced by words used independently without any expressed syntactic relationships. This does not mean that communication is less complete or less exact; it is aided by facial expressions, by gestures, by intonations of the voice. In this type of discourse, almost any word may have independent capacity for communicating an idea or an emotion. Since these expressions do not involve questions of syntax, they have not been studied in detail. But to form some idea of the frequency of such uses, an effort was made to record the independent uses of substantives.

2.91 In conversation.

2.911 Direct address. JOA 33 ¡ *Hijo de mi alma!* **(46–1722)**

2.913 Exclamations and exclamatory questions. SAS 13 ¡ *Qué cosa bárbara!* **(39–555)**

2.915 Incomplete or interrupted expressions. LLA 26 *Estoy medio adormida. No sé ... Una cosa nueva ...* **(36–115)**

2.917 Answers to questions. SEC 38 ¿ *Qué ha sucedido ?* — *Una tragedia.* **(22–238)**

2.93 In the abbreviated style of telegrams, newspaper headlines, advertisements, etc. ABC 40 *Dantzig, en manos de los hitleristas.* (7–299)

2.95 The independent subject of the sentence. A characteristic trait of Spanish is the use of a substantive at the beginning of the sentence to present emotionally the theme of interest. This substantive, which is always followed by a pause, is syntactically independent of what follows. But it may be logically the subject or object of the following sentence.

In extreme cases, it may even have no logical relationship with the following discourse.

2.95 The substantive precedes a direct question and is the subject of the verb of the question.   MUJ 7 *¿ Tú qué sabes ?*   (26–66)

2.97 The substantive precedes a statement or command.

2.971 It is the logical subject of a following indirect question.   JOA 26 *También ese doctor yo no sé qué doctor será.*   (3–4)

2.972 It is the logical subject of a following subject clause.   FAL 17 *Miloshin, se veía que quería convencer a María.*   (11–16)

2.973 It is the logical subject of a following object clause.   RAN 15 *La revolución supongo que, igual que hace siete años, será una cosa inminente.*
(6–7)

2.975 It is the logical subject of an adverbial clause.   IGN 27 *Yo hacía varios años que no le veía.*   (6–6)

2.977 It is the logical subject of a following relative clause.   IBA 32 *Yo, señor, — continuó el viejo — lo que más siento es que no veré en qué acaba todo esto.*   (4–7)

2.98 It is a logical object of a following clause.

2.981 Of a main verb.   RIC 272 *— Los versos, déjalos — dijo Silda.*   (4–4)

2.985 Of a subordinate verb.   ZAM 27 *Los suyos, los que su padre le compró, claro es que los tiene en su casa.*   (3–4)

2.99 Substantives in an absolute construction.   Substantives are used with adjectival expressions, adjectives, and participles in absolute constructions which are independent of the rest of the sentence and whose relation to the other elements of the sentence is understandable only in the light of the context.   These constructions are discussed under adjectives and participles and need not be further illustrated here;   see 25.39 and 38.54.

NOUNS

3. A word which is used as the name of a person, thing, or abstraction is called a noun. Nouns are in function substantives. As a matter of identification, it may be said that words which are adjectivally modified are nouns. Thus an adjective, an infinitive, or a clause, if modified by the article, becomes a noun.

3.1 Gender. All nouns have gender, either masculine or feminine. Since any attempt to add to the materials on gender which are found in dictionaries would have made it necessary to list the gender of all nouns, the present study has nothing to contribute on the subject.

3.2 Number. Nouns may be singular or plural.

3.21 Special uses of the singular.

3.223 A noun modified by the indefinite adjective *alguno* sometimes has the force of a plural. BEN 62 *Alguna vez se recoge lo que se arrojó al viento.* (19–26)

3.23 Special uses of the plural.

3.231 A plural noun has the force of a singular. This group includes only nouns which have a truly singular force and does not involve collectives of the type of *los cabellos.* RET 128 *Gutierre murió por fatal* quid pro quo *de galantería y de celos.* ([42]–132)

The commonest nouns are: *amores* (8–17), *celos* (14–26), *cielos* (3–3), *fuerzas* (3–3), *horas* (9–16), *mientes* (4–4), *noches* (8–10).

3.233 The plural of an abstract noun usually has the force of a concrete illustration of the abstraction, distributed over a series of acts or expressions, or observed in a series of persons or cases. SIE 30 *Déjese usted de locuras.* (22–43)

3.235 The plural of a masculine noun may stand for a masculine and feminine singular. STE 19 *Entró a la casa de sus tíos.* (26–70)

3.24 Distributive use. When it is necessary to indicate that a given singular notion is applicable to each one of a group, Spanish usually uses the singular, especially if the notion involved is a part of the body. With notions more remotely associated with a person, such as articles of clothing or other personal attributes, physical and mental, the plural is sometimes used.

3.241 With the singular. FOM 25 *Varios de los chicos empezaron a jaranear cierta noche, produciendo truenos de ventosidad con la boca.* (29–69)

3.243 With the plural. ABU 194 *Creo notar una agitación de cosas blancas, como si me saludaran con los pañuelos.* (4–4)

3.3 Uses of nouns. The regular uses of nouns have already been discussed under substantives. The present section is concerned with a few special uses of nouns.

3.31 "Cognate accusative." An intransitive verb sometimes is used with a noun as object which expresses the same idea as the verb. This type of object is called an "inner object" or cognate accusative. PAT 18 *Vivía una vida inquietante.* (8–10)

3.311 Similarly with a noun of closely related meaning to the meaning of the verb. UGA 8 *Los jóvenes y los niños dormían la siesta.* (9–13)

The only common verb is *dormir* (*la siesta*) (8–10).

3.313 With transitive verbs, the use of an object of cognate meaning is merely a matter of style. DEB 55 *Cantaba aquella canción melancólica.*
(Not counted)

3.5 Nouns used in apposition.

3.51 The same noun, modified, is repeated. A stylistic device, common in some writers. NER 45 *Verán la onda, la onda incansable que va y viene.* (7–24)

3.52 Noun in apposition, introduced by *de.* The use of *de* to connect two nouns of place or time which are in reality identical has long been established in Spanish. RET 35 *La ciudad de Montevideo.* (*)

3.521 With nouns referring to persons. LLA 11 *El ángel de la señorita Veneranda.* (8–16)

3.523 Similarly in direct address and in exclamations. ZAM 50 *¡Qué lástima de hombre!* (3–9)

3.53 As a predicate appositive introduced by *de.* LIN 94 *No lo parecía de soltero.* (14–34)

For a similar use of adjectives, see 25.371.

3.6 Nouns used adjectivally. Nouns and adjectives are closely related and often identical in form. Any attempt to distinguish between the two must rest upon an arbitrary assumption that the normal use of a given word is as a noun or as an adjective. With some words this is simple; with others, like *amigo,* it must be a matter of opinion. At least it is important to point out the dual functions which some of these words perform.

3.61 Unmodified, as attributives. PEL 464 *Las Rimas del pintor poeta.* (37–120)

3.62 Unmodified, as complement. A noun used as subjective or objective complement is regularly adjectival when it indicates the class to which the subject or object belongs. IDO 116 *Se conoce que usted es artista.* (*)

For details, see 35.5.

3.63 After *desde, después de.* RUB 23 *Desde niño quedó huérfano.* (5–9)

For a similar use with adjectives, see 25.373, 25.375.

3.64 Modified by an adverbial expression.

3.641 Positive. VIG 71 *Don Fermín, el anarquista místico, algo discípulo de Rosseau.* (25–38)

3.643 Comparative. OCC 194 *¿ No serán hombres más hombres ?* (10–12)

3.645 Superlative. RAN 103 *Lo más siglo XIII de Santiago es el viaje.* (3–4)

3.7 Nouns used adverbially. Nouns are often used, particularly when modified, to express adverbial notions of time, place, etc.

3.71 Extent or measure of space. REY 104 *Arrastran unos metros la embarcación.* (14–16)

3.72 Definite or indefinite point of time. PAT 204 *Se amaban como el primer día.* (60–579)

3.73 Duration of time. SON 38 *Calló y estuvo largo espacio con los ojos cerrados.* (50–266)

3.731 The duration may be indicated as prior to or subsequent to the action or state by an adverb or preposition. UNA 89 *Pocos días después se celebraba el matrimonio.* (45–127)

The commonest expressions are: *antes* (14–20), *antes de* (7–9), *atrás* (6–9), *después* (**32–68**), *después de* (6–9), *más tarde* (10–10).

3.74 Price or value. DIV 10 *Cuesta quince mil quinientos francos.* Chiefly with *costar* and *valer.* (15–20)

PERSONAL PRONOUNS

4. The personal pronouns have preserved to a greater extent than any of the other substantives the original Latin distinctions of case. They must therefore be studied in three different functions, each with corresponding differences of form: stressed, as subject of the sentence; stressed, as object of a preposition; and unstressed, as direct or indirect object of a verb.

As Subject of a Verb

4.1 Forms. The regular forms for the subject pronouns, with their corresponding frequencies, are: *yo* (**57–1956**), *tú* (**46–914**), *él* (**58–534**), *ella* (**54–422**), *ello* (**22–31**), *nosotros* (**46–116**), *vosotros* (**26–50**), *ellos*, (**34–78**), *ellas* (**30–48**).

4.2 Substitutes for the regular forms. The regular forms for the first and second person are frequently replaced by other devices.

4.3 First person.

4.31 First person plural for first person singular. In literary style, particularly in newspapers (if they can be called literary), it is the practice to use the first person plural instead of the first person singular, the author modestly hiding his identity in the group. ALT 186 *Indicamos más arriba los abusos de algunos oficiales.* (Not separately counted)

4.32 un servidor. Only in colloquial style. ARN 52 *Por lo tanto un servidor ha amainao y entro en la calle de Fuencarral.* (6–10)

4.33 servidor de usted. Only in answers to a question, in the sense of "it is I (or me)". IGN 52 *Usted, el señor Sambenítez, ¿ verdad ? — Servidor de usted.* (4–5)

4.34 uno (una). Only in colloquial style. SJQ 118 *Ha de saber usía que aunque una viste de pañolón, una es decente.* (4–9)

4.4 Second person. Forms of address. To illustrate more fully the various forms of address, examples of the use of *tú* and *vosotros* are included with the substitutes for the second person.

4.41 *tú*. *Tú* is the intimate form of address; it is used in all cases in which in English a speaker would use the Christian name of the person whom he was addressing. Differences of address dependent upon differences of social station no longer are current in Spanish. But there is a very real difference between the intimacy conveyed by *tú* and the formality conveyed by *usted*.

4.411 Between equals. JES 25 *Tienes razón, chico. Tú llegarás lejos.*

4.412 Addressing a servant. ZAM 76 *¿ Tú también tienes familia ? — Sí, señorita. — Les querrás mucho. — Sí, señorita, ¡ figúrese usted !*

4.413 Addressing a child. IBA 383 *¡ Al papá, Isidrito! ¡ salúdale!*

4.414 Addressing an animal. PAT 214 *Ven al regazo de tu Meg; puss, puss.*

4.415 In lofty literary style, approaching the diction of poetry. MGR 37 *¡ Oh, tú, silencio sublime, que cubres con tu manto los sollozos del dolor!* (This is from a newspaper.)

4.416 In prayers. FOM 223 « *Padre nuestro, que estás en los cielos . . .* »

4.42 *vosotros.* In origin, *vosotros* referred only to a class (like French *vous autres Américains*). It is now used to address two or more persons who would be addressed with *tú* as individuals. In Spanish America *vosotros* is almost unknown in current speech, even the plural of *tú* being *ustedes.*

4.421 Addressing two persons. IGN 26 (*Carolina y Natalia casi se desvanecen.*) — *¿ Vosotras le conocéis ?*

4.423 Addressing more than two persons. LUG 367 *No nos felicitéis, amigos. Los dichosos sois vosotros.*

4.425 Addressing an audience or imaginary readers of a book. PEQ 163 *Vosotros os sentáis en un terrero.*

4.426 Occasionally even in advertisements. MGR 42 *Pedid detalles al Director, calle de Floridablanca, número 119.*

4.43 *usted* (*ustedes*). *Usted* is the formal form of address. It is used in all cases where in English the speaker would use the family name of the person whom he was addressing.

4.431 Addressing a superior, respectfully. IBA 35 *No hay que enfadarse, caballeros; tómenme ustedes el nombre.*

4.432 Addressing an equal, courteously. ORR 95 *Veo que usted me conocía, señora.*

4.433 Addressing a servant, aloofly or considerately. LIN 11 *Lléveselo usted a su cuarto ahora mismo.*

4.434 Addressing the reader in advertisements. This is the regular form. BYN 4 *Use hojas Gillette legítimas.*

4.436 In Spanish America, as a plural of *tú*. UGA 23 *¿ Cuándo te casas ?*

— preguntó Melián. — Eres el más feliz de los Tenorios — concluyó García.
— No me hablen ustedes de cosas tristes — contestó.

4.437 Even in address to imaginary readers. NER 22 *La medium era*
parlante. (*Ustedes saben que hay mediums* auditivos, videntes, *etc.*)

4.439 Alternation of *tú* and *usted*. The changing form of address is often
a subtle indication of changes in the state of mind of the speaker, as in
the following passage in which a married woman discovers a former
lover of hers making love to her daughter. SIE 85 *¿ Usted ? . . . ¿ Tú ? . . .*
Caballero, no sé con qué derecho se atreve usted a venir a esta casa. (Total
of all expressed forms of *usted* and *ustedes:* **48–2104**)

4.44 usté. This is the normal pronunciation of *usted*, but it is so written
only in reproductions of colloquial style. WAS 6 *¿ Usté quería comprar*
un poco de pan ? (11–199)

4.45 ustés. Even more colloquial. ART 6 Ustés *se pasan las horas del calor*
a la sombra. (4–18)

4.46 vos for *tú*.

4.461 In Argentina and Uruguay *vos* is the common form of address in
colloquial style. Object pronouns and possessives remain *te, tu,* etc.
The verbs, with special exceptions, end in *–ás, –és, –ís,* in the indicative
and in *–á, –é, –í,* in the imperative. URU 21 *¿ De qué te reís, vos ?*

4.462 In imitations of the archaic style, *vos* is still occasionally found
in Spain. The object pronouns and possessives are *os, vuestro,* etc.
SON 30 *¿ Vos, sin duda, sois el enviado de Su Santidad . . . ?*

(Total: 6–137)

4.471 First person plural for second person singular. A form of indi-
rection common in all the modern languages. MUJ 15 *Oye, hijita, supongo*
que ya estamos preparando el equipaje.

4.473 Third person plural for second person singular. Another loose
avoidance of direct address. JOA 76 *No sé cuando se me va a perder la pa-*
ciencia a mí. — Cuando te mueras. — Fíjense cómo está todo esto. — La
culpa es tuya. — Tienes razón.

4.475 Reflexive for second person singular. PIN 20 *¡ Cuidado con lo que*
se replica y llégate a chillar con las mujeres !

4.481 su excelencia (su merced, su señoría). Still occasionally used in
addressing titled personages or. public officials. SON 120 *Vengan por aquí*
sus Excelencias. (7–8)

4.483 vuecencia. An abridged form of *vuestra excelencia.* ABU 404 *Nada*
tiene Vuecencia que agradecernos. (4–6)

4.485 *el señor* (*el señorito*). Used by servants in addressing their employer. TRI 131 *¿ No va el señor con madama ?* (14–29)

4.487 *la señora* (*la señorita*). Like *el señor.* SAS 71 *¿ Cómo dijo la señora ?* (6–9)

4.49 General commands. Commands and instructions which are issued to a group (readers, listeners, etc.) are usually expressed either by the reflexive or by an infinitive.

4.491 Reflexive. VIG 35 *Recuérdese el buen ejemplo de Charles Maurras.* (23–40)

4.492 Infinitive. ABU 409 (*Gregoria, golpeando la puerta.*) — *Abrir ... Abre, Senén.* Illustrating the difference between an indefinite command: "Open, somebody, anybody," and a specific command addressed to an individual. Negative. MGR 44 *No fiarse de nombres imitados.* (10–20)

4.493 Second plural. The following advertisement illustrates three forms of general command. MGR 21 *Hipofosfitos Salud. Bebed de este manantial. Cuando trate usted de combatir anemia, no dude en utilizar el poderoso jarabe. Pídase en farmacias.*

4.495 Third plural. PAT 197 *Espero una carta importante — advirtió Alberto. — Pues que se la envíen a mi casa.* (14–25)

5. Uses of the subject pronoun. The subject pronouns are used as subject of a finite verb, as subject of an infinitive, and in many constructions without a verb, elliptical, explanatory, or absolute.

5.1 As subject of a finite verb. Since Spanish has preserved the personal endings of finite verb forms, the subject pronouns are not normally necessary to determine the meaning of the sentence. ABU 18 *Puede que aciertes. Ya son grandecitas.* (*)

5.11 When the subject pronouns are expressed they are therefore always emphatic, that is to say, stressed forms. The most frequent situation in which they require emphasis is when there is a contrast of subjects, expressed or implied. There is little evidence of the use of subject pronouns to avoid ambiguity, except that *usted* (*ustedes*) are more frequently expressed than any other form. In this case, the practice may be due as well to courtesy. ZUN 47 *Yo, en cambio, al salir a la calle, me he encontrado a un conocido mío.* IBA 33 *¿ Ven ustedes esta prenda ?* (60–3696)

5.12 The subject is compound, one or both the subjects being a personal pronoun. URU 40 *Usted y yo vivimos dos vidas completamente distintas.* (33–79)

5.13 A subject expressed with the imperative.   SEC 21 *Pregunta tú.*
(24–60)

5.131 Rarely also with a negative command in the second person.   JOA
83 *No me atormentéis más vosotros, hijos.*   (3–4)

5.135 For the use and omission of *usted* (*ustedes*) in commands in the
subjunctive, see 29.183.

5.14 A subject of the third person, not referring to a person, is expressed.

5.15 *él, ella,* etc. referring to a thing.   There is usually an element of
personification in the sentence.   ROD 14 *Conviene mantener viva en nuestra
alma la idea que ella está en perpetuo aprendizaje.*   (11–18)

5.16 *ello.*

5.161 Summing up an unnamed idea which is conveyed by a preceding
clause.   NER 38 *Donde había un tesoro había un alma en pena.   Ello era
elemental.*   (16–20)

5.162 In the set phrase *ello es que,* "the fact is that".   UNA 86 *Y ello
fué que al pasar un día Tristán, se le vino encima el agua del riego.* (6–7)

5.2 The subject pronoun is modified.

5.21 By *mismo.*   RAN 84 *Me la tuvo que dar él mismo.*   (**38–94**)

5.211 With a reflexive verb, *mismo* may modify the subject, rather than
a stressed form of the reflexive object pronoun.   BRA 158 *Necesitamos en-
gañarnos nosotros mismos.*   See also 6.221.   (7–11)

5.213 In dialect, the old form *mesmo* is still preserved.   TIG 20 *¿ Sábeslo
tú mesmo ?*   (3–5)

5.23 By an indefinite adjective.

5.231 *solo.*   DEB 12 *¿ Pero yo solo voy a almorzar ?*   (**20–27**)

5.233 *todo.*   ZUN 35 *Casi todas ellas sabían a aceite.*   (**24–40**)

5.24 By an appositive qualifying adjective or past participle.   LIN 26
Yo, enamorado, prescindiría de todo.   (4–9)

5.25 By a parenthetical relative clause.   PEL 32 *Yo, que te lo debo todo,
estoy obligado a ser liberal contigo.*   (**46–169**)

5.26 By a noun in apposition.   ORT 77 *Por tierras de Sigüenza he hecho
yo, Rubín de Cendoya, un viaje sentimental.*   Especially in the type
nosotras las mujeres. (5–5)   (19–27)

For the use of a noun in apposition with an unexpressed subject, see
36.8.

5.3 A subject pronoun used for emphasis when the subject is expressed by a noun or another pronoun.

5.31 With a noun subject. The subject pronoun is usually modified. JIM 83 *Y Platero tiembla de nuevo todo él.* (5–5)

5.32 With a relative pronoun subject. OCC 188 *Alejarse de los cuidados que uno lleva arraigados en sí y que ellos, nada más que ellos, constituyen la totalidad de nuestro ser.* (3–3)

5.35 Two subject pronouns, each modified by an adjective or participle, are in apposition with an expressed subject. JIM 116 *Pasaron las alegres parejas, ellos alegres, valientes ellas.* (8–11)

5.4 With non-finite forms of the verb.

5.41 As subject of an infinitive.

5.411 The infinitive replaces a subordinate clause. UNA 153 *¿ Me quieres por mí o por ser yo cosa tuya ?* (26–45)

5.412 The infinitive is used in an exclamation. MUJ 20 *Aquí se vivía, ¡ y yo sin verlo !* (7–7)

5.42 In absolute constructions, with a participle or adverb.

5.421 With a present participle. MUJ 6 *Estando tú, sobran los libros.* (13–18)

5.422 The pronoun expressed with the participle is identical with the subject of the main verb. STE 22 *Por detrás asoman muchos otros, mirando también ellos con gran interés.* (3–3)

5.425 With a past participle. The subject may be identical with that of the main verb. IBA 363 *Ahora, retirado él, tenía una tiendecita en el cerro de los Corvos.* (4–4)

5.427 With an adverb. TRI 41 *Pasaron el fumadero, ella delante.* (3–3)

5.5 As subjective complement. RUS 139 *El primero que te ha de guardar soy yo.* Especially without expressed subject of the type *soy yo.* For the agreement of the verb, see 36.7. (31–94)

5.6 Used without a verb, in elliptical expressions.

5.61 In coordinated expressions.

5.611 After a copulative. ABC 27 *Su señoría defiende a los patronos, y yo a los obreros.* (25–54)

5.612 After an adversative. IGN 44 *Yo no soy nadie, ¡ en cambio ella !* (5–6)

5.615 Without connective. URU 67 *Lo decía él, yo no.* (11–14)

5.62 After expressions of exception.

5.621 *menos.* SIE 84 *En esta casa todos me quieren mal. — Menos yo.* (4–6)

5.623 *sino.* FOM 98 *¿ Quién, sino él, podía adivinarlo ?* (3–3)

5.63 After expressions of comparison.

5.631 *como.* RUB 17 *Tú, como ellas, eres llama del infinito amor.* (**52–146**)

5.64 *que.*

5.641 After a comparative adjective or adverb. MGR 37 *Te sentiste más pequeño que ellos.* (**36–98**)

5.643 After *antes.* JIM 38 *Si te mueres antes que yo, no irás a la marisma inmensa.* (9–9)

5.645 After *el (lo) mismo.* LUG 146 *Aquí le jugamos para entretenernos. — Lo mismo que yo.* (7–7)

5.647 After other expressions implying comparison (*contrario, primero, igual, otro*). ORT 120 *Yo hallo ante mí algo como distinto y otro que yo.* (5–6)

5.65 After a relative pronoun. ART 32 *Diera cuanto poseo por lograr de Amelia lo que usted.* (4–5)

5.7 In exclamations.

5.71 In questions and answers, in conversation. STE 23 *¿ Cuántos años tienes ? — ¿ Yo ? . . . Voy a cumplir seis.* (**36–270**)

5.72 Modified by an adjective. LLA 64 *Yo he hecho siempre lo que he querido. — ¡ Dichoso usted!* Compare with this construction *¡ Pobre de mí!;* see 6.9. (6–7)

5.8 After *entre.* After the preposition *entre* a personal pronoun with another substantive normally has the subject form. This construction is probably derived from the use of *entre* to introduce a real subject; see 2.113. REY 106 *Entre Diz y yo hemos llenado el fogón de tablas.* (6–9)

5.9 *tú* as a substantive. In a number of expressions (*hablar de tú, tratar de tú,* etc.) *tú* is used after a preposition as a substantive, meaning "the name of *tú*". PAT 208 *Quiero que me trates de tú.* (5–6)

PERSONAL PRONOUNS USED AS OBJECT OF A PREPOSITION

6. The personal pronouns used as object of a preposition are always stressed. They are used after both simple and compound prepositions.

6.1 Forms. In form, they are identical with the personal pronouns used as subject, except in the first and second person singular. There is also a special form for the reflexive pronoun. IBA 363 *Me preguntó por ti.*

The frequencies of the different forms are as follows: *mí* (**56–544**), *ti* (**42–200**), *usted* (**43–448**), *usté* (9–49), *usía* (3–18), *vos* (for *ti*) (3–32), *él* (**58–548**), *ella* (**60–448**), *ello* (**44–104**), *sí* (singular and plural) (**34–172**), *nosotros* (**42–160**), *vosotros* (**20–45**), *ustedes* (**31–89**), *ellos* (**56–222**), *ellas* (**46–134**).

6.11 *él* (*ella*, etc.) used for *sí*. Theoretically, *sí* is used whenever the pronominal object of the third person is identical with the subject of the verb. There are, however, occasional examples of the non-reflexive form. VIG 115 *No quiere darles madrastra en ella misma.*   (8–8)

6.16 Special forms with *con*. Instead of *con mí, con ti, con sí,* Spanish developed from Latin *mecum*, etc. special forms.

> **conmigo.** JIM 28 *Vente tú conmigo.*   (**41–103**)
> **contigo.** MAY 11 *Sólo me casaré contigo.*   (**22–70**)
> **consigo.** ALT 185 *El Fuero general no trajo consigo la unificación jurídica.*   (**10–11**)

6.2 General uses.

6.21 The pronoun is modified. The personal pronoun may be modified by an intensive adjective, by an indefinite adjective, or by a noun used in apposition.

6.22 By an intensive adjective.

6.221 *mismo.* Especially with reflexive forms. BEN 40 *Heliodoro vive en sí mismo.*   (**37–81**)

6.223 Less often with non-reflexive forms. IDO 110 *De su homenaje a Teresa Alberto se enorgulleció, como si lo rindieran a él mismo.*   (18–27)

6.225 *propio.* JES 146 *Acaso estoy viendo visiones — se dijo para tranquilizarse a sí propio*   (11–14)

6.23 By an indefinite adjective.

6.235 *solo.* ROM 103 *Ésta, por sí sola, sobrepuja a todo lo antes aquí citado.*   (13–19)

6.237 *todo.* UGA 10 *En todo ello había quizá cierta condescendencia.*   (17–18)

6.238 A numeral. UNA 157 *Ahí les dejo a ustedes dos solos.*   (4–4)

6.239 The definite article may replace the personal pronoun, forming an indefinite pronoun. IGN 57 *Entre los dos se estableció una gran corriente de simpatía* (instead of *entre ellos dos*). (3–4)

6.24 By a noun in apposition. TRI 119 *D'Annunzio es el exquisito novelista de nosotros los* sportsmen. The noun is normally a noun of class. (4–7)

6.4 Special uses of the pronoun of the third person.

6.41 The masculine and feminine forms for the third person refer to both persons and things. WAS 3 *En la pálida cara de él advertíase la fatiga de una larga jornada.* SON 187 *Abrí el pliego y pasé por él una mirada.* (*)

6.421 *ello*. The neuter *ello* normally sums up an idea expressed in a preceding clause. PAL 18 *Yo estaba en el Paraíso, me hallaba absolutamente convencido de ello.* (42–77)

6.423 Less frequently its antecedent is a neuter pronoun. RUS 29 *Como no lo haces, teniendo poder para ello, tienes el mismo goce.* (5–5)

6.5 Special uses after *a*. The personal pronouns are used after *a* not only to indicate the goal of motion (persons or places), but also as the stressed forms for the direct and indirect object. In the latter case, they are usually accompanied by the unstressed forms of the personal object pronoun, although they may be used alone, especially in the case of *usted*. They are also used in elliptical constructions and in conversational style, without an expressed verb.

6.51 Expressing destination or goal of motion.

6.511 Persons. LIN 52 *¡Pues a mí podía venir un señor marido con esos tonos!* (25–57)

6.513 Places. REY 150 *¿Queréis que intentemos huir, cuando lleguemos a ella* [*la isla*]? (19–23)

6.6 As object, direct or indirect, of an expressed verb.

6.611 With an unstressed form of the pronoun. URU 42 *Me aflige a mí también.* (60–255)

6.613 Especially with *usted* (*usté*, etc.). PAT 197 *Nancy, Meg y Ben le están esperando a usted.* (33–228)

6.614 The object is compound and the unstressed pronoun sums up the two objects. IGN 17 *Conchita nos llevó al Golf a Natalia y a mí.* (8–12)

6.621 Without an unstressed pronoun, alone. ROD 20 *Cada tribu del Ática ha contribuido a él.* Rare with antecedent which is a person. (12–15)

6.623 With *usted* (*usté*, etc.). FOM 94 *Papá y mamá me envían a saludar a ustedes.*   (21–47)

6.63 As indirect object, when the direct object is a personal pronoun, not of the third person, especially when the verb is used reflexively. SON 31 *De niño te parecías mucho a ella, ahora no.*   (25–40)

6.7 As object, direct or indirect, without an expressed verb.

6.71 In elliptical expressions.

6.711 In coordinated expressions. SIE 53 *¿ No te hace gracia? Ni a mí tampoco.*   (9–13)

6.715 After comparatives. *como.* SEC 39 *A nadie como a ti son aplicables los divinos versos del maestro Garcilaso.*   (6–8)

6.716 *que.* SJQ 46 *No se la dé a nadie más que a mí.*   (7–9)

6.72 In conversational style.

6.721 In questions and answers. ART 45 *¿ Qué te ha parecido la comedia? — ¿ A mí?*   (23–63)

6.723 In exclamations. TIG 28 *¡ A ella! ¡ A ella!* Usually used to incite or urge to action.   (8–13)

6.8 Dependent on a word other than the verb.

6.81 Dependent on an adjective. RIC 19 *Sentíase superior a sí mismo.*
(14–15)

6.82 Dependent on a past participle. LLA 82 *¿ Dónde iré yo, que no vayan conmigo mis tormentos, tan pegados a mí como la joroba?*   (5–5)

6.9 *¡ pobre de mí!* The stressed personal pronoun is sometimes used with *de* after an adjective or interjection in exclamatory expressions. The construction is a type of apposition. PIN 76 *¡ Pobre de mí!* (13–23)

PERSONAL PRONOUNS USED AS DIRECT OR INDIRECT
OBJECT OF A VERB

7. The personal pronouns used as direct or indirect object of a verb are unstressed forms which are now always attached to the verb, either as proclitics or as enclitics. The forms are derived from the Latin accusative and dative cases, but a variety of forces, particularly that of analogy, has tended to wipe out original distinctions of case, with the result that it is often difficult to determine whether a given form is used as a direct or an indirect object. And this difficulty is increased by the identity of form for the direct and indirect objects referring to persons when nouns are used, both being expressed by *a*, so that it is impossible to determine whether a given verb is transitive or intransitive. Since the particular functions of each pronoun are so closely related to its forms, it is necessary to analyze the use of each of the forms.

7.1 Use of the different forms.

7.11 First person. In the first person a single form serves for both direct and indirect object.

7.111 Singular, direct object. *me.* REY 134 *Todos me temen.* **(57–1254)**

7.113 Indirect object. *me.* BEN 14 *No me hables.* **(60–1941)**

7.115 Plural, direct object. *nos.* JIM 82 *Lo lejano nos vuelve a lo real.*
(54–348)

7.116 Indirect object. *nos.* ALT 10 *Ofrécenos este ejemplo.* **(56–354)**

7.12 Second person. Again there is no distinction in form between direct and indirect object.

7.121 Singular, direct object. *te.* MAY 8 *Yo te adoro.* **(54–495)**

7.123 Indirect object. *te.* URU 53 *Voy a serte sincero.* **(48–758)**

7.124 As direct or indirect object with *vos* as subject. URU 21 *¿ De qué te reís, vos ?* Colloquial in Argentina and Uruguay. **(4–123)**

7.125 Plural, direct object. *os.* LIN 46 *Mi mujer os llevaba al palco de la Marquesa.* **(24–96)**

7.126 Indirect object. *os.* RUB 84 *Thermidor os enseñará su región.*
(26–112)

7.13 Third person. The pronouns of the third person present a number of special problems. In the earliest period of Spanish, the direct objects were *lo, la, los, las,* and the indirect objects, *le, les.* But the identity of form for direct and indirect objects in the first and second persons, lead to the use of *le* (like *me, te*) as direct as well as indirect object. And similarly in the plural, *les* became a direct as well as an indirect object form. But here the analogy of *nos, os* tended to preserve the use of *los* as direct object. Finally, the need for a specifically feminine form for the indirect object, lead to the use of *la, las* as indirect as well as direct feminine forms. In all cases, the neuter object is expressed by *lo.*

7.131 At the present time, there are three types of usage common in Spanish. In the first, *le* is used as a direct object with masculine antecedents, whether they be persons or things. This type is largely limited geographically to the north of Spain. In the second, *lo* is used as a direct object with masculine antecedents, whether they be persons or things. This is the primitive construction and is most widely used in Andalusia and in Spanish America. Finally, in the third type, *le* is used when the antecedent is a masculine person, and *lo* when the antecedent is a masculine thing. The usage is never a rule; if the name of a thing is personified, it may be represented by *le;* if the name of a person is "depersonalized" by a verb which is normally used with a thing as object, it may be represented by *lo.* Moreover stylistic considerations of sound, variety, and the like may determine the choice of form. This type of usage is the most widely current of the three. In the use of *la* and *las* as indirect object, the practice appears to be a personal matter, the forms appearing sporadically in all parts of Spanish-speaking territory. In the plural, *los* is everywhere the predominant form for the direct object; when *les* is used, it normally refers to persons, and not to things.

7.14 Direct object, referring to singular masculine persons.

7.141 *le.* WAS 21 *Yo había nacido para hombre de negocios, — dijo a quien le quiso oír.* **(58–942)**

7.142 The antecedent is *usted.* ART 34 *Le juzgo como usted merece.* (25–99)

7.145 The antecedent is a male animal. BYN 1 *El Rey macedonio puso en libertad al enorme elefante apresado y le consagró al sol.* (6–10)

7.149 *se le ve.* With a reflexive indefinite subject. PEL 468 *Se le abruma con los grandes nombres de Góngora y Quevedo.* Note that this is the regular construction and that *se lo* is not found referring to persons. (21–30)

7.151 *lo.* VIG 115 *El viudo se enamora de ella y ella lo rechaza.* **(48–444)**

7.152 The antecedent is *usted.* SJQ 31 *Soñaba este hombre con tenerlo a usted aquí siquiera quince días.* (11–30)

7.155 The antecedent is a male animal. BYN 1 *La criada de Molière era la encargada de llevar al teatro al animalito y de cuidarlo.* (10–26)

7.16 Referring to plural masculine persons.

7.161 *les.* ZAM 65 *Les conozco; unos botarates aficionados al juego.* (25–52)

7.162 The antecedent is *ustedes.* BRA 48 *Les encantará a ustedes.* (6–9)

7.164 The antecedent is compound and both masculine and feminine. ZAM 76 *¿ Les querrás mucho [a tu madre y tus hermanos]?*   (7–10)

7.165 The antecedent is a group of male animals.   PIN 96 *¿ Ha visto, ni en sueños, que las liebres les muerdan a los galgos ?*   (3–3)

7.169 *se les ve.* This is the regular construction, and not *se los ve.* JAN 103 *Allí se les trató con bondad y confianza.*   (8–11)

7.171 *los.* LIN 96 *A los hombres hay que tratarlos como hombres.* **(52–226)**

7.172 The antecedent is *ustedes.*   URU 56 *Me da mucha pena verlos a usted y a Julio como si fueran extraños.*   (6–7)

7.174 The antecedent is compound and both masculine and feminine. BEN 7 *En todas partes los tomaban por padre e hija.*   (7–12)

7.18 Referring to singular feminine persons.

7.181 *la.* IBA 368 *Feli iba muy mal; no la había visto.*   **(57–876)**

7.182 The antecedent is *usted.*   UGA 32 *Me parece que es usted divina y que merece que la quieran mucho.*   **(20–70)**

7.186 *se la ve.* DEB 91 *Y así se la veía siempre.*   (11–12)

7.188 *le.* FAL 168 *Aquel amigo de su hermano le atraía. La excitaba el saber de aquellas confidencias simples.* This use of *le* for *la* marks the complete assimilation of *le* to the pattern of *me, te.*   (8–8)

7.19 Referring to plural feminine persons.

7.191 *las.* SON 32 *Las saludé a todas.*   **(43–134)**

7.192 The antecedent is *ustedes.*   LUG 154 *¡ Dios nuestro Señor las acompañe, señoritiñas!*   (3–4)

7.21 Referring to singular masculine things.

7.211 *le.* ABC 26 *Es el medicamento que usted necesita. Si le toma esta misma noche, conseguirá el descanso de un sueño tranquilo.*   **(21–62)**

7.213 *lo.* RIC 269 *¿ Serán estos libros malos ? — preguntó, cogiendo uno, sin atreverse a abrirlo.*   **(60–615)**

7.22 Referring to plural masculine things.

7.221 *los.* IDO 5 *Si quitaba los ojos del paisaje, los ponía en el hermano sentado junto a él.* With a compound subject, masculine and feminine. MUJ 28 *Tráeme toca y abrigo. — Los traje ya.*   **(60–285)**

7.223 *les.* REY 116 *Se dedican a secar los fusiles y las armas por si les ha atacado la humedad.* Masculine and feminine as well as masculine. (4–4)

7.23 Referring to singular feminine things.

7.231 *la*. FOM 90 *Voy a traer una tacita de café. — No, iré a tomarla yo mismo.* (60–588)

7.239 *se la ve*. PEL 245 *Esta poesía resulta empalagosísima, cuando se la ve reunida en un libro.* (3–3)

7.24 Referring to plural feminine things.

7.241 *las*. PAL 130 *Arranqué dos peras, las oculté en el bolsillo y vuelvo rápidamente.* (47–184)

7.25 Referring to an unnamed antecedent and hence neuter. The only form is *lo*. The chief uses are as follows.

7.251 The antecedent is a general idea expressed in a preceding clause. PEQ 35 *Todos los días le llevaban del pueblo unos periódicos; yo lo recuerdo.* (60–759)

7.252 Especially after *decir, saber*, etc. MAY 11 *Ya lo sé, respondió.* (42–308)

7.253 Occasionally *lo* is omitted in this situation. JES 30 *Pero un poco . . . ¿Cómo diré? . . . un poco masculina.* (6–7)

7.254 The antecedent is a neuter pronoun. ROD 16 *¿Por qué lo que así respetas en el juego, lo desconoces en la acción?* (44–140)

7.255 The antecedent is a series of nouns, often summed up by *todo*. LLA 4 *Mis libros, mis papeles, mis pasos, todo lo espías.* (3–4)

7.256 The antecedent is a single feminine or plural noun. This is probably not a case of lack of agreement in the logical sense, but a mental transfer which replaces the specific noun with an unnamed condition or state. FOM 92 *La esposa confesaba su postración, achacándolo a la caminata del día antes.* (5–5)

7.257 Anticipates a general idea expressed in a following clause. ROM 21 *Digámoslo de una vez, ninguna de ellas está completa.* (19–39)

7.26 With indefinite force, no antecedent expressed or implied.

7.261 *la*. SIE 26 *A un hombre soy capaz de perdonarle lo que sea; ¡pero mujer que me la hace, me la paga!* (16–22)

7.262 *las*. ORR 170 *San Juan se las daba de Tenorio.* (17–29)

7.265 *lo*. ABU 412 *Pues, señor, D. Carmelo lo ha tomado con gana.* (18–36)

7.27 With partitive force, in the sense of "one," "some," "any," etc. The construction is found only with *tener* and impersonal *haber*, and is most common in the negative.

7.271 *la.*   IGN 89 *Yo tengo plena confianza en usted. — Pero yo no la tengo en mí, querido duque.*   (13–16)

7.272 Modified by an adjective.   RET 138 *En el edificio puede verse una colección de yesos tan bella que no la tiene igual ninguna ciudad de Alemania.*   (3–3)

7.273 *las.*   ABU 418 *¿ Tabernas ? Por aquí no las hay.*   (11–14)

7.274 Modified.   PAX 343 *No las hay mejores en toda la plaza.*   (4–5)

7.275 *lo.*   UNA 97 *Pero lo que no sabemos es quién sea su padre, ni si lo tiene.*   (7–10)

7.276 Modified.   LIN 34 *¿ Os habéis olvidado del paño ? — No lo hay negro.*   (4–6)

7.277 *los.*   ZUN 28 *Me encontré a un tal D. Pascasio Bonetillo, hombre beato si los hay.*   (14–26)

7.278 Modified.   MGR 34 *Los hay altruistas.*   (9–15)

7.31 Indirect object, referring to masculine persons.

7.311 *le, les.*   IBA 30 *Si ves al chico, dile que venga.*   (**60–1914**)

7.312 The antecedent is *usted, ustedes.*   SAS 7 *¿ Qué le parece a usted ?*   (**38–331**)

7.313 *le* is used for *les.*   RAN 27 *Ni las mujeres le dan tanta importancia a los hombres.*   (13–19)

7.318 *se* (in the combination *se la, se lo,* etc.).   LIN 14 *Después se los cuento a Pepe.*   (**42–128**)

7.319 The antecedent is *usted, ustedes.*   CAT 8 *Dios se lo pague, Dⁿ. Cosme.*   (17–45)

7.32 Referring to feminine persons.

7.321 *le, les.*   WAS 132 *Ella no había preguntado por él, pero le dijeron que el mozo andaba en la ciudad.*   (**57–507**)

7.322 The antecedent is *usted, ustedes.*   JAN 303 *Le repito, señorita Lucrecia, váyase tranquilita.*   (**36–114**)

7.323 *le* is used for *les.*   JIM 43 *Le contaban a las flores lo que habían visto en África.*   (3–3)

7.324 *la, las.*   FOM 224 *No tengas miedo, — la decía Crispín.*   (**31–91**)

7.325 The antecedent is *usted, ustedes.*   BRA 184 *Quiero decirla a usted que todo eso es verdad.*   (4–5)

7.328 *se* (in the combination *se la, se lo,* etc.).   IMP 17 *Es preciso — se dijo a sí mismo al decírselo a ella.*   (36–98)

7.329 The antecedent is *usted, ustedes.*   LUG 157 *Nada dejé allí, doña Segunda. ¡ Se lo juro a usted por lo más sagrado!*   (9–11)

7.33 Referring to a neuter antecedent.

7.331 *le.*   JOA 10 *A todo le encuentras defectos.*   (17–24)

7.34 As subjective complement, with *ser, estar, parecer,* etc.   The neuter pronoun *lo* is often used with a copulative verb to sum up a preceding noun of class or adjectival expression.   In English this pronoun is not usually expressed, although " so " and " it " are sometimes used.

7.341 Representing a noun.   STE 29 *Porque todos los hombres de su raza fueron hombres de campo, lo fué él también.*   (27–65)

7.342 The pronoun may be modified by an adjectival phrase with *de.*   PEQ 25 *Digo que aquellas emociones debían de ser de pena, y que éstas debían de serlo de alegría.*   (13–18)

7.35 Representing an adjectival expression.

7.351 An adjective.   TIG 6 *¡ Eso no es caballeroso! ¿ Lo es, acaso, asesinar a una mujer de esa manera ?*   (31–76)

7.355 A past participle, used as an adjective.   LIN 94 *¡ Qué pesado es! No lo parecía de soltero.*   (3–5)

7.356 Especially with *estar..*   SJQ 77 *¿ No está usted encantado con esta familia, como ya por suerte lo estoy yo ?*   (9–12)

7.358 An adjectival phrase.   RUS 11 *Las personas son de bien o no lo son.*   (3–3)

7.41 Elided forms of the personal object pronouns.   In popular speech the object pronouns which ended in *–e (me, te, le, se)* were in older Spanish frequently elided before a verb form which began with a vowel. Before an unstressed *e–* this elision is of course universal in speech, although the full form is regularly written.   Before *a–,* in reproductions of colloquial style, elision is still occasionally found.   CAT 9 *¿ Qué ta pasao, Bartolo ?*   (4–21)

7.49 Reciprocal and reflexive object pronouns.   The forms of the reciprocal and reflexive object pronouns, unstressed, are, in the first and second persons, identical with the regular object pronouns, whether direct or indirect object.   In the third person, a special unstressed pronoun *se* is used for direct or indirect object in both singular and plural.

For examples and discussion of the use of the reflexives and reciprocals, see 27.3–27.7.

7.5 Combinations of two object pronouns. When two object pronouns are used together, they fall into two definite patterns: if the direct object is a pronoun of the third person, it regularly follows the indirect object; if one of the two pronouns is the reflexive pronoun *se*, it regularly precedes the other pronoun.

7.51 The direct object is of the third person.

7.511 *me lo*. BEN 6 *Me lo habían dicho.*   (41–225)

7.512 *te lo*. MAY 68 *Deseaba decírtelo.*   (33–146)

7.514 *se lo* (for *le lo*, *les lo*). REY 123 *Se lo ofrece al primer ministro.*
(53–282)

7.515 *se lo* (indirect reflexive). JIM 79. *Por miedo de que se lo comieran los gatos.*   (41–104)

7.517 *nos lo*. TRI 218 *¿ Por qué no nos lo presenta?*   (19–28)

7.519 *os lo*. LLA 43 *Papá os lo contará ahora.*   (6–8)

7.52 One of the pronouns is reflexive *se*.

7.521 *se me*. ROD 209 *Tierra y mar se me representan como una inmensa tumba.*   (46–134)

7.522 *se te*. UNA 151 *Se te habían quitado las alucinaciones.*   (23–37)

7.523 *se le*. URU 24 *Cuando se le dice algo, empieza a inventar historias.*
(56–242)

7.524 *se nos*. PAT 201 *Se nos va a hacer tarde.*   (21–27)

7.525 *se os*. NER 92 *Se os atribuirán todas las cualidades.*   (4–4)

7.526 *se les*. REY 100 *No estaría de más que desde aquí se les hiciera fuego.*   (34–66)

8. Uses of the object pronoun.

8.1 As direct object. The personal object pronouns appear as direct object of the verb in the same constructions as other substantives. These uses have been illustrated in the preceding sections. Special uses of the pronouns in the partitive sense and as subjective complement are discussed in 7.27 and 7.34. At this point we shall discuss a few special situations.

8.11 An object pronoun is the object of two coordinated verbs.

8.111 The pronoun may be repeated with the second verb.   IGN 61
Déjeme que lo piense y lo estudie.   (35–76)

8.112 Or the pronoun may be understood with the second verb.   STE 30
Sus peones le respetaban y querían.   There appears to be no difference in
meaning; the distinction is one of stylistic preference.   (30–90)

8.13 If a noun object follows a verb and is also the object of a second
coordinated verb, it is regularly replaced after the second verb by the
proper object pronoun.   MUJ 20 *Tengo obligación de ver sus lágrimas y
de enjugarlas.*   (15–30)

8.14 A direct object may be modified by an indefinite adjective.

8.141 *los dos.*   TIG 21 *En sus manos está el que se venga abajo y nos aplaste
a las dos.*   (6–7)

8.145 *todos.*   PAX 15 *Ahí está en el centro de aquel grupo, haciéndolos reír
a todos.*   (25–35)

8.149 Other adjectives (*ambos, a los tres,* etc.).   JAN 107 *A ambos los
abrumaban a preguntas.*   (5–5)

8.15 Modified by a noun of class.   LIN 22 *A los nobles os decapitaban.*
                                                                (5–5)

8.16 Omission of an object pronoun.   The direct object is omitted after
dispensar and *perdonar* in expressions of courtesy.   ZUN 24 *Usted dispense.*
                                                                (20–49)

8.2 Indirect object.   In general the indirect object indicates a person
to whom the action or state of the verb is of interest.   The relationship
may be close, as when one is the person to whom something is given, or
the relationship may be remote.   In the second case, the indirect object
may be said to modify the whole sentence, rather than the verb itself.

8.21 The indirect object is in close relation to the verb.   This situation
occurs with transitive verbs which have a direct object as well, with
impersonal intransitive verbs, of the type of *gustar,* and with other intransitive verbs, reflexive or non-reflexive.

8.211 With transitive verbs.   REY 93 *Tengo que decirle francamente que
no sé lo bastante para eso.*

The commonest verbs are: *aconsejar* (14–19), *advertir* (19–37), *agradecer*
(15–25), *anunciar* (15–19), *asegurar* (**23–32**), *causar* (16–27), *comunicar* (10–11),
conceder (13–14), *contar* (**37–90**), *contestar* (13–19), *costar* (11–18), *dar* (**58–504**),
deber (**22–41**), *decir* (**65–844**), *dejar* (**32–60**), *devolver* (13–15), *echar* (12–17),
enseñar (**28–48**), *entregar* (12–20), *enviar* (11–16), *escribir* (17–25), *explicar* (18–
24), *hacer* (**44–180**), *imponer* (14–17), *indicar* (11–12), *leer* (10–11), *llevar* (12–15),

mandar (16–29), *mostrar* (13–18), *negar* (12–18), *ofrecer* (**28–48**), *pagar* (11–20), *permitir* (**20–31**), *poner* (19–33), *presentar* (17–30), *prestar* (14–20), *prometer* (**21–31**), *proponer* (10–11), *recordar* (12–20), *regalar* (18–22), *responder* (10–10), *revelar* (11–13), *tener* (10–12), *traer* (**29–55**).

8.213 With intransitive verbs of impersonal type or used with inanimate subject.   MUJ 15 *Vamos a cambiar de conversación, si te parece.*

The commonest verbs are: *bastar* (19–23), *convenir* (17–29), *doler* (17–28), *estar* + a complement (12–15), *faltar* (**28–58**), *gustar* (**41–146**), *importar* (**27–71**), *interesar* (10–10), *ocurrir* (12–25), *parecer* (**54–284**), *pasar* (**25–72**), *quedar* (**28–40**), *ser* + a complement (**35–78**), *sobrar* (12–15), *tocar* (16–29).

8.215 With reflexive intransitives.   OCC 132 *La aguja de la torre, la vela marina se nos presentan.*   ([32]–70)

The only common verbs are: *aparecerse* (6–6) and *presentarse* (6–7).

8.217 With other intransitive verbs. This group is difficult to identify because of the identity of form for direct and indirect objects.   PAT 24 *Ha venido usted a hablarme de amor.*

A very large number of verbs appear sporadically with objects which appear to be indirect. When a writer is a confirmed *loísta* it is possible to determine which objects he considers direct and which indirect, but it must be remembered that neither *la*, *las*, nor *los* are assuredly direct objects, nor are *le* and *les* assuredly indirect objects. The verbs which are most certainly used with indirect objects are: *contestar* (19–28), *dar* (in the sense of " strike " or " take a fancy for ") (**26–74**), *escribir* (12–20), *hablar* (**46–116**), *mirar* (12–24).

8.22 The indirect object modifies the whole sentence. In many cases the relationship of the indirect object to the verb is so remote that it may more properly be said to modify the whole sentence. Grammarians have used a wide variety of names for this type of indirect object: dative of reference, dative of interest, dative of advantage, ethical dative, and the like. In all these cases the indirect object refers to a person who is in some way, either through ownership or habitual association or psychological bent, concerned with some particular thing mentioned in the sentence. While any attempt to define the particular concern must be somewhat arbitrary, it seems worth while to set up a few classes in which a particular interest dominates. It should be remarked that the use of the sentence dative is far more common in colloquial style than in formal discourse.

8.23 Possession. The idea of possession is likely to be prominent when nouns habitually associated with persons are involved.   FOM 9 *Me ha agarrado las piernas.* For the use of the article, see 18.65.   (**54–546**)

8.231 The idea of possession may be reinforced by the use of the possessive adjective.   JOA 15 *Si yo te toco tus cosas es porque tú me tocas las mías primero.*   (8–9)

8.24 Separation or deprivation. Even here the idea of possession is sometimes present. FAL 210 *Le daba cuanto dinero le pedía.* ([57]–**411**)

The commonest verbs are: *arrancar* (12–16), *arrebatar* (7–7), *comprar* (6–7), *escaparse* (9–13), *exigir* (6–9), *impedir* (5–5), *ocultar* (8–8), *oír* (6–10), *pedir* (**41**–**126**), *preguntar* (**41**–**96**), *quitar* (**30**–**53**), *robar* (7–12), *rogar* (**23**–**42**), *sacar* (8–12), *suplicar* (11–13).

8.25 Advantage or interest. This is the loosest of the groups. In its most extreme use, it is not always easy to decide the particular implication of the indirect object or ethical dative. But no attempt is made here to subdivide the possible varieties. MAY 4 *La madre le preparó un benéfico alojamiento.* SAS 91 *No me llore* (the *me* must imply that the weeping would be annoying to the speaker). (**59**–**520**)

8.27 The indirect object expresses place.

8.271 Destination or goal. RET 134 *Nos llegaban ambas cosas.* (**29**–**43**) Also expressed by the stressed pronoun with *a*, see 6.51.

8.273 Place in which or on which. ORR 92 *Luego le pusieron el sombrero.* (**33**–**73**)

8.275 The place is indicated by an adverb. JAN 13 *Sintió venírsele varias dificultades encima.* (**25**–**34**)

8.29 The indirect object may be modified by an indefinite adjective.

8.291 *todos.* BEN 8 *Así arruinó su casa y nos dió a todos tantos disgustos.* (7–7)

8.4 Agreement of the object pronouns.

8.41 Simple agreement. The object pronouns agree with their antecedent in gender and in number. IGN 41 *Aspiro a la fortuna de mi tío. Pero la quiero para mí solito.* (*)

8.42 Complex agreement. With a compound antecedent, the pronoun may agree with the nearest antecedent or become a masculine plural.

8.421 Agrees with the nearest antecedent. MGR 47 *Apoplejía, parálisis, arterioesclerosis, la evita y cura « Antiapoplético Berdaguer. »* (5–5)

8.423 Masculine plural. ROD 80 *Pero a la raza le eran precisos nuevo ambiente, tierra nueva, y los tuvo.* (4–8)

8.5 Redundant uses of the object pronouns with an expressed noun or pronoun object. One of the characteristic traits of Spanish expression is the use of object pronouns, even when the object of the verb is expressed by a noun or another pronoun. When a noun or pronoun object precedes the verb, the object pronoun may serve as a device for indicating the function of the preceding noun or pronoun; when the noun or pronoun follows the verb, the personal pronoun must either be an anticipation of the substantive object or the object must be an appositional modifier of the personal pronoun. In both situations the use of the redundant pronoun is more frequent with an indirect than with a direct object, but this is probably to be explained by the fact that persons are more likely to be the indirect than the direct object of an action.

8.51 The direct object precedes the verb. In this situation, the use of the redundant pronoun is somewhat more common than its omission. In general, it may be said that if the direct object is closely bound to the verb, so that it is pronounced in a single breath group with the verb, the personal pronoun will be omitted. In this case an expressed subject of the verb follows the verb. But if the direct object is followed by a pause, the redundant pronoun is usually expressed. In this case the subject or other elements may intervene between the object and the verb. With the stressed forms of the personal pronoun the use of the redundant pronoun is the regular usage.

8.52 The redundant pronoun is not used, in main clauses.

8.521 The direct object is a noun modified by stressed adjective. RUS 71 *Buenas pruebas te doy.* **(25–49)**

8.522 Stressed noun. ROM 88 *Razón tenía Villegas.* (13–23)

8.523 Noun modified by an interrogative adjective. TIG 13 *¿Qué disparate habrá pensado?* (*)

8.524 Interrogative pronoun. ZAM 141 *¿A quién llamas?* (*)

8.525 Demonstrative pronoun. RUB 17 *Esto vió el mundo.* (19–28)

8.526 Indefinite or negative pronoun. JOA 68 *Algo ha comido.* **(29–55)**

8.53 In subordinate clauses.

8.531 A relative pronoun is object. IGN 110 *Esa mujercita a quien adoro.* (*)

8.534 A noun is object in a relative clause. PEL 19 *Aquella ciudadanía que tan altos ejemplos dió de amor patrio.* (13-13)

8.535 A noun or pronoun is object in an adverbial clause. STE 21 *Si algo necesita, no tiene usted sino tocar tres veces la campanilla.* (7–8)

8.54 The redundant pronoun is used, in main clauses.

8.541 The direct object is a noun. TRI 127 *El arquetipo, yo lo he vislumbrado en Josefina.* **(48–152)**

8.543 The direct object is a personal pronoun. PIN 138 *A ellos los enterré.* **(34–68)**

8.544 The direct object is a demonstrative or other pronoun. ART 70 *Esto no puedo yo evitarlo.* **(32–68)**

8.545 The direct object is *todo*. It is probable that this use of *todo* was in origin adjectival; see 8.145. ABU 20 *Todo lo sabe el indino.* (17–35)

8.55 The direct object is a simple relative pronoun. This construction, which is now largely colloquial, is probably due to a desire to identify the relative object more accurately.

8.551 *que.* ARN 52 *Mi mujer, que ya la conocéis, se empeñó en darme caza.* In this, as in many similar cases, there is a possibility that the *que* should be considered a causal conjunction. **(15–28)**

8.56 The indirect object precedes the verb.

8.57 The redundant pronoun is not used, in main clauses.

8.571 The indirect object is a stressed noun. ROM 103 *Al mismo Sr. Pulido debo varias que él recibió de Viena.* **(20–29)**

8.572 The indirect object is a stressed personal pronoun. RET 33 *A ellos puede agregarse el colombiano José Asunción Silva.* **(5–8)**

8.574 Other element. PAX 23 *A las satisfacciones del trabajo suceden el terror, la zozobra.* **(9–11)**

8.579 In subordinate clauses. PEL 233 *Rengifo admite hasta treinta maneras de canciones, a las cuales todavía añade dos Vicens.* **(10–15)**

8.58 The redundant pronoun is used.

8.581 The indirect object is a noun. RUS 22 *A cada hijo o nieto que me nace le abro cuenta corriente.* **(44–99)**

8.582 The indirect object is a stressed personal pronoun. ORT 136 *A mí me acontece pensar lo contrario.* **(41–200)**

8.583 An interrogative pronoun. SIE 54 *¿ A quién le debes tú ese dinero ?* **(6–6)**

8.585 A relative pronoun. NER 48 *Imaginaos un hombre a quien le duele pensar.* Chiefly *a quien.* **(11–16)**

8.587 Other pronoun. IMP 206 *A otro le sería dable posar su mano en la azucena.* **(18–25)**

8.61 The direct object follows the verb. In this case, the omission of the redundant pronoun is the rule. With a noun object referring to a thing, the use of the pronoun is rare.

8.62 The redundant pronoun is not used.

8.621 The object is a noun. BRA 19 *¿ Quién quiere a Laurita ?* (*)

8.622 The object is a stressed personal pronoun. All the examples are *usted, ustedes.* LLA 74 *¡ Nuestra nobleza no nos permite engañar a usted!* (4–4)

8.63 The redundant pronoun is used.

8.631 With a noun, normally referring to a person. URU 49 *¡ Lo quiere tanto a Julio!* (16–36)

8.632 With a stressed personal pronoun. SIE 25 *No le envidio a usted, amigo.* (**43–151**)

8.633 With other pronouns. RAN 40 *A veces le atropellan a uno los chauffers.* (11–14)

8.634 With *todo.* Probably adjectival. MGR 16 *Un incendio amenazaba destruirlo todo.* (**47–118**)

8.635 With *todos.* Like *todo.* BEN 32 *Usted nos ha conocido a todos.* (17–25)

8.637 The direct object is a clause. JES 29 *Ya lo creo que los encontraré.* (5–9)

8.64 The indirect object follows the verb. The use of the redundant pronoun is far more common than with the direct object.

8.65 The redundant pronoun is not used.

8.651 The indirect object is a noun. ZAM 116 *Esos viajes sentimentales suelen costar a las mujeres muchas lágrimas.* (*)

8.653 The indirect object is a stressed personal pronoun. ZUN 13 *Aseguro a ustedes que me dejaron maravillado.* Only with *usted, ustedes.* (4–7)

8.66 The redundant pronoun is used.

8.661 With a noun indirect object. ABC 48 *Esto les ocurre solamente a las personas que no utilizan los productos Pedykur.* (**51–330**)

8.662 With a stressed personal pronoun. ABU 25 *¿ Qué les importa a ustedes, ni qué me importa a mí ?* (**44–273**)

8.665 With other pronouns. BEN 6 *¡ Qué poco le ayudan a una !* (**23–48**)

8.7 The redundant pronoun may sum up two objects. If the objects are of different person, a combination involving the first person will require a redundant pronoun in the first person plural.

8.71 *nos.* BEN 9 *Pudo salvarnos a su hijo y a mí.*   (6–6)

8.72 At times, the redundant pronoun refers only to the first of two coordinated objects. LIN 112 *¡ Las cosas que le he dicho al simón y al caballo.* It is possible that this is an example of the use of *le* for *les*; see 7.313.   (5–7)

POSITION OF THE OBJECT PRONOUNS

9. The object pronouns are unstressed forms and are always attached, in speech, to the verb. In writing, they are written as separate words when they precede the verb, but are attached to the verb when they follow. The modern practice may be stated simply, by saying that they regularly precede finite forms of the verb in all types of discourse, except in affirmative commands, and that they follow the verb in affirmative commands and also follow the infinitive and present participle. There are variations and complications of this general practice, which will be discussed in the following paragraphs. Combinations of two pronouns and reflexive or reciprocal pronouns follow the same practice as single object pronouns.

9.1 The pronoun precedes the verb in statements, questions, and exclamations. JIM 42 *Ahí la tienes.*   (*)

9.2 The pronoun follows the verb in statements, questions, and exclamations. In the older language, the pronoun followed the verb regularly when it began a new breath group. This occurred most frequently when the verb began the sentence, when it followed a coordinating conjunction, and when it followed a subordinate clause. In contemporary Spanish, the use of the pronouns after the verb is almost wholly literary, the only expressions occurring in speech being fixed phrases of the type of *dijérase.* For the most part, modern writers follow the older tradition of using postposition only at the beginning of a group or after a pause, but with a few writers the use of this order is merely a mannerism unrelated to any feeling for the rhythm of the sentence, as a result of which they may use postposition even in subordinate clauses.

9.21 The verb begins a sentence. SON 26 *Hallábanse francas todas las puertas.*   **(33–183)**

9.22 The verb follows a coordinating conjunction. RIC 255 *Callaron los dos y quedáronse pensativos.*   (18–35)

9.23 It follows a subordinate clause. SON 49 *Cuando juzgó que los había mirado a todo sabor y talante, acercóse.*   (16–33)

9.24 It follows an adverbial phrase. PAT 8 *En esto, oyóse otra voz femenina desde dentro.*   **(21–60)**

9.25 It follows an adverb. SON 108 *Desgraciadamente, quedéme sin superarlos.*   (7–11)

9.26 It follows an absolute construction. DEB 92 *Una vez bien ordenadas mis ideas, quedéme en grata contemplación del jardín.*   (6–7)

9.27 It follows a present participle. RIC 257 *Dando de mano a sus ambiciones de artista, acogióse en Santillana.*   (5–6)

9.28 It follows the subject. FAL 221 *David lanzóles amenazadoras miradas hacia el suelo.*   (18–74)

9.29 It follows the object. ROM 10 *Esta doctrina apoyábala Fauriel.*
                                                                (9–15)

9.31 It follows a subordinating conjunction. IMP 10 *Era como si sorprendiérale la mujer.*   (7–12)

9.5 Commands and wishes.

9.51 The pronoun precedes the verb.

9.511 In negative commands. PEQ 76 *No os estremezcáis.*   (*)

9.512 In affirmative commands or wishes introduced by *que*. CAT 5 *¡ Que se la toque el demonio!*   (17–37)

9.513 In affirmative commands or wishes when the subject or other stressed element precedes the verb. TIG 32 *¡ La Virgen nos ampare!*
                                                                (14–22)

9.52 The pronoun follows the verb in direct commands, expressed in the imperative or in the subjunctive replacing the imperative. SEC 9 *¡ Déjame!* WAS 144 *Y hágame el bien de darme un poquito de árnica.* **(57–621)**

9.6 The pronoun follows the infinitive. PAL 13 *Me precipité hacia ellos para abrazarlos y besarlos.*   **(60–1509)**

9.7 The pronoun follows the present participle. JIM 48 *Un elemento nuevo lo aislaba, dejándolo sin razón.*   **(60–825)**

9.8 The pronoun follows a non-verbal expression. The only situation

of this type which survives is the use of the pronoun after the interjection
he. ROD 19 *Henos aquí en Atenas.*   (4–4)

10. Position of the pronoun with compound forms.

10.1 Finite forms.

10.11 The pronoun normally precedes the auxiliary verb, as with a
simple form. VIG 27 *Se han revuelto múltiples pasiones.*   (*)

10.12 Rarely, the pronoun is placed after the auxiliary.

10.121 When the verb begins the sentence. IDO 115 *Hánse observado
largos eclipses.*   (5–10)

10.122 The verb follows another element of the sentence, after a pause.
ALT 10 *Internamente, habíanse relajado mucho todas ellas.*   (6–9)

10.4 With the perfect infinitive. The pronoun is regularly placed after
the auxiliary *haber.* ABC 42 *Debía haberlo conseguido.*   **(37–72)**

10.5 With the perfect active participle. The pronoun is regularly placed
after the auxiliary *habiendo.* RAN 24 *Habiéndonos citado a las ocho, veo
que usted comparece a las ocho y media.*   (3–4)

10.6 With complex forms.

10.61 With progressive tenses, formed with *ir* (*estar*, etc.) and the present participle. With these forms, usage is divided in contemporary
Spanish, not between author and author, but in the writings of individual
authors. In general, the two tendencies may be described as follows.
If the progressive tense is felt to be a unit, that is to say, if *está mirando*
is considered as the equivalent of *mira*, the pronoun will be placed before
the auxiliary *está.* But if the two elements are considered as forming
two distinct expressions, the pronoun will be placed after the participle,
as *anda buscándolo.* The auxiliaries which most frequently form a unit
tense are *ir* and *estar;* see 34.9. There is a slight preponderance of cases
in which the pronoun precedes the auxiliary.

10.62 The pronoun precedes the auxiliary verb. OCC 188 *Se están divir-
tiendo.*   **(48–178)**

10.63 The pronoun follows the participle. SEC 77 *Estaría desayunán-
dose.*   **(46–111)**

10.64 Rarely, the complex form is inverted and the pronoun follows the
participle. SJQ 82 *Diciéndole estaba yo a mi tío que usted lo buscaba.* (3–3)

10.65 When there are two pronoun objects, they are usually placed
before the auxiliary. ARN 70 *Me la está friendo.*   (6–6)

10.66 If there is a second coordinated participle which has a pronoun object, the pronoun is naturally placed after that participle.   ALT 185 *Seguían dándose o confirmándose fueros municipales.*   (3–3)

10.67 When the progressive form is an infinitive, there is an alternative, as with finite forms.

10.671 The pronoun may follow the auxiliary.   FAL 160 *Los hombres que parecían irla siguiendo se metían en un estanco.*   (7–8)

10.672 Or the pronoun may follow the participle.   MGR 19 *Es menester ir sometiéndose poco a poco a los rayos solares.*   (3–3)

10.7 With complex forms consisting of a verb and a complementary infinitive.

10.71 The pronoun is object of the main verb.   In this case, the pronoun regularly precedes the main verb.   IBA 27 *Las veía pasar.* **(57–296)**

10.711 The dependent infinitive may also have an object which is placed after the infinitive.   CAT 4 *¡ Conque no se atrevió a tocarle la cresta!*
                                                        (30–78)

10.72 The pronoun is object of the dependent infinitive.   Usage in this situation, as with the progressive tenses, depends on the degree to which the combination of verb and dependent infinitive is felt to be a unit.   If the main verb is an auxiliary verb of aspect, mood, or tense (see 34.), it may be considered as forming a unit of expression.   Thus *voy a hacer* may be the equivalent of *haré* and in this case the pronoun will precede the auxiliary: *lo voy a hacer.*   On the other hand, the dependent infinitive may be felt as expressing a notion which is distinct from that of the main verb and in this case the pronoun will follow the infinitive.   With verbs which are not auxiliaries, this is the regular construction.   It is also the predominant construction even with auxiliary verbs.

10.73 The main verb is an auxiliary verb of aspect, mood, or tense.

10.731 The object pronoun precedes the auxiliary.   PEQ 80 *La acabo de leer.*   **([60]–586)**

The commonest auxiliaries are: *acabar de* (12–13), *deber* (11–24), *empezar a* (6–6), *haber de* **(27–52)**, *ir a* **(41–196)**, *poder* **(40–155)**, *querer* **(24–64)**, *saber* (10–12), *soler* (4–4), *tener que* (14–21), *venir a* (5–6), *volver a* (16–22).

10.733 There may be two pronoun objects, both dependent on the infinitive.   LLA 27 *Ni yo misma me lo sé explicar.*   **(21–34)**

10.734 One of two pronoun objects may be dependent on the main verb and one on the infinitive.   ART 40 *La realidad vive en el personaje y se lo* *hace a una vivir por entero. (se,* object of *hace,* for *le; lo,* object of *vivir*). (9–12)

10.735 The dependent infinitive may itself be that of an auxiliary verb followed by another infinitive; a pronoun object of the second infinitive may still precede the main verb. RUS 74 *No le quiero volver a ver.* (5–5)

10.74 The pronoun follows the dependent infinitive. DIV 177 *Podría citarse, por ejemplo, la de la sesión del 3 de abril.* ([60]–1464)

The frequencies for the commonest auxiliaries are: *acabar de* (19–37), *comenzar a* (8–16), *deber* (**45–113**), *deber de* (6–9), *dejar de* (11–16), *empezar a* (13–21), *haber de* (**43–99**), *hay que* (**26–48**), *ir a* (**50–193**), *llegar a* (17–21), *poder* (**57–424**), *querer* (**48–209**), *saber* (22–33), *soler* (14–18), *tener que* (**34–91**), *venir a* (**30–64**), *volver a* (**30–50**). It will be noted that *ir a* is the only auxiliary which shows an actually greater frequency of position before the auxiliary. This was in the older language the preferred construction with all auxiliary verbs.

10.75 With verbs other than auxiliary verbs followed by a complementary infinitive. The pronoun regularly follows the infinitive. JES 154 *Santa trataba de distraerlo.* ([54]–299)

Typical verbs are: *acabar por* (8–8), *decidir* (5–5), *desear* (**21–21**), *entrar a* (5–6), *intentar* (7–7), *lograr* (12–16), *necesitar* (10–19), *parecer* (15–20), *pensar* (8–14), *pretender* (7–8), *procurar* (8–8), *tardar en* (5–6), *temer* (8–8), *tratar de* (12–17).

10.751 With both auxiliary verbs and other verbs, there may be two pronoun objects after the infinitive. RUS 32 *No querría usted empeñármelos.* (10–11)

10.753 If the second of two coordinated dependent infinitives has a pronoun object, it naturally follows the infinitive. PAL 16 *Él se encargó de enganchar los dos más fuertes y domarlos.* (11–17)

10.79 The pronoun follows the main verb. The only usage which is common is that in which the object pronoun is object of the main verb.

10.791 In statements and questions. LUG 147 *Y púsose a estudiar en voz alta.* (5–12)

10.793 In direct commands. PIN 65 *Déjame salir.* (13–22)

10.795 Both main verb and dependent infinitive may have objects. TIG 12 *Mándeme tirarme al pilón de la plaza y allá voy de cabeza.* (3–3)

10.8 With non-finite forms of the auxiliary verb.

10.81 The auxiliary verb may itself be an infinitive.

10.82 The object pronoun depends on the auxiliary verb and follows it. ORR 179 *Hubiera querido hacerle ver el fondo de su espíritu.* (18–29)

10.821 Both auxiliary verb and dependent verb have objects. LUG 154
Hay que acercarse a saludarlas.   (3–3)

10.83 The pronoun is object of the second infinitive.

10.831 It may follow the auxiliary verb. IGN 29 *Eso es para poderlas
dar besos.*   (28–41)

10.833 Or with equal frequency it may follow the dependent infinitive.
DEB 44 *Parecía querer justificarse.*   Especially with reflexive verbs.
                                                                       (26–44)

10.85 The auxiliary verb may be a present participle.

10.86 The object pronoun depends on the auxiliary verb and follows it.
ZUN 50 *Adormece al interesado haciéndole soñar las mayores delicias.*
                                                                       (12–16)

10.87 The pronoun is object of the dependent infinitive.

10.871 It may follow the auxiliary verb. SAS 143 *Queriéndome pegar sin
razón.*   (10–13)

10.873 Or it may follow the dependent infinitive. MUJ 31 *Volviendo a
sentarse.*   Especially with reflexive verbs.   (14–17)

DEMONSTRATIVE PRONOUNS

11. The demonstrative pronouns are used to point out a specific individual in space or time. In form and meaning they are identical with the demonstrative adjectives. But the demonstrative pronouns, except the neuter forms, regularly bear an accent when written. The regular forms are: *éste* (*–a, –os, –as, esto*), *ése* (*–a, –os, –as, eso*), *aquél* (*–élla, –éllos, –éllas, aquello*).

11.1 In addition to the regular demonstrative pronouns, there are a number of usages in which *el* (*la, lo, los, las*) are demonstrative pronouns. Those in which *el* is followed by a phrase with *de* are included in the present chapter. Cases in which *el* is followed by a relative are discussed under Substantive relative pronouns, as are uses of the regular demonstrative pronouns with a relative clause; see 15.3. Cases in which *el* is followed by a stressed possessive adjective or a phrase with *de* + a personal pronoun are treated under Possessive pronouns, see 12.

11.2 Regular uses of the masculine and feminine forms. The demonstrative pronouns are distinguished by their types of reference to the persons involved in a sentence or to the time involved in a state or action. Roughly they may be said to correspond to the first, the second, or the third person.

11.21 *éste.* The demonstrative of the first person: indicating persons or things related to the speaker, or to the present in time. PEQ 143 *Éste es el mayor encanto.* Especially common as subject of *ser* followed by a noun as subjective complement. **(60–474)**

11.22 *ése.* The demonstrative of the second person: indicating persons or things related to the person addressed, or falling within his experience in time. ORR 103 *Ése es el jefe de los Macucos.* **(26–59)**

11.221 More frequently referring to things than to persons. URU 38 *¿ Y ésa es la cara con que se presenta usted ?* **(40–124)**

11.23 *aquél.* The demonstrative of the third person: indicating persons or things unrelated to or remote from the speaker and the person addressed, or distant in time. ZAM 130 *Sólo aquélla, a pesar de su pobreza, reaparece en mi memoria.* The pronominal use of *aquél* is relatively rare. **(31–57)**

11.3 Special uses of the masculine and feminine forms.

11.31 As substitutes for the personal pronoun of the third person. The personal pronouns of the third person are likewise demonstrative in origin and it is natural that the other demonstratives should replace them in this function.

11.311 *éste*.   FOM 10 *¡ Y es éste el que amenaza con tragarse frito al Gobierno!*   **(33–93)**

11.312 *ése*.   ARN 12 *Ése coge una cestita, una botella vacía.*   (12–30)

11.313 *aquél*.   RUB 14 *Aquélla no es la Diana sagrada de las incomparables flechas: es Hécate.*   (9–13)

11.32 Indicating " the former " and " the latter."   When there are two antecedents, *éste* refers to the nearer, that is " the latter," and *aquél* to the more remote, that is " the former." They are used in pairs or individually.

11.321 *éste . . . aquél*.   VIG 109 *Éstas son el polvo grueso que queda sobre el cedazo; aquélla, el fino, el sutil, el depurado.*   (8–12)

11.322 *aquél . . . éste*.   JIM 86 *El hombre y el mono se rascan, aquél la greña, y éste las costillas.*   (4–4)

11.325 *éste* alone.   ROD 85 *Se escapa el agua que humedece los cabos de las flores y éstas se marchitan.*   **(38–141)**

11.326 *éste último*.   UGA 21 *Melián y García conocían a todos, sobre todo este último.*   Possibly influenced by French *ce dernier*.   (9–12)

11.328 *aquél* alone.   ORT 136 *El estilo de un escritor, es decir, la fisonomía de su obra consiste en una serie de actos selectivos que aquél ejecute.*   (11–15)

11.33 With depreciative force.

11.331 *ése*.   JOA 10 *A mi me gustan los hombres varoniles y que fumen, y no los hombres que se perfuman y se peinan . . . como ése.*   (9–17)

11.333 *éste*.   IGN 50 *¡ Un hipócrita y un farsante, que te has puesto de acuerdo con éste para robarme!*   (4–5)

11.34 Indefinite feminine use.   TIG 67 *¡ Ese pobre Tigre Juan va a morir de ésta!*   (8-13)

11.35 In a partitive phrase with *de* modifying an indefinite noun.   IMP 73 *¿ Qué prefieres? ¿ Navegar en una lancha de ésas o que tomemos un coche?*
(10- 14)

11.4 Modified by *mismo*.   STE 251 *Máximo, ¿ cuál es tu religión? — Ésa misma: la de tu mamá.*   (3–3)

11.5 Modified by a phrase with *de*.

11.51 *éste* (*ése, aquél*) *de*. BYN 75 *A mí me encantan las corridas de pueblo, pero algo mejor organizadas que ésta del domingo en Las Navas.* (12–12)

11.52 *el* (*la, los, las*) *de*.

11.521 With a noun or pronoun. BEN 8 *Ya que la salud del cuerpo parece asegurada, atendamos a la del alma.* (58–472)

11.523 *la de González* " the wife of González," " the González woman." ZAM 95 *Sí, es la de González.* (4–6)

11.524 *la*, indefinite feminine. FOM 236 *Aquello fué la de Dios es Cristo.* (4–4)

11.525 With an infinitive. SJQ 33 *Este muchacho adolece de un defecto gravísimo: el de poner su corazón al alcance de cualquier mujer que lo mire.* (19–26)

11.526 With a substantivated adverb, usually of time or place. ABU 16 *¡ Qué caer los de arriba, y qué empinarse los de abajo!* (16–30)

11.53 *todos los de*. PAL 20 *En el sofá dormiríamos todos los de la familia sin molestarnos.* (5–5)

11.54 Special functions of *el de*.

11.541 As subjective complement. STE 249 *Su respuesta fué la del médico al enfermo.* (20–25)

11.543 In apposition with a noun or pronoun. PEL 246 *Un solo nombre, el de cierta Dª. Isabel, suena en estas poesías.* (21–47)

11.545 Coordinated with a noun. JES 236 *Después sentó al chico en la baranda, entre su cuerpo y él de Durán.* (12–28)

11.55 In the same functions, the demonstrative is sometimes omitted.

11.551 As subjective complement. ALT 189 *La pena generalmente aplicada era de destierro y confiscación.* (5–5)

11.6 *el* (*la, los, las*) used as a demonstrative with past participles which have verbal force. RET 32 *Los llamados modernistas.* It is possible that *los* in this and similar cases should be considered an article which makes a noun out of the participle. But the difference between *los llamados* and a non-verbal participle, like *los enamorados*, is obvious; see 25.431. (28–100)

11.7 Neuter forms.

11.71 Regular uses. The neuter demonstrative pronouns are used to point to an unnamed idea expressed in a preceding clause or about to be expressed in a following clause. They all have a tendency toward collective value, summing up not only general notions but also specific groups of individual objects, whether expressed or implied. Thus *esto* may mean "this place," summing up the house, the garden, the furniture, etc.

11.72 Individual forms.

11.721 *esto*. MAY 67 *Ni esto es un despoblado.* (60–369)

11.723 *eso*. RUS 10 *Nosotros no nos fijamos en eso.* *Eso* is the most frequently used of all the demonstrative pronouns. (**56–604**)

11.725 *aquello*. SIE 61 *¿ Dónde está todo aquello?* *Aquello* is the least frequently used of all the demonstrative pronouns. (**30–55**)

11.73 Types of antecedent.

11.731 Sums up an idea conveyed by a preceding clause. IDO 116 *Viene un crítico y dice de una estatua que es una obra maestra, y eso basta: los demás lo repiten.* (60–822)

11.732 Sums up a group of ideas expressed by a series of nouns. SJQ 38 *La cerveza, la copa de coñac, el café, todo eso lo toma en una cervecería servida de camareras.* (3–3)

11.733 Sums up a group of ideas not explicitly expressed. ZAM 89 (A servant brings in the luggage) *¿ Puedo dejar esto aquí un momento?* (Not separately counted)

11.734 Sums up an idea expressed by an individual noun. This construction is most common when a number of other ideas have intervened and the gender of the particular noun used has been forgotten. It is naturally most frequent in conversational style. LIN 46 *Vuestro padre tiene el honor de dirigirte la palabra y . . . no os ha dirigido más que eso en toda su vida.* (9–12)

11.735 Sums up an idea which is conveyed by a following clause or phrase. VIG 41 *Gran escritor, no sólo en sentido literario, sino, sobre todo, y esto es más importante, en sentido humano.* (15–18)

11.737 Sums up an idea expressed by a following infinitive. ORT 118 *Y eso que tienen de común no es más que esto: constituir la meta de nuestra conciencia.* (3–3)

11.8 Special uses of the neuter pronouns.

11.81 Used alone in exclamations. REY 157 *¿ Os gustan las chicas guapas, con la nariz bien chata? — ¡ Sí, sí! ¡ Eso, eso!* (7–8)

11.82 Modified by an indefinite adjective.

11.821 *esto mismo.* RUS 8 *Por eso mismo, ya debían ustedes tenerle cariño.* (5–5)

11.822 *esto solo.* ORR 174 *Eso solo ya daba el sello particular de buen gusto sobrio.* (3–3)

11.825 *todo esto.* IMP 23 *A todo esto llevaban ya una hora callejeando.* (34–70)

11.83 Modified by a phrase with *de.*

11.84 *esto (eso, aquello) de.*

11.841 With a noun or pronoun. RIC 260 *Aunque siempre fuí muy poquita cosa, soñé con llegar a mucho en esto de la música.* (23–46)

11.842 *a eso de (las seis).* CAT 23 *Despertóse a eso de la madrugada.* (3–3)

11.845 With an infinitive. TRI 49 *Es horrible, horrible esto de saber que lleva una en su sér tanta vergüenza.* (9–10)

11.847 With a substantive clause. PAX 10 *¿ Cree usted que sea pura galantería o una tradición muy antigua eso de que se sirvan las señoras antes que los hombres ?* (5–5)

11.849 *todo esto de.* SJQ 80 *Todo esto de la poesía de la naturaleza es una pura farsa.* (3–3)

11.85 *lo de.*

11.851 With a noun or pronoun. IGN 41 *Aunque lo de las cinco mil no haya dado resultado.* (25–49)

11.855 With an infinitive. BEN 35 *Lo de calumniar siempre, sacar a relucir historias.* (4–4)

11.858 With a substantivated adverb, usually of time or place. ART 77 *¡ Llamar! ¿ A qué voy a llamar ? A que me respondan lo de siempre: « No sé ».* (8–9)

11.859 *todo lo de.* TIG 31 *Ya sabe que todo lo de esta casa es suyo.* (3–3)

11.86 *lo* used with past participles which have verbal force. ROM 103 *Esta sobrepuja a todo lo antes aquí citado.* Compare also 11.6. (3–3)

11.87 *éste* and *esto* before *ser* + a complement. When a demonstrative pronoun is used as subject of *ser* followed by a noun, the pronoun may agree with the following noun, or may be neuter. The neuter naturally makes the thing pointed out vaguer, more collective in character.

11.871 The pronoun agrees with the predicate noun. PEQ 143 *Éste es el mayor encanto.* (33–75)

11.873 The pronoun is neuter. FOM 225 *Aquello era una ciudad de cementerio.* (36–85)

DEMONSTRATIVE ADVERBS

11.9 A number of adverbs are demonstrative in origin and still retain their function of pointing out a manner, place, quantity, or time. These demonstratives readily become substantives and adjectives, as in such expressions as *el dia de hoy* or *es así.* The demonstrative adverbs are listed with the other adverbs (39.61), but it will be well to point out here the chief classes.

11.91 Manner. *así;* correlative to *como.*

11.92 Place. *aquí, acá; ahí; allí, allá.* The demonstratives of place correspond in their use to that of the demonstrative adjectives and pronouns: *aquí, acá,* like *este,* referring to things near the speaker; *ahí,* like *ese,* referring to things near the person addressed; and *allí, allá,* like *aquel,* referring to things remote from both speaker and person addressed. All are correlative to *donde.*

11.93 Quantity or degree. *tanto, tan;* correlative to *cuanto* (or *como*).

11.94 Time. *ahora, entonces, hoy.*

POSSESSIVE PRONOUNS

12. The possessive pronouns are formed with the demonstrative pronoun *el* (*la, lo, los, las*) and the stressed form of the possessive adjective. They are found in both masculine or feminine and in neuter forms.

12.1 Masculine and feminine.

12.11 Forms. The only frequent forms are: *el mío* (**31–85**), *el tuyo* (18–32), *el suyo* (**46–94**), and *el nuestro* (18–26).

12.2 Uses. The possessive pronouns may be used in any function in which other substantives are used.

12.21 Subject or object of a verb, or object of a preposition. UNA 160 *¡ Mi vida, mi vida por la suya!*   (**42–128**)

12.22 As subjective complement. SAS 47 *¿ Por qué estoy en esta tierra que no es la mía ?* It should be noted that as subjective complement, the possessive pronoun distinguishes between a number of objects possessed, in contrast with the possessive adjective, which distinguishes between a number of possessors. See 19.6.   (10–10)

12.3 Without an expressed verb.

12.311 In elliptical expressions. After *como*. ORT 140 *Temperamentos tales tienen que fracasar en una época como la nuestra.*   (3–4)

12.313 After *que*. IMP 73 *Este mar parece más denso que el nuestro.* (3–3)

12.32 In exclamations in conversational style. WAS 20 *¡ Qué amigos los suyos, tío Pepablo!*   (14–19)

12.4 Special uses.

12.41 The pronoun may be modified.

12.42 By an intensive adjective.

12.425 *propio,* placed after the adjectival element. STE 35 *Su dolor fué un triple dolor: el de sus padres, el suyo propio, también el de ella.* (3–3)

12.43 By an indefinite or qualifying adjective. ABU 415 *Sigue tu camino lleno de luz, y déjame en el mío tenebroso.*   (3–3)

12.44 By an adjectival phrase. RUS 12 *Mire usted qué pañuelo es el mío de boda.*   (4–4)

12.5 The adjective element may be replaced by a prepositional phrase with *de* and a personal pronoun, in the third person. BRA 161 *Es el retrato de don Lorenzo el joven, no el de usted.*   (14–17)

12.6 Feminine indefinite forms.

12.61 Singular. TIG 34 *Ha de salirse siempre con la suya.* (5–5)

12.62 Plural. JOA 56 *No tendría más remedio que hacer una de las mías para hacer un escarmiento.* (3–3)

12.7 *los suyos.* The masculine plural forms are used as nouns in the sense of "my folks," "his men," "our troops," etc. In this case *los* is the definite article. RIC 37 *Su padre amaba a los suyos tiernamente.*

(**24–31**)

12.8 Neuter forms. The neuter possessive pronouns, like other neuters, refer to a notion which has not been expressed by a noun. OCC 196 *A cada* quisque *lo suyo.* (9–18)

12.81 The neuter pronoun may be modified by an adjective, usually indefinite. LLA 49 *Todo lo tuyo me importa.* (3–3)

INDEFINITE PRONOUNS

13. The indefinite pronouns are limiting or restricting expressions of quantity, quality or class. The present list of indefinites includes not only those which are strictly or exclusively pronominal, but also all indefinite adjectives used as pronouns, including forms of such adjectives modified by *lo,* and combinations of an adjective and a noun which are used with pronominal force.

13.1 The various pronominal expressions are arranged alphabetically, combinations being entered under the significant word in the group. Under each word, combinations of that word with other words are arranged in the following order: Definite article, indicated by *el* or *lo;* Demonstrative adjective, indicated by *este;* Possessive adjective, indicated by *mi;* Indefinite article, indicated by *un;* Combinations of two indefinites, entered under the first, except that *solo* and *todo* used with another indefinite are regularly placed with the other. When the adjective *algún* is used with an indefinite pronoun, the entry is under the pronoun. Singular and plural forms are generally listed separately.

For negative indefinite pronouns, see 40.65.

13.2 *algo* (**44–280**), — *algo de (eso)* (3–3), *algo de (bueno)* (6–6), — *algo de (la vida)* (17–26), — *algo que* (10–18), — *algo más* (5–5); **alguien** (**33–56**); **alguna cosa** (8–8); **alguna cosilla** (3–3), **alguno** (12–15), — *alguno* (for *alguien*) (4–5), — *algunos* (**28–38**), — *alguno de* (7–9), — *alguno de* (for *uno de*) (3–4), — *alguno de* (with plural force) (4–4), *algunos de* (13–16); **ambos** (**21–38**); **bastante** (12–17); **ca** (for *cada*) — *ca uno* (3–8), **cada** — *cada cual* (16–27), — *cada uno* (**37–58**), *cada uno de* (12–17); **cualquier cosa** (13–16); **cualquiera** (17–21), — *cualquiera de* (13–14), — *un cualquiera* (always pejorative) (6–8); **demás** — *lo demás* (19–26), — *todo lo demás* (7–9), — *los demás* (**35–71**), — *todos los demás* (6–6); **demasiado** (6–7); **dos** — *los dos* (**41–142**); **entrambos** (7–8); **fulano** (4–5); **gente** (7–14); **infinidad de** (3–3); **más** (masculine or feminine) (9–10), — *más* (neuter) (**43–114**), — *más de* (+ a noun) (5–5); **menos** (masculine or feminine) (3–5), **menos** (neuter) (**23–32**); **mismo** — *el mismo* (**37–69**), — *los mismos* (10–12), — *lo mismo* (**41–118**); **muchísimo** (3–3); **mucho** (neuter) (**21–29**), — *muchos* (**26–35**), — *muchos de* (9–13); **no sé qué** (9–10); **otra cosa** (**21–35**); **otro** (**55–163**), — *otra* (indefinite feminine). SEC 27 *Ésa es otra.* (5–5), — *otros* (**36–78**), *el otro* (**44–120**), *los otros* (**30–52**), — *los otros dos* (7–7), — *este otro* (15–20), — *estos otros* (3–5), — *otro de* (6–7), — *otro cualquiera* (4–4) — *otro tanto* (4–4), — *otros (dos,* etc.) (5–5); **par** — *un par de* (11–11); **parte** — *la mayor parte de* (9–13); **pico** — *y pico* (after numerals) (3–3); **poco** (neuter) (**24–40**), — *pocos* (9–9), — *un poco* (13–27), — *un poco de (agua)*

(30–61); *poquito* — *un poquito de* (4–4); *porción* — *una porción de* (4–5); *propio* — *lo propio* (" the same thing ") (3–3); *resto* — *el resto de* (4–4); *solo* — *un solo* (3–4); *tal* (6–7), — *el tal* (3–3); *tanto* (neuter) (19–25), — *tanto . . . como* (8–9), *tantos* (9–10), *tantos otros* (3–3); *todo* (neuter) (60–532), — *todos* (60–507), — *el todo* (6–7), — *y todo* (" 'n everything ") (5–12); *todo el mundo* (26–47); *último* — *el último* (10–16); *una cosa* (4–5); *único* — *el único* (21–32), — *lo único* (20–29), *uno* (52–138), — *uno que* (15–19), — *uno a uno* (3–3), — *uno de* (55–250), — *uno de* (after form of *ser*) (29–41), — *uno solo* (6–8), *unos cuantos* (3–3); — Combinations of *uno* and *otro; uno . . . otro* (20–32), — *unos . . . otros* (26–34), — *uno . . . el otro* (when two individuals are involved) (8–12), — *el uno . . . el otro* (12–20), — *los unos . . . los otros* (5–6), — *uno y otro* (8–10), — *unos y otros* (8–8); *varios* (4–4), *varios de* (3–3).

INTERROGATIVE PRONOUNS

14. The various interrogative expressions which are used to introduce a question or exclamation may be pronouns, adverbs, or adjectives. Their forms are identical with those of the relatives. In general, the same forms are used in both direct and indirect questions. But Spanish, like other languages, frequently uses a relative form of expression in indirect questions, instead of an interrogative form. Where both types are used to express the same notion, the relatives are included with the interrogatives, to facilitate comparison. Because of their use in conversation, the interrogatives are often used without a verb, either in exclamatory utterance or in elliptical expressions implying a verb.

14.1 Referring to persons.

14.11 In direct questions, singular.

14.111 *quién.* As subject, subjective complement, or object of a preposition. MAY 115 *¿ Quién la llamó?* **(54–234)**

14.112 *a quién.* As direct object. ZAM 141 *¿ A quién llamas?* (12–14)

14.115 Without a verb. LUG 5 *¡ Y usted es el peor de todos! — ¿ Quién, yo?* **(25–45)**

14.12 Plural.

14.121 *quiénes.* LLA 80 *¿ Quiénes más han quedado?* (7–13)

14.122 *quién.* This is a survival of the Old Spanish construction. REY 154 *¿ Quién sois vosotros para negar la armonía de nuestras leyes?* (3–3)

14.15 In indirect questions, singular.

14.151 *quién.* As subject, subjective complement, or object of a preposition. BYN 56 *Ignoramos quién fuera el autor.* **(36–81)**

14.152 *a quién.* As direct object. BEN 31 *Que sepan a quién socorren.* (3–3)

14.155 Without a verb. MUJ 36 *Lorenzo está en casa y sabe Dios con quién.* (5–5)

14.16 Plural.

14.161 *quiénes.* ALT 465 *Procuró que no pudiese adivinar quiénes eran los testigos.* (6–7)

14.2 Referring to persons or to things with distinguishing force, " which ? ", " which one (ones) ? ".

14.21 In direct questions.

14.211 *cuál.* CAT 16 *Tengo campanas de todo tono.* ¿ *Cuáles prefiere usted?*
(12–15)

14.213 *cuál de.* Used when the group within which the distinction is made follows the interrogative. ROD 83 ¿ *A cuál de las semillas estará vinculado el nuevo árbol?* (6–9)

14.22 In indirect questions.

14.221 *cuál.* ROM 17 *Distinguirá bien cuáles versos son de Lope y cuáles tradicionales.* The first *cuáles* is an adjective. (6–6)

For *a cuál más,* see 26.595.

14.3 Referring to an unnamed neuter concept, " what ? ".

14.31 In direct questions and exclamations. *qué.*

14.311 As subject, object of a verb, or object of a preposition. IBA 370 ¿ *Y qué han hecho de ella?* Especially common in exclamations without a verb. ART 36 *De ahí que goce la estimación de usted.* — ¿ *Y qué? ¿ Se hace camino ?* **(57–735)**

14.32 As subjective complement.

14.321 The subject is a neuter pronoun. JIM 91 ¿ *Qué es eso, Platero ?*
(32–65)

14.322 The subject is a noun. ABC 22 ¿ *Qué es Digestónico ? — Es una medicación.* Neuter *qué* regularly asks for a definition of a noun; in the same construction *cuál* (adjective) asks for a distinction; see 22.221.
(10–13)

14.323 The subject is a masculine or feminine pronoun. NER 25 ¿ *Qué es usted ?* (4–5)

14.325 *¡ qué diablo (demonio, etc.) !* In exclamations *qué* may be reinforced by a mild oath. RIC 253 *Tú necesitas ordenar tu vida y ¡ qué diablo ! . . . ser útil para algo.* (10–13)

14.33 *qué cosa.* ORT 111 ¿ *Qué cosa son los dioses ?* Asking for a definition.
(3–3)

14.34 In indirect questions. *qué.*

14.341 As subject, object of the verb, or object of a preposition. ORR 176 *No sé qué será de nuestros hijos.* **(26–40)**

14.342 As subject complement, with a noun as subject. OCC 133 *No podríamos decir qué son las cosas que vemos.* (3–5)

14.35 Followed by an infinitive. FOM 22 *No sabía qué pensar.* (19–26)

14.38 *lo que.* That there was in origin a distinction between relative *lo que* and interrogative *qué* seems clear, because of the demonstrative element in *lo que* which gives to it a definiteness which is lacking in *qué*. But it is often impossible to find any distinction between the two in contemporary usage. Their close relationship is revealed by the fact that when the pronoun *lo que* is introduced by a preposition, it precedes *lo*, although it is logically the introducer of the relative *que*.

14.381 As subject or object of a verb. BRA 106 *No sé lo que me pasa.* (32–76)

14.382 As object of a preposition. BYN 57 *No quieran ustedes saber a lo que huele.* (6–8)

14.385 As subjective complement with a neuter pronoun as subject. ARN 14 *No sé lo que es eso.* (22–38)

14.386 As subjective complement with a noun as subject. JAN 112 *Ni siquiera sabe lo que es amor.* (6–8)

14.39 In exclamations. JAN 21 *¡ Lo que dirán los que no nos conocen!* (6–7)

14.4 With quantitative force, " how much ? ", " how many ? "

14.41 Referring to persons or to things.

14.411 *cuánto(s).* PAL 17 *¡ Ay, cuántas se me habrán escapado a mí!* (10–10)

14.42 Referring to an unnamed neuter concept.

14.421 *cuánto.* RAN 17 *No sé cuánto le habrá dado.* (12–18)

14.43 *lo que.*

14.431 In indirect questions. ORR 96 *No recordó lo que ese hombre hubiera podido sufrir por ella.* (5–7)

14.432 In exclamations. ARN 14 *Hija, lo que saben algunas.* (5–7)

INTERROGATIVE ADVERBS

14.5 The interrogative adverbs express relationships of cause, manner, place, purpose, quantity, and time. In form, they are identical with the relative adverbs. Like other interrogatives, they are often used in exclamatory as well as interrogative discourse, and they are often used in elliptical expressions without a verb.

14.51 Cause.

14.511 *por qué.* URU 54 *¿ Por qué te pones así ?* With an exclamatory infinitive. JAN 10 *¿ Por qué no divertirse un poco?*   **(57–300)**

14.514 *cómo.* SIE 58 *¿ Has terminado ya de pruebas ? — Sí. ¿ Cómo no has subido?* Equivalent to *¿ Cómo es que . . .?*   **(4–5)**

14.6 Manner.

14.61 *cómo.* TRI 220 *Hola, ¿ cómo va?*   **(60–324)**

14.611 Followed by infinitive. DEB 94 *No sé cómo demostrársela.* (17–17)

14.612 With exclamatory infinitive. UGA 41 *Pero ¿ cómo salir de ese mundo ?*   **(4–5)**

14.613 Without a verb. LIN 18 *A veces, y sin saber cómo, dices unas cosas que tienen sentido común.*   **(9–11)**

14.615 As an exclamation, meaning "how ? ". TIG *¿ Qué es lo que he de impedir yo ? — Mi boda. — ¿ Cómo ? — Escapando.*   **(10–13)**

14.616 As an exclamation meaning "what ?", and implying that the speaker does not understand. PAX 15 *Lo siento, sobre todo por Roberto. — ¡ Cómo ! . . . esta noche está tan alegre.*   **(18–29)**

14.617 As an exclamation meaning, "what do you mean ?", and followed by a word or phrase which has just been spoken. SAS 31 *¿ Y en su pueblo ? — ¿ Cómo pueblo ? — Bueno, en su Madrid. ¿ Hacía usted lo mismo ?*   **(4–6)**

14.618 *¡ cómo no !* "of course !" SEC 38 *¿ No recuerdas ? — ¿ Cómo no ?*   **(12–17)**

14.62 *qué.* As an exclamation, meaning "what do you mean by saying ? " and followed by an expression which has just been spoken. TIG 18 *No me defenderé. — ¿ Qué te has de defender tú, blanco?*   **(7–12)**

14.63 *qué tal.* In origin, *qué tal* was an adjectival expression, a variant of *cuál*, but it has now become adverbial. RAN 19 *¿ Qué tal le va?* It is most commonly used alone, asking for an expression of opinion or evaluation. JOA 27 *Y qué tal, ¿ es bueno?* Rarely there is the possibility that it is still an adjective. ART 76 *¿ Qué tal sigue?*   **(13–23)**

14.7 Place.

14.71 *dónde.* Place in which. UNA 160 *¡ Dios ! ¿ Dónde está Dios?*   **(40–124)**

14.711 Place to which. PAL 13 *¿ Dónde vas ? — le pregunté.*   **(6–9)**

14.713 Followed by an infinitive. TIG 27 *No sabe dónde encontrar a usted.* (6–8)

14.72 *adónde* (*a dónde*). Place to which. IMP 79 *¿ Adónde iría?* Without a verb. SJQ 39 *¿ Cómo que me agarre? ¿ Adónde?* (24–40)

14.73 *de dónde.* WAS 20 *¿ De dónde viene este hombre?* (15–20)

14.74 *en dónde.* OCC 262 *¿ En dónde está la cantera?* (6–7)

14.76 *hasta dónde.* URU 41 *Te he escuchao para ver hasta dónde llegaba tu desvergüenza.* (7–7)

14.79 *por dónde.* ABU 418 *¿ Por dónde se va al Infierno?* (11–12)

14.8 Purpose.

14.81 *a qué.* Most frequently after expressions involving motion. ART 77 *¡ Llamar! ¿ A qué voy a llamar?* (18–26)

14.82 *pa qué.* Colloquial only. CAT 9 *Yo mesmo la saqué de su casa, pa qué mentir.* (4–6)

14.83 *para qué.* PEQ 37 *¿ Por qué es tarde? ¿ Para qué es tarde?* (31–66)

14.85 Quantity. The commonest forms are *cuánto, qué* and *lo que.* It will be well to distinguish between adverbs modifying verbs and those modifying adjectives and adverbs.

14.86 Modifying a verb.

14.861 *cuánto.* DEB 14 *¡ Cuánto nos alegramos de verle por aquí!* (21–35)

14.865 *cómo.* IBA 367 *¡ Cómo te lo agradezco!* The confusion between manner and quantity is widespread; it is most clearly revealed in the use of *tanto . . . como,* instead of *tanto . . . cuanto.* (3–6)

14.867 *lo que.* In indirect questions. ZUN 32 *No sabe usted lo que le consideran todos los profesores.* (12–13)

14.868 *lo que.* In exclamations. RUS 130 *Un día hasta me pegó. ¡ Lo que lloré!* (8–15)

14.87 Modifying an adjective or adverb.

14.871 *qué.* FOM 23 *¡ Qué bella era la vida!* (42–222)

14.872 *cuán* (apocopated form of *cuánto*). VIG 107 *¡ Qué tremenda diferencia! ¡ Cuán distintas sus luchas!* (16–27)

14.881 *lo* (adjective) *que.* In indirect questions and exclamations only. PIN 141 *Cuanto dicen de la abundancia del dinero en América y de lo fácil que es ganarlo, es una vil engañifa.* See 18.97. (6–11)

14.883 *lo* (adverb) **que.** ORT 88 *Se lamenta de lo mal que andan las cosas en nuestro país.* (4–4)

14.89 Modifying an adjectival or adverbial phrase. *qué.* SIE 16 *¡ Si vieras qué a destiempo has venido!* (3–3)

14.9 Time.

14.91 *cuándo.* PEL 31 *¿ Pero cuándo recibió sus lecciones?* (26–47)

14.911 *desde cuándo.* IGN 88 *Hasta ignoraba desde cuándo formaban parte de su servidumbre.* (5–8)

14.92 For the uses of *si,* "whether," in direct and indirect questions, see 42.8.

14.98 Interrogative adverbs used as nouns. IDO 5 *Veían todos el porqué de su aire pálido.* Especially *por qué (porqué).* (7–8)

RELATIVE PRONOUNS

15. Relative pronouns fall into three main classes: restrictive relatives, introducing a clause which is essential to the identification of the antecedent; parenthetical relatives, introducing a clause which adds a qualification which is not essential to the identification of the antecedent; and substantive relatives, which involve their own antecedent, either in a single word or in a combination. All relative clauses are adjectival modifiers.

RESTRICTIVE RELATIVES

15.1 The commonest restrictive relative pronoun, in all functions in the sentence, with all types of antecedent, is *que.* Only after a preposition, with a personal antecedent, is it regularly replaced by *quien;* with other antecedents, after a preposition it may be replaced by *el cual* or *el que.*

15.11 As subject of its clause, with either a person or thing as antecedent. ***que.*** ORT 77 *Soy un hombre que ama verdaderamente el pasado.*
(60–2820)

15.12 As object, with either a person or thing as antecedent. ***que.*** MAY 4 *Venía recordando la última temporada que pasó en Asturias.* (60–1224)

15.14 As object of a preposition.

15.15 The antecedent is a person.

15.151 *quien.* RUS 17 *Tú eres el sobrino a quien más quiero.* (23–37)

15.152 *quienes.* RAN 80 *Los primeros amigos a quienes vi prorrumpieron en ayes lastimeros.* (15–20)

15.155 *el cual.* Especially after dissyllabic or compound prepositions. ORR 178 *Había comprendido a la mujer delante de la cual se hablaba.* (4–6)

15.157 *el que.* FAL 25 *El juez le miró como a un estafador con el que tendría que ver algún día.* (7–18)

15.16 The antecedent is a thing.

15.161 *que.* Especially with monosyllabic prepositions. SJQ 43 *Bien sabe usted el dolor por que estoy pasando.* (60–420)

15.165 *el cual.* Especially with dissyllabic and compound prepositions. TIG 38 *Lo que sientes ahora es vértigo. Una atracción contra la cual quieres oponer tu voluntad.* (23–41)

15.167 *el que.* Especially with dissyllabic and compound prepositions. DEB 88 *Hay tendencias contra las que no se puede luchar.*   (15–23)

15.17 The relative is followed by an infinitive. ZAM 134 *Tengo tantas, tantas cosas que decirte.* For discussion, see 37.483.

PARENTHETICAL RELATIVES

15.2 The commonest parenthetical or explanatory relative is again *que.* But in this usage, *quien, el cual,* and *el que* compete with *que* in all functions of the relative in the sentence, particularly after a preposition. It should be remarked that a parenthetical relative is found most frequently after a specific antecedent, that is to say, one that needs or permits no further identification, such as a personal pronoun, a proper name, or a noun modified by a determinative.

15.21 As subject or object of its clause, with either a person or a thing as antecedent.

15.211 *que.* The antecedent is a personal pronoun. SIE 24 *Dichoso usted, que tiene tales seguridades.* The antecedent is a proper noun. PEL 8 *Las escribió Boschá, que fué Cónsul de Barcelona.* The antecedent is a specific noun. URU 56 *Sea franca con su padrino, que tanto le quiere.*
(60–1354)

15.213 *quien.* IGN 59 *Telegrafió a Madrid para que fuera el doctor Bustamente, quien llegó al día siguiente.*   (15–28)

15.214 *quienes.* STE 32 *¡ Si es un muchacho! — observó la mamá de dos bonitas niñas, quienes sonreían, sin saber por qué.*   (9–13)

15.215 *el cual.* The antecedent is a person. STE 242 *Elvirita prendióse de uno de los brazos de su tía y del otro la Perla, la cual destacábase espléndida entre todos los demás.*   (14–22)

15.216 The antecedent is a thing. ORT 128 *Me refiero a ciertos objetos únicos e inconfundibles, los cuales no están presentes ante mí.*   (10–12)

15.217 *el que.* SAS 57 *Yo tengo todas tus cartas, las que me acostumbraron a tu ternura.*   **(21–26)**

15.22 As object of a preposition.

15.221 *que.* The antecedent is a thing; only after monosyllabic prepositions. LUG 365 *¿ Quiere usted absolverme de aquel pecado, de que estoy sinceramente arrepentido?*   (18–42)

15.223 *quien.* The antecedent is a person; the preposition is normally monosyllabic. MAY 68 *Se muestra gozosa de aprovechar la blandura de su amigo, a quien sigue convenciendo.* **(36–83)**

15.234 *quienes.* The antecedent is personal; the preposition is normally monosyllabic. PAX 11 *Hacía ademanes a las dos señoras, con quienes sostenía una conversación animada.* (5–8)

15.235 *el cual.* The antecedent is a person or a thing. After a monosyllabic preposition. JAN 304 *Es un funcionario celoso, al cual debemos consideración.* **(31–88)** After a preposition of more than one syllable. ROD 9 *Su potestad, bajo la cual cabe todo lo creado, se ejerce sobre las almas.* (15–26) After a compound preposition. FOM 98 *Seguía su misma vida alegre, dentro de la cual Eva Luz significaba una contrariedad.* (9–11)

15.237 *el que.* The antecedent is a person or a thing. After a monosyllabic preposition. ALT 193 *Para la regulación de las Juntas se dictaron varias Ordenanzas, de las que son notables las de 1417.* **(30–98)** After a preposition of more than one syllable. JIM 34 *Me ponía mi mano sobre su corazón, sobre el que el pecho joven subía y bajaba.* (7–7)

15.24 With a neuter ántecedent. The antecedent is a notion conveyed by a preceding clause.

15.241 *que.* RAN 31 *Luego dice dónde ha nacido, que es: o en el barrio de maravillas, o en Granada.* (18–26)

15.245 *lo cual.* REY 113 *Es posible que cada uno quiera tirar por su lado, lo cual sería un grave inconveniente.* (13–22)

15.246 After a preposition. IMP 88 *Haré cuanto pueda por conocerle, a lo cual te pido que me ayudes.* (9–12)

15.247 *lo que.* JOA 20 *Y tú te ríes sin decir nada, lo que quiere decir que piensas lo mismo que yo.* (16–24)

15.248 After a preposition. WAS 3 *Cubríale la cara una barba tupida y corta, por lo que podía sospecharse que poco tiempo antes se afeitaba totalmente.* (8–9)

15.25 Neuter *que* used as a subjective complement to sum up a noun or adjective expressing class. This use of *que* is exactly parallel to that of the personal object pronoun *lo* as a subjective complement; see 7.34.

15.251 Summing up a noun. PIN 151 *Te esperaré pa que salgamos los últimos, como dos pastores que somos.* (8–9)

15.255 Summing up an adjective. TIG 14 *Abra los ojos y mire bien lo fea y vieja que soy.* **(25–45)**

15.27 *El cual* (*lo cual*) used with the force of a conjunction. The relative pronoun *el cual* (*lo cual*) is always used to give additional information concerning the antecedent, and from this basic usage is derived its use, once very common but now relatively rare, as the equivalent of a coordinating copulative conjunction, with the force of "and it" or "and this."

15.271 *el cual*. Usually after a preposition. ART 19 *Ese silencio es una respuesta. — O una requisa. — De la cual sacará usted las más dolorosas consecuencias.* (3–3)

15.273 *lo cual*. VIG 69 *Expresión tan digna de Hamlet como del amante veronés. Lo cual sugiere el sentido dramático de duda que hay en el verdadero amor.* (5–6)

15.274 After a preposition. RAN 38 *Pero ¿ con qué objeto ? — le preguntaba yo. A lo cual el* chauffer *hacía un gesto vago.* (5–6)

15.275 *todo lo cual*. Only after a preposition. UGA 23 *Eres el más feliz de los Tenorios — concluyó García. A todo lo cual respondió el héroe — No me hablen ustedes de cosas tristes.* (3–3)

SUBSTANTIVE RELATIVES

15.3 Substantive relatives are those which involve their own antecedent. They may be expressed by a single word, as *quien* or *cuanto*, or may consist of a demonstrative pronoun followed by a restrictive relative, as *el que* or *eso que*. In the second type, it is possible to conceive of the combination as two independent elements, but since the combination is used as an exact equivalent of the simple forms, it has seemed best to group them together.

15.31 *el que*.

15.311 Referring to definite persons or things. JIM 23 *Los que estábamos en ellas nos gritábamos cosas de ingenio mejor o peor.* (54–438)

15.312 With indefinite force. PIN 119 *Le dará cinco mil duros al que me prenda.* (18–31)

15.315 With quantitative force. REY 161 *No tenemos agua. — ¿ Y el río ? Con una cuerda y un cubo podemos sacar la que queramos.* (3–3)

15.32 *con el que* for *el con que*. If the relative element of the combination is the object of a preposition, the preposition is normally placed before the demonstrative element. BEN 5 *Sí, señora; por el otro Zurita, que es al que dicen todos el malo.* (4–4)

15.33 In partitive expressions with *de*.

15.331 As an attributive modifier of an indefinite noun. PEQ 144 *Era una polacra vieja de las que transportan petróleo.* (11–16)

15.333 As a predicate modifier. ART 81 *No soy de las que llevan a un duelo al hombre adorado.* (3–4)

15.34 In apposition with a noun. This construction is unquestionably the source of the use of *el que* as a simple relative of the parenthetical type and it is often impossible to distinguish which is the predominant function. PAT 216 *Me quedan unas diez mil pesetas, las que presté a Manolo.* The sense here seems clearly to be "those that" and not "which." (12–19)

15.35 As subjective complement, instead of neuter *lo que*. This construction involves a sort of attraction in gender. MUJ 21 *Es la jaulita la que se ha de abrir. La que* cannot mean "the one that"; it is "the thing that." See also 15.45. **(27–44)**

15.36 As objective complement, instead of *lo que*. UNA 13 *En un poema la realidad no es la del que llaman los críticos realismo* ("of what the critics call . . ."). (4–4)

15.37 After *como*. FOM 97 *Solían nacer mujeres y hombres carentes de afectividad, tan dignos de lástima como el que nace loco.* (12–19)

15.38 After *que*. Always in comparisons between notions of the same category and never with quantitative force; see 26.421. URU 40 *Usted sobre mí no tiene más autoridad que la que mi cariño quiere concederle.* (9–13)

15.39 Modified.

15.391 *todo el que.* RUS 34 *Esos monos son la risa de todo el que los mira.* (4–5)

15.392 *todos los que.* ORT 17 *Así pasa con todos los que tengo aquí.* **(22–28)**

15.4 *lo que.* It is not always possible to distinguish between relative uses and uses in indirect questions with *lo que*. In the present study *lo que* is considered as interrogative only when it introduces a clause after a verb which expresses or implies a question; see 14.38.

15.41 Regular uses. BEN 6 *De la gente ya sabe uno lo que puede esperar. Saber* is considered as introducing an indirect question only when it is negative or interrogative. **(60–711)**

15.42 *con lo que* for *lo con que*. If the relative element of the combination is the object of a preposition, the preposition is normally placed before the demonstrative element. MGR 18 *¡ Un millón de dólares es en lo que tasa esa mujer al marido!* **(20–22)**

15.44 In apposition with a neuter concept. As with *el que*, this is the origin of the use of *lo que* as a simple relative; see 15.247. RAN 29 *El ascensor carecía de letrero, lo que me hizo pensar muy mal del servicio.* Either "a fact which" or "which."   (4–4)

15.45 As subjective complement. ABU 29 *El lujo es lo que sostiene la industria.* Compare 15.35.   (31–44)

15.46 As objective complement. RET 40 *Las nuevas tendencias culminaron en lo que Lugones llamó "la conquista de la independencia intelectual."* Compare 15.36.   (3–3)

15.48 After a comparative.

15.481 Introduced by *de* in quantitative comparisons. BRA 14 *Pero podríamos vivir mejor de lo que vivimos.*   (17–18)

15.485 Introduced by *que* in comparisons of identical categories. PAL 16 *Me lamía la cara acaso más a menudo que lo que hubiera aconsejado la decencia.* The *lo que* clause is used adverbially and compared with the adverb *a menudo*.   (6–6)

15.49 Modified.

15.491 *todo lo que.* LLA 17 *Todo lo que no es hermosura en el mundo, no debe existir.*   (30–56)

15.5 Another demonstrative pronoun replaces *el (lo).*

15.51 *aquel que.*

15.511 Regular uses. SON 123 *Aquel que caminaba detrás mostraba al pueblo la sentencia de Pilatos.*   (11–18)

15.514 In apposition with a noun. JES 25 *Me estoy preparando para la cátedra auxiliar de Biología, la que dejó vacante el viejo Ruani, aquél que no creía en los microbios.*   (5–6)

15.517 *aquel con quien.* If the relative element is the object of a preposition and refers to a person as antecedent, *quien* normally replaces *que.* It should be remarked that *aquel* normally replaces *el* when the relative is object of a preposition even when the antecedent is a thing. But see 15.32. CAT 22 *Érase un individuo muy metido en política y perseguido por aquellos a quienes hacía la oposición.*   (10–10)

15.519 Modified. *todos aquellos que.* ART 17 *Tiene en usted un gran admirador. — En mí y en todos aquellos que la tratan.*   (3–4)

15.52 *aquello que.* ROD 84 *El valor de aquello que se hace o se dice, ¿quién lo calculará con fijeza?*   (9–9)

15.53 *ese que.*

15.531 Regular uses. LLA 43 *¿ Qué muertos son esos que resucitan?*
(12–14)

15.532 *ese con quien* (*el cual*). If the relative element is object of a preposition, *que* may be replaced by *quien* or *el cual*. ORR 178 *No era de esas con las cuales siquiera se puede tratar el tema siempre peligroso del amor.*
(3–3)

15.533 In a partitive construction with *de.* ARN 55 *Me compré un Mapa de esos que vendían en la Puerta del Sol.*
(12–15)

15.54 *eso que.*

15.541 Regular uses. UNA 13 *Nada hay más ambiguo que eso que se llama realismo en el arte literario.*
(17–20)

15.549 Modified. ***todo eso que.*** ABU 28 *Será cuento todo eso que se dice de tu señora.*
(3–4)

15.7 *quien.* *Quien* differs from *el que* in that it contains its own antecedent. Functionally therefore, each of the elements, antecedent and relative, must be examined separately. *Quien* always refers to persons.

15.71 The relative element is subject of its clause.

15.711 The antecedent is also subject of the main clause. NER 38 *Quien enterraba su oro, mataba casi siempre al excavador del pozo.*
(**25–43**)

15.713 The antecedent is subjective complement. ART 45 *¿ Es usted quien habla?*
(**30–56**)

15.72 The antecedent is direct object.

15.721 *quien* is introduced by personal *a.* IMP 16 *Era virtud de Celia envolver a quien estaba cerca de su corazón en un vaho de ternura.* (6–8)

15.723 More frequently *a* is omitted, especially when the main clause is negative. IGN 31 *Arturo no tiene un cuarto ni quien se lo dé.* (19–30)

15.725 The antecedent is indirect object. *Quien* is regularly introduced by *a.* WAS 21 *Yo había nacido para hombre de negocios, — dijo a quien le quiso oír.*
(9–10)

15.727 The antecedent is object of a preposition. IDO 5 *Respiraba la satisfacción de quien está bien hallado en el mundo.*
(14–25)

15.76 The relative element is object of a preposition. In this situation the antecedent element is usually the object of the same preposition. RUS 92 *La casaré con quien la tenga que casar.*
(4–4)

15.77 After *como*. FAL 13 *El extranjero le sacudió el brazo como quien tira de la campanilla en la casa que no abren.* (13–16)

15.79 *quienes*. If it is necessary to express the notion of a group of individuals, *quienes* is used instead of *quien*. Its constructions are identical with those of *quien*. ABC 38 *Quienes mandan desde entonces son los socialistas.* (14–24)

15.81 *cuanto*. As a substantive relative pronoun, *cuanto* originally involved as its antecedent *tanto*. But it is now used as an equivalent of *todo lo que*. It may refer to persons and things, or it may be neuter.

15.811 Referring to persons and things. VIG 67 *Augusto Pérez resucitará para seguir viviendo en el recuerdo de cuantos lean Niebla.* (10–12)

15.815 As a neuter pronoun, "all that." UGA 32 *Lisandro sacó su cartera, donde había reunido cuanto tenía.* **(25–51)**

15.816 Reinforced by *todo*. ORR 98 *Sintió convicción de que todo cuanto le habían referido era calumnia.* (7–8)

15.85 *que*. The only situation in which *que* is now used as a substantive relative is in elliptical expression with an expressed or implied infinitive.

15.851 The infinitive is expressed. STE 252 *Ya tengo qué dejarte en recuerdo, padrino querido.* *Que* here has the force of "something which". See also 37.485. (18–23)

15.855 The infinitive is implied, especially when *que* is object of a preposition. TIG 18 *Págame la deuda, y si no tienes con qué, por mi propia mano me cobro.* The use of the written accent in these constructions must not be interpreted as indicating an interrogative pronoun; it merely reveals that the pronoun is a stressed form. (5–6)

15.91 Generalizing, indefinite relatives. There are a number of generalizing, indefinite relatives, formed by affixing *quiera que* to a simple relative, which have the force of concession of indifference. The only form in common use is *cualquiera (cualquier) que*, used either as a pronoun or as an adjective.

15.911 Used as a pronoun. *cualquiera que*. SJQ 38 *Cualquiera que lo oiga, pensará que estamos en un desierto.* (5–6)
The verb is regularly in the subjunctive; see 29.645.

15.915 Used as an adjective. *cualquier . . . que*. JAN 22 *Lo peor es que cualquier tipo que compra una estampilla de a cinco, se cree con derecho a enamorar a las empleadas.* (3–3)

15.95 Special uses of relatives.

15.951 Relative pronouns and adverbs are sometimes used introducing elliptical expressions without a verb.

15.956 *lo que.* RIC 269 *Y a mi hermano le va a pasar lo que a Don Quijote de la Mancha.* *Lo que* is almost the equivalent of *lo mismo que.* (9–13)

15.957 *que.* TRI 218 *No tenía Gabriel para qué adoptar los aires doctorales que en Villalón.* *Los aires* is almost the equivalent of *los mismos aires.* (3–3)

15.96 A noun modified by a relative clause may be used in conversational style instead of a complete sentence. ARN 67 *Entro, y plum, el Califa y el Tirones que estaban allí.* **(23–54)**

RELATIVE ADVERBS

16. Relative adverbs, like relative pronouns, fall into three main classes: restrictive, parenthetical, and substantive. It is from the last usage, in which the antecedent is involved in the relative, that the use of *como* and *cuando* as subordinating conjunctions has developed. In the following discussion, only those uses which are clearly relative are included. The main types of adverbial modification are: manner, place, quantity and time.

16.1 Manner. *Como* is still found sporadically with an expressed antecedent or dependent upon a preposition. But the only uses which are in any way common, where it is properly a relative adverb rather than a conjunction, are when it is in the predicate position.

16.11 Involving its own antecedent, in the predicate position. UNA 95 *Déjame solo, que es como quiero estar* ("the way in which"). (4–5)

16.2 Place. The common relative adverb of place is *donde*. It is found alone and introduced by a preposition in all types of relative usage.

16.21 *donde.* Usually indicating place in which, but occasionally also place to which.

16.211 Restrictive. ROD 82 *El fruto donde se esconde el germen preferido es arrancado del árbol por una mano codiciosa.* **(42–152)**

16.212 Parenthetical. NER 36 *Había nacido en la Barca, donde su tío era alcalde.* **(42–132)**

16.213 Substantive. SIE 84 *¡ Tengo un hambre de decirte todo lo que te quiero donde nadie nos oiga!* **(32–55)**

16.215 Expressing place to which. Common only as a substantive relative. JAN 108 *Ni siquiera tenían libertad para ir donde quisieran.* (6–11)

16.217 With an adverb as antecedent. The relative is attributive. ABU 197 *Este D. Pío, aquí donde le ves, tan suavecito, es un tigre.* (14–15)

16.218 The relative is predicate. TRI 132 *Allí era donde se bañaba por las tardes.* (3–3)

16.22 *adonde* (also written *a donde*). Usually of place to which.

16.222 Parenthetical. PAT 16 *Habían vuelto los dos del Puerto de los Pinares, adonde habían subido en compañía de unos amigos.* (8–13)

16.223 Substantive. RUS 96 *Pero me volvería adonde antes estaba.* (17–22)

16.23 *de donde.*

16.231 Restrictive. IDO 11 *Desviaron sus pensamientos hacia la distante ciudad europea de donde él venía.* (3–3)

16.232 Parenthetical. WAS 11 *Debía estar en las proximidades de la casa de don Pedro, de donde partía un camino mejor.* (10–12)

16.233 Substantive. UGA 18 *No puedo vivir lejos de donde ella está.* (5–7)

16.24 *en donde.*

16.241 Restrictive. MGR 44 *Puede Ud. obtener ahora la pura Cera Aseptina en la Farmacia o Perfumería en donde compre habitualmente.* (7–12)

16.242 Parenthetical. PAX 333 *Salen a una planada cubierta de árboles, en donde el río Blanco y el río Negro se encuentran.* (14–19)

16.25 *por donde.*

16.251 Restrictive. BRA 189 *Y aparece silenciosamente Laura en la puerta por donde se marchó.* (10–12)

16.252 Parenthetical. RAN 90 *¡ La campiña arcádica, por donde los ríos se deslizan mansamente!* (8–10)

16.253 Substantive. SJQ 45 *Vamos por donde digas.* (5–5)

16.29 **Relative adverbs of place followed by an infinitive.** The antecedent is usually expressed. JES 227 *En busca de un establo donde alquilar caballos.* See also 37.493. (7–7)

16.3 **Quantity.** The only relative adverb of quantity which is still in use is *cuanto*, in expressions of proportionate comparison. LLA 5 *Cuanto más tiempo esté con mi mujer, mejor.* See also 26.74. (9–15)

16.31 If the *más* which follows *cuanto* modifies a masculine or feminine noun, *cuanto* agrees with the noun. MUJ 30 *Cuantas más vueltas le doy, más imposible me parece.* (4–4)

16.32 lo que. The quantitative force of *lo que* is such that it may be used to replace *cuanto* or *tanto como*. ZAM 158 *No hay mujer que distraiga lo que un libro bueno.* (7–8)

16.321 todo lo que. DEB 93 *Bien sabe Dios que soy dichosa, todo lo que se puede ser en la vida.* (3–3)

16.4 Time. The regular relative adverb of time, *cuando*, has become a subordinating conjunction and has been replaced, when an antecedent is expressed, by *que;* see 16.615. A trace of its original use is found, however, when it is introduced by a preposition. SAS 51 *Me acuerdo de cuando eras chiquito* (" the time when "). (9–10)

16.5 Generalizing, indefinite relative adverbs. As with pronouns, *quiera que* may be added to a relative adverb to form a generalizing indefinite. DEB 52 *Dondequiera que sea, tal vez pases el tiempo mejor que nosotros.* (8–10)

The only common adverb is *dondequiera que* (3 3).

RELATIVE ADVERB *que*

16.6 Probably the most difficult word in Spanish to analyze adequately is *que*. Some of its functions are clear: as relative pronoun, as annunciative subordinating conjunction, as correlative of expressions of comparison of superiority and inferiority. But there remain a large number of cases in which it is difficult, if not impossible, to determine exactly the function which it performs in the sentence. Perhaps the simplest solution would be to say that for the Spaniard *que* is a connective, coordinating or subordinating as the context demands. In some of its uses, however, the presence of an antecedent makes it clear that it is used as a relative adverb.

16.61 With an expressed antecedent.

16.611 Expressing manner. IMP 74 *De cualquier modo que fuese, el suceso le pinchaba como una espina en el corazón.* Perhaps this type belongs below in 16.62, or perhaps *de cualquier modo que* should be considered a generalizing indefinite of manner, equivalent to *comoquiera que*. (4–4)

16.612 The antecedent is a superlative adverb. LUG 359 *Lo más amablemente que supo, invitó a callar a los estudiantes.* (5–7)

16.613 The antecedent is an adverb introduced by *por* (*por bien que, por más que,* etc.) or by *lo* (*lo bien que,* etc.) TIG 47 *La voz de lo requetebien que lo hace.* (13–20)

16.615 Expressing time. ABU 34 *El día que se las lleven me ha de costar algunas lágrimas.* The use of *que* for *cuando* in this construction is clear evidence that *cuando* is felt to be a conjunction, rather than an adverb. (35–92)

16.62 An identical preposition used with the antecedent is not repeated before *que.* FOM 105 *Del amor al estudio se contagió doña Josefa en los límites que le era dable* (that is: *en los límites en que*). (12–12)

16.63 The first element of an expression of the type *allí es donde* is the relative adverb *que,* before *como, donde, cuanto* (*lo que*), or *cuando.* UNA 95 *Déjame solo, que es como quiero estar.* (3–3)

16.65 Other uses of *que.*

16.651 *hace mucho tiempo que está aqui.* *Que* is probably in origin a relative adverb of time; see 16.615, 32.12.

16.652 *alguna que otra vez.* *Que* is considered a coordinating alternative conjunction; see 42.76.

16.653 *tengo que* (*hay que*) *hacerlo.* *Que* was probably in origin a substantive relative pronoun, but it has now lost all independent force and is merely a part of the auxiliary verb.

16.654 *por bueno que sea* (*lo bueno que es*). *Que* is considered a neuter relative pronoun, summing up the preceding adjective, as does the object pronoun *lo;* see 15.25.

III. ADJECTIVES

17. A word which is used to modify a substantive is called an adjective. Adjectives are divided into two classes: limiting and qualifying. A limiting adjective is one which restricts the application of a noun or other substantive in quantity or in quality. Limiting adjectives may be determinative, identifying specific individuals, as the demonstratives, the definite article and the possessives; or indefinite, as the indefinite article, the indefinite and negative adjectives, the interrogatives, and the numerals; or relative. A qualifying adjective is one which distinguishes a substantive from other substantives of its class or which adds to an already identified substantive a description of its appearance, character, or value.

17.01 In addition to words which are normally classified as adjectives, other elements of the sentence are used adjectivally. Verbal participles, present or past, are regularly adjectival. Most nouns may be used as adjectives. Relative clauses are always adjectival modifiers. Prepositional phrases, particularly those introduced by *de*, are often adjectival. And adverbs, particularly demonstrative adverbs, are often used as adjectives.

DEMONSTRATIVE ADJECTIVES

17.1 The demonstrative adjectives are used to point out, in space, time, order, etc., a specific individual or individuals. In form and in basic meaning they are identical with the demonstrative pronouns, including a neuter: *este* (*-a, -o, -os, -as*), *ese* (*-a, -o, -os, -as*), *aquel* (*-ella, -ello, -ellos, -ellas*). When written, they never bear the accent.

17.2 Other expressions used as demonstratives.

17.21 *dicho.* " This," in the sense of " the aforesaid." ABC 34 *Se da el nombre de usted para dicha cartera.* (6–27)

17.22 *el tal.* " This," in the sense of " the said." ABU 20 *La tal Condesa es persona de grandes influencias.* (11–15)

17.23 *tal.* Like *el tal*, but rare. ORR 95 *Tal respuesta desazonó a Elisa.* (3–3)

17.3 Regular uses.

17.31 *este*. The demonstrative of the first person: indicating persons or things related to the speaker in space, to the present in time. PEQ 20 *En esta soledad, entre estos volúmenes, parece que resurge en mí toda mi vida de niño.* SAS 125 *¿ Por qué no vienes esta noche ?* **(60–1971)**

17.32 *ese*. The demonstrative of the second person: indicating persons or things related to the person addressed, expressions which he has used or which he has just heard, or events which in time fall within his experience or which have just been called to his attention. LLA 51 *No, no abras esos ojos pasmados.* LIN 66 *Es que estoy comprometida para ir.— Sabes que debo estar en Santander durante esos días.* **(60–1239)**

17.33 *aquel*. The demonstrative of the third person: indicating persons or things unrelated either to the speaker or the person addressed, in space, or remote from the present in time. ZUN 24 (a woman is watching a bullfight) *¿ Quién es aquel torero del traje azul ?* ALT 9 *Los caballeros del Templo pueden considerarse como uno de los grados sociales superiores de aquellos tiempos.* **(54–1194)**

17.4 Special uses.

17.41 As definite article. A remnant of the primitive use of the demonstratives, particularly *ese*, as definite article is found in a number of fixed phrases in the plural. RIC 30 *Tal era la mozuela que le empujó a salir de aventuras por esos mundos de Dios.* **(5–7)**

17.42 With depreciative force. Both *este* and *ese* are used with expressions of dislike or scorn; the latter more frequently.

17.421 *este*. PAT 12 *¡ Puaf, esta gentuza !* **(3–5)**

17.423 *ese*. PAL 136 *Ya te he dicho que no quiero que hables con ese mequetrefe.* **(19–52)**

17.43 *esto, eso, aquello* as neuter adjectives. Like the definite article *lo*, which was demonstrative in origin, the demonstrative adjectives are occasionally found as neuter adjectives modifying an adjective or past participle. The only phrases which survive in use are *esto poco, esto último.* IMP 23 *Si Celia optaba por esto último, podía colegirse que deseaba ver al mirón.* **(3–3)**

17.6 With two coordinated nouns. The adjective is normally repeated with two coordinated nouns. OCC 261 *Muy curioso es ver cómo defiende ese mundo y esa vida del intelectual.* **(16–21)**

17.61 But if the two nouns are considered as forming a unit, the adjective is not repeated.   UNA 27 *Estas señoras y señoritas.*   (7–13)

17.7 Position.   The adjective usually precedes the noun.   PAT 7 *El habitual silencio de la población se profondiza por aquella parte.*   (*)

It should be noted that the demonstrative adjective is always stressed, even though it precedes a noun.

17.71 For special stress, the adjective is often placed after the noun. SJQ 129 *¡ Bendita sea la madre que parió al señorito ese!*   (19–40)

THE DEFINITE ARTICLE

18. The definite article is a limiting adjective which is used to indicate a specific individual, person, or thing, whose identity has already been established or is about to be established. In origin it was a demonstrative, and it is still demonstrative, although it can no longer make distinctions in space or time, like the other demonstratives.

18.1 Forms.

18.11 Regular forms. The regular forms of the article, *el, la, lo, los, las* are adequately illustrated in the following sections.

18.12 Special forms.

18.121 *er,* for *el.* Dialect only (Andalusia, Spanish America). CAT 7
Er río.   (3–22)

18.123 *el,* for *la,* before feminine nouns beginning with stressed *a–* (*ha–*). The form is not a masculine form, but an elided form of Old Spanish *ela,* feminine.

18.124 Before *a–.* CAT 6 *El alma.*   ([51]–239)

  The commonest nouns are: *agua* (**35–70**), *ala* (13–16), *alba* (5–7), *ansia* (5–5), *alma* (**41–109**).

18.125 Before *ha–.* REY 113 *El hambre.*   (11–16)

  The only common noun is *hambre* (5–7).

18.13 Contracted forms. In combination with *a* and *de,* the masculine forms are regularly *al* and *del: al aire, del señorito.*   (*)

18.131 *ar,* for *al.* Dialect only. CAT 8 *Me lo trujo ar chico.*   (5–7)

18.135 *a el, de el,* not contracted before proper names beginning with the article. BYN 50 *de* El Eco Saboyano.   (11–14)

18.2 Uses of the definite article. The basic use of the article to indicate a particular identified individual is still its most frequent usage. But this use has been extended in a number of ways. The most important development has been its use to express collectives, which easily became identical with classes. A further extension of the collective use is found in its employment with abstract nouns and with nouns of material. Another important field is its use with personal attributes to express possession, replacing the possessive adjective. The use of the definite article must also be studied from the point of view of the function of the noun modified in the sentence. For the primitive use of the identifying article began with its use to modify the subject of the sentence and its use in other situations has been a slow development. Even to-day the use of the article with a noun used after a preposition or used as a complement or appositive is far rarer than its use with a noun which is subject.

18.21 The article with demonstrative force. A few cases survive in which the article is still used with demonstrative force.

18.213 With the force of *el mismo*. ARN 38 *Entre estas y otras chirigotas por el estilo, se nos sienta en la mesa.* Chiefly in the phrases *a la vez* and *por el estilo.* (25–48)

18.22 Regular uses. JIM 19 *El camino sube.* IBA 24 *Bebió de un golpe la copa que le ofreció la tabernera.* (*)

18.23 With general nouns of class. ORT 98 *El vino exalta los corazones.* (50–688)

18.24 With abstract nouns. SON 115 *Nada tiene que ver con la religión.* (60–1458)

18.241 Omitted after prepositions. IBA 368 *Repetíanse con frecuencia los ataques.* Regular, when the prepositional phrase is an adjectival or adverbial unit. (*)

18.245 Personified abstractions. A number of abstract notions are personified and become almost proper nouns. They are regularly accompanied by the article. ABU 34 *Su institutriz es la Naturaleza.* (49–201)
   Typical nouns in this group are: *amor, fortuna, guerra, muerte, naturaleza, ocasión, suerte.*

18.25 With infinitives. The infinitive is an abstraction of the notion expressed by the verb. For discussion, see 37.11.

18.26 With clauses. SEC 11 *Debías agradecerle el que se haya echado por ahí a buscar quien nos sirva.* The use of the article with a clause indicates that the notion expressed by the clause is presented as a generalized abstraction, not as a fact. See also 29.519. (8–13)

18.27 With appellatives of unique objects. The article is regularly used with nouns which indicate a unique object. They, again, are almost proper nouns. SJQ 45 *Hay algunos santos en el cielo.* (*)
   Typical nouns in this group are: *cielo, demonio, diablo, iglesia, infierno, luna, mundo, paraíso, sol, tierra.*

18.28 With names of materials and mass nouns. ABU 13 *Se juntarán aquí el agua y el fuego.* (Counted under nouns of class)

18.283 Even after *como.* WAS 22 *Un agua fría como el hielo.* (4–5)

18.285 Omitted after a preposition. DEB 9 *Un mar de oro.* (27–170)

18.29 With names of diseases. MGR 5 *La tristeza engendra la neuras-
tenia.* (14–25)

18.31 With names of games. SON 43 *Jugaban a la rueda.* (18–50)

18.311 Omitted. OCC 188 *Se jugaba a carambolas.* Especially after *una
partida de.* (10–16)

18.32 With names of languages. RIC 29 *Con estas palabras traducidas
del francés engañan al vulgo.* (7–9)

18.321 The noun is direct object of a verb. MUJ 15 *Se ha empeñado en
dominar el español.* (3–3)

18.325 Omitted after *de.* ZUN 40 *Un profesor de inglés.* (11–22)

18.327 Omitted aften *en.* RUB 83 *Una frase en griego.* (13–27)

18.329 Omitted after a verb. MUJ 10 *Hoy tienes alemán.* (4–6)

18.33 With names of meals. DEB 91 *Después del almuerzo.* (11–13)

18.34 With nouns of measure or rate. ABC 50 *Ganan $75 a la semana.*
(7–11)

18.35 With expressions involving a cardinal numeral.

18.351 Expressions of age. After *a.* ORR 176 *Los niños fuman a los
cinco años.* (14–22) After *de.* SON 128 *Tenía la petulancia de los veinte
años.* (7–7) After *desde.* SIE 13 *¡ Desde los nueve!* (4–4) After *cumplir.*
LLA 35 *Cuando cumplió Miguelillo los catorce, murió la madre.* (4–4)

18.353 Expressions of time. After *a.* WAS 11 *A las dos horas de marcha
el caballo perdió una herradura.* (10–16)

18.355 Parts of a total. The only common form is *mitad.* SJQ 35 *Pasas
aquí la mitad del año.* (9–9)

18.36 With expressions involving an ordinal numeral.

18.361 The ordinal precedes the noun. JOA 41 *Cuando subimos la primera
vez, te empezaste a hacer la graciosa.* (10–20)

18.362 Omitted. ALT 472 *En primer lugar.* **(23–33)**

18.365 The ordinal follows the noun. The article is usually omitted.
PAL 12 *Allí había yo visto por vez primera la luz del día.* (12–12)

18.37 With nouns referring to persons.

18.371 Collectives. BEN 6 *De la gente ya sabe uno lo que puede esperar.*
(26–155)

18.373 General nouns of class.   URU 26 *A los padres nos da rabia que los hijos nos traten como a iguales.*   **(48–296)**

18.374 Omitted, after a preposition.   PIN 57 *Escandalizar es cosa de mujeres.*   **(6–7)**

18.375 Peoples or nationalities.   OCC 192 *Las chinas, al bañarse en público, sólo ocultan el rostro.*   **(23–106)**

18.377 Professions.   IDO 14 *En la profesión misma del abogado algo le seducía.*   **(18–41)**

18.38 Proper nouns referring to persons.

18.381 Normally without the article.   IDO 11 *Alberto volvió los ojos.* (*)

18.382 But the article is used with Arabic titles.   PEL 460 *El romancero del Cid.*   **(5–7)**

18.383 Also with the names of some foreign writers, particularly Italian. VIG 5 *El Petrarca fué el primer* humanista.   **(9–21)**

18.385 In popular style, nicknames of both men and women are used with the article.   Men.   ARN 67 *Entro, y plum, el Califa y el Tirones que estaban allí.*   **(8–60)**

18.386 Women.   ARN 14 *Ahora me he conchavao con la Pelitos.*   **(23–112)**

18.388 Proper names of persons, modified.   The article is regular. IBA 149 *A la pobre Feli le temblaba el corazón.*   **(37–137)**

18.389 Omitted in direct address and in exclamations.   STE 243 *Pobre Alex, ¿ por qué . . . por qué ?*   **(20–42)**

18.39 With a title.   IBA 149 *El señor Vicente.*   **(60–378)**

18.391 Omitted in direct address.   REY 207 *¿ Verdad que no le molesto, señor de Guzmán ?*   **(28–210)**

18.393 Omitted with proclitic title.

> **don, doña.**   SON 35 *Don Antonino juntó las manos.*   **(51–786)**
> **fray.**   RET 123 *Encabezados por Fray Martín de Valencia.*   **(6–24)**
> **monseñor.**   SON 27 *La cámara donde agonizaba Monseñor Estéfano Gaetani.*   **(3–6)**
> **San, Santa.**   ABC 22 *A la Sacramental de San Justo.*   **(44–214)**
> **so.**   ARN 16 *Haberla pegao, so primo.* Usually with adjectives. (3–7)
> **Mr.**   BYN 57 *Ya me dirán lo arbitrario de esta clasificación de Mr. Duran.*   **(4–31)**

18.41 With names of kinship.   The article is used.   PIN 125 *Me quedo con el tío Ramón.*   **(11–33)**

18.411 But the article is also frequently omitted in conversational style. URU 64 *¡ Y mama Rita no es manca!* (8–22)

18.42 Proper nouns used in the plural. The article is regularly used, but the noun is sometimes in the singular, sometimes in the plural. The numerous nouns ending in *–ez* are assumed to be singular, perhaps unjustifiably.

18.421 Singular form. JIM 54 *Vi el eucalipto de las Velarde.* (11–38)

18.423 Plural form. ALT 6 *Los Guzmanes contra los Ponces.* (10–17)

18.43 Appellatives. A large number of common nouns are used as the specific names of persons. As proper nouns, they are often capitalized in writing. They are usually accompanied by the article. PEL 240 *La corte del Rey Católico.* **(47–349)**

18.431 With names of kinship thus used, the article is often omitted. LLA 43 *Papá os lo contará ahora.* (7–34)

18.433 In direct address, the article is regularly omitted with appellatives. ARN 11 *Señorito, una limosna.* **(44–566)**

18.434 Rarely, the article is used even in address. RUS 29 *¡ Hola tío, y la compañía!* (3–3)

18.437 An appellative may be added to a proper name, as in *Guzmán el Bueno.* The construction still exists in popular speech. ARN 97 *Mariano el Pajero.* (13–27)

18.438 In the learned forms *Alejandro Magno* and *Carlomagno,* the article is not used. NER 70 *Carlo Magno aún no aparecía en la historia.* (4–4)

18.44 With nouns referring to place.

18.441 Cities. The article is not normally used. JAN 103 *Se fueron a Valparaíso.* **(54–225)**

18.442 When modified by a qualifying adjective, the article is used. TRI 117 *La práctica intuición del vivir del gran París.* (9–12)

18.443 But modified by a limiting adjective, the article is omitted. DIV 351 *Todo París.* (3–3)

18.444 A few city names involving an adjective have become fixed in a form without the article, as *Buenos Aires* and *Veracruz.* (5–12)

18.445 On the other hand, a number of cities and towns are regularly used with the article, even when unmodified. PAL 22 *Se pasa al camino de la Fuente.* (13–17)

Typical towns are: *la Coruña, el Escorial, la Habana.*

18.45 Countries, continents, provinces, etc.   Normally without the article.   ORT 89 *España, don Rubín, es un rosal.*   (13–80)

18.451 Especially after a preposition.   DEB 4 *Las capitales de Francia y España.*   **(50–398)**

18.452 But the article is sometimes found, even after a preposition. TRI 117 *La conciencia misma de la Europa.*   The use of the article gives the noun a collective, all-embracing character.   (10–24)

18.455 When modified by a qualifying adjective, the article is normally used.   BYN 43 *Remonta al antiguo Egipto.*   **(23–57)**

18.456 But, as with cities, some names which are modified are used at times without the article.   BYN 27 *Algunas de las casas que hoy construye América del Norte.*   (8–18)

18.458 Some names of countries are normally accompanied by the article even when unmodified.   ROM 212 *Un romancero comparable al publicado del Brasil.*   **(22–99)**

   The names most frequently found are: *la China, la India, la Argentina, el Perú, el Ecuador.*

18.459 But even with these names, the article is sometimes omitted after a preposition.   ROM 195 *Posee las principales publicaciones hechas sobre literatura popular en Brasil, Portugal, España y otras naciones.*   (6–8)

18.46 Islands.   The only names commonly found include the word *isla* (*islas*), which is modified by the name and is regularly used with the article.   RIC 30 *A las Islas Hawai.*   (3–7)

18.47 Mountains.   Regularly with the article.   ART 11 *Los Dioses del Olimpo.*   (15–32)

18.48 Points of the compass.   Usually with the article.   ABC 38 *Con pequeña brisa del Suroeste.*   ([31]–66)

18.481 After a preposition, the older terms *Levante, Occidente, Oriente, Poniente* are sometimes found without the article.   ALT 9 *Dando lugar al gran Cisma de Occidente.*   (4–6)

18.49 Rivers.   Regularly with the article.   RET 35 *La ribera opuesta del Plata.*   (16–27)

18.491 The word *río* is expressed.   PAX 333 *En donde el río Blanco y el río Negro se encuentran.*   (4–6)

18.51 Seas, oceans, bays, etc.   Regularly with the article.   BRA 115 *El Cantábrico.*   (5–17)

18.511 With the word for sea expressed.   BRA 178 *El mar Rojo.*   (3–3)

18.52 Squares, streets, etc. The word for the particular unit is usually expressed and the article is normally used. ⌐ ZAM 46 *En la calle de Alcalá.*
(34–136)

18.521 In prepositional phrases, the article is sometimes omitted. JIM 87 *El coche se va, calle Nueva arriba.* (10–14)

18.53 Other names, as of cafés, public buildings, theatres, etc., used as appelatives and normally accompanied by the article. ZAM 64 *Yo no voy a la Zarzuela.* (16–46)

18.531 But the name may become a real proper noun and be used without the article. ZAM 54 *También hay que ir a Eslava.* (5–18)

18.54 With expressions of time.

18.541 If a temporal noun is modified, it is regularly accompanied by the article. RET 128 *Al año siguiente fundaron un colegio.* (30–54)

18.55 Date of the month. The article is normally used when the date is used adverbially without a preposition. IGN 58 *El 28 de Junio llegó la condesa.* (17–42)

18.551 After *a*, the article is sometimes omitted. PAX 11 *Estamos a primero de Enero.* (5–6)

18.553 Similarly after *en*. ALT 10 *Dió en 13 de Mayo de 1312 una bula.* (8–28)

18.555 If the date is in apposition with another expression of time, the article is omitted. LUG 11 *Este mismo día, 29 de Septiembre.* (5–14)

18.56 Day of the week. As subject or used as an adverb, without a preposition, the article is used. BYN 74 *El domingo torearon Iglesias y Sussoni.* (14–31)

18.561 As subjective complement or after a preposition, the article may be omitted. PAT 18 *Hoy es jueves.* (5–6)

18.563 Similarly when in apposition with another temporal expression. LUG 155 *Mañana, sábado, es fiesta.* (4–4)

18.57 Festivals, holidays, etc. The article is normally used. UGA 42 *El Carnaval era una movilización de turbulentas alegrías.* Especially when a modified noun is involved. JIM 32 *Esta mañana del Sábado Santo.* Or when the name includes *el día de*. VIG 38 *Conocemos cuántas fueron muertas el día de San José.* ([10]–14)

18.571 But after a preposition, the article is frequently omitted. PAT 136 *Las vacaciones de Navidad.* ([13]–20)

18.58 Hour of the day. The article, feminine, is regularly used.   LIN 8
A las nueve y tres segundos.   ([45]–158)

18.581 In pairs, after prepositions, the article is occasionally omitted.
TRI 224 *De dos a tres por las tardes.*   (6–15)

18.583 With *mediodía.*   The article is used.   RAN 22 *¿ El mediodía?*
                                                                    (10–14)

18.584 But the article is sometimes omitted, especially after prepositions.
JIM 97 *A mediodía, cuando el sol quema más.*   (8–11)

18.585 With *media noche.* The article is sometimes used.   REY 149 *A la
media noche Ugú se acerca a Paradox.*   (4–5)

18.586 It is also sometimes omitted.   FOM 10 *Su risa disonaba a media
noche.*   (6–8)

18.59 Months. Regularly without the article. The names of the months
rarely are used alone as subject or object, being introduced by the phrase
el mes de.   SJQ 35 *Desde Mayo hasta Octubre.*   (27–111)

18.61 Seasons of the year. As subject, or adverbial, without a preposition, with the article.   MUJ 16 *Llega el verano.*   (11–16)

18.611 Even after a preposition, the article may be used.   RUS 17 *En
el invierno.*   (12–18)

18.612 But after a preposition the article is more frequently omitted.
SAS 82 *En verano.*   (18–35)

18.62 Years. The article is used.   OCC 263 *Ese vocablo es el eje del
pensamiento del 98.* Especially with *el año de.*   (16–57)

18.63 With the names of works of art, books, operas, paintings, etc.
LLA 78 *El Tristán.*   (18–79)

18.631 But with the names of foreign works, sometimes with other
works, the article may be omitted.   PAT 199 *Y David Copperfield, de
Dickens.*   (9–108)

18.64 With the names of fields of knowledge. The article is sometimes
used.   FOM 106 *Su intermitente apego a la Astronomía.*   (12–47)

18.641 The article is also sometimes omitted.   PAL 306 *La carrera de
Jurisprudencia.* The article is more likely to be omitted if the phrase
in which it falls has a definitely adjectival force.   (10–47)

18.65 The definite article is used to express possession. With words
which indicate notions which are habitually associated with persons the
definite article frequently is used to express the possessor. In a sense

there is no possessive connotation in the article itself; the context makes clear that the particular object or attribute indicated by the article is the one which belongs to the subject, or some other person, of the sentence. For this reason the true possessive adjective is used whenever it is desirable to avoid ambiguity or to stress the element of possession. The notions which are most often associated with a person are parts of the body, articles of clothing (or tools of a trade), mental or non-material attributes (*la memoria, la voz,* etc.), and members of the family.

18.66 The possessor is the subject of the sentence. This is the situation in which the use of the article is the most natural. ZAM 57 *Yo pierdo el seso.* **(52–636)**

18.661 *tiene los ojos azules.* After *tener* the expression becomes almost the equivalent of a phrase with *ser.* DEB 11 *Tenía el rostro noble.* (10–20)

18.663 *lleva la cabeza inclinada.* ORR 102 *Llevaba el bigote caído.* (3–7)

18.665 In absolute constructions. STE 20 *La viajera permanecía muda, entumecidos el cuerpo y el alma.* **(27–100)**

18.667 Even when the possessor is the subject, the possessive adjective is often used, particularly when it modifies the object of a preposition. STE 21 *La viajera levantó sus ojos.* **(42–206)**

18.668 When the article is used, a reflexive pronoun with the verb often shows that the article refers to the subject. ZUN 14 *¿ Qué le pareció? — me preguntó, retorciéndose las guías del bigote.* **(36–154)**

18.67 The possessor is different from the subject. In this case, the identification of the possessor is less obvious; when the article is used it is accompanied in the majority of cases by a personal pronoun which makes clear to whom the possession is referred.

18.671 The word modified is subject of the sentence. JES 151 *Le radiaban los ojos con brillo fosfórico.* **(42–106)**

18.672 The possessive adjective is used. JAN 5 *Su rostro blanco carecía de finura.* **(46–172)**

18.673 The word modified is object. SAS 55 *Tu crueldad me llena el alma.* **(50–234)**

18.674 The possessive adjective is used. LLA 15 *Prefiero besar tus manos.* **(35–82)**

18.675 The word modified is object of a preposition. JOA 64 *Cuando se te cae algo de las manos.* **(49–214)**

18.676 The possessive adjective is used. LUG 151 *En un rinconcito de su corazón manteníase viva la imagen.* **(50–230)**

18.678 A personal pronoun indicates the possessor when the article is used. LUG 13 *Don Juan le estrechó la mano.* **(55–356)**

18.679 Very rarely a personal pronoun is used even with a possessive adjective. IDO 219 *Ajándole y estrujándole sus ropas.* **(8–9)**

18.68 Types of personal attributes. The use of the article is predominant with parts of the body, mental and non-material attributes, and articles of clothing. With names of kinsmen, the possessive is far more frequent.

18.681 Parts of the body. With the article. IDO 11 *Al oírlos volvió los ojos.* **(52–970)**

18.682 With a possessive adjective. IBA 26 *Maltrana fijó sus ojos en la más pequeña.* **(42–394)**

18.683 Mental attributes. With the article. JOA 12 *Me tocas el amor propio.* **(42–109)**

18.684 With a possessive adjective. PEQ 79 *Estas sensaciones que bullen en mi memoria.* **(18–33)**

18.685 Articles of clothing. With the article. ZUN 16 *Llevaba en el bolsillo dos caramelos.* **(30–90)**

18.686 With a possessive adjective. JAN 5 *Fué a tomar su sombrero.* **(12–19)**

18.687 Members of a family. With the article. DEB 12 *Me senté; la tía y Agustín sentáronse a su vez.* **(16–45)**

18.688 With a possessive adjective. SAS 23 *Pues de él y de Jesús está celosísimo mi primo.* **(30–252)**

18.7 Uses of the definite article as influenced by the function of the noun modified. We have already commented on the fact that the article is most frequently used with the subject of the sentence. And in the discussion of the different type of nouns we have had occasion to point out the relative rarity of its use after prepositions. There are, however, other functions of the noun modified which have a clear effect on the use of the article. For when a noun is a complement, subjective or objective, or in apposition, or used in elliptical expressions of comparison, it may indicate either a specific individual or it may indicate a class. In the first case, the definite article is used; in the second, the noun becomes adjectival in force and the article is omitted.

18.71 The noun modified is subjective complement.

18.711 The article is used. REY 90 *Que sea él el capitán.* (**56**–**304**)

18.713 The noun may be an adjective used as a noun. IDO 117 *Será usted siempre el bienvenido.* (19–39)

18.715 The article is not used. PEQ 92 *Fué rector del colegio.* (**42**–**78**)

18.72 The noun modified is objective complement.

18.721 The article is used. PAL 19 *Una gran sala que llamaban la sala nueva.* (3–5)

18.723 The article is not used. ROD 14 *La antigüedad imaginó hijas de la Justicia a las Horas.* (6–11)

18.73 The noun modified is in apposition with another substantive.

18.731 The article is used. MAY 64 Xiraldes, *los cohetes voladores de Asturias.* (**60**–**411**)

18.733 The article is not used. REY 121 *La ciudad de Bu-Tata, capital del reino de Uganda.* (**50**–**218**)

18.74 The noun modified follows an expression of comparison.

18.741 After *como.* The article is used. SON 27 *Su perfil destacábase sepulcral, como el perfil de las estatuas yacentes.* (**46**–**114**)

18.743 The article is not used. PEQ 26 *Yo, como hijo del alcalde, recibía una lección especial.* (16–30)

18.745 After *que.* The article is used. VIG 103 *Las novelas son más inverosímiles que la vida.* (7–11)

18.75 With pairs or series of nouns. The definite article is frequently omitted with pairs or series of nouns in which the identity of the individuals is merged in the group, which is felt as an indefinite plural. IDO 4 *Casas, árboles, peñascos evocaban en su espíritu un enjambre de recuerdos.* (**28**–**54**)

18.81 Use of the article with coordinated nouns. When two or more coordinated nouns are used with the definite article, the article is repeated with each noun, if each of the nouns represents an independent notion. IDO 6 *El mar y el distante horizonte marino.* (**57**–**588**)

18.82 If the pair, or series of nouns, is considered as forming a unit, the article is not repeated. BYN 31 *La fortaleza y rectitud del santo Monarca castellano.* ABC 24 *Los anunciantes, productores, comerciantes, profesionales, que anuncian.* (**50**–**225**)

18.9 The neuter article *lo* is used with adjectives and past participles, or with other words, such as nouns and adverbs, which are used adjectivally. In general, *lo* indicates either a collection of unnamed illustrations of the quality expressed by the adjective, or a single unnamed illustration of that quality. In other words it is collective or illustrative. It does not in itself express an abstraction; that is expressed by an abstract noun. But when used with an adjective expressing an abstract quality, it may closely approach an abstraction.

18.91 As a collective. SIE 81 *¡ Lo bueno cuesta, hijo!* (37–100)

18.911 To stress the collective force, *todo* may be used with *lo*. JES 30 *Consideraba todo lo terrible de esta organización.* (15–20)

18.92 As an illustrative. TIG 17 *Me empuja a hacer lo contrario de lo que deseo.* (60–358)

18.921 Frequently in prepositional phrases. RAN 39 *En lo sucesivo haré todo cuanto esté en mis manos.* (22–36)

18.922 After *a*, with the force of "in the style of." PAT 21 *Lacio el bigote, a lo tártaro.* (5–5)

18.93 The adjective may be in the superlative. VIG 110 *En lo más hondo de su ser.* Usually illustrative. (44–144)

18.931 In prepositional phrases. ART 33 *Tendrá otros planes . . . Y a lo mejor . . . otros amores.* (7–9)

18.94 With past participles. MGR 14 *Volvía a desandar lo andado.* (34–47)

18.941 Modified by *todo*. ROD 9 *Todo lo creado.* (4–4)

18.943 In prepositional phrases. LLA 3 *Es lectura importante por lo visto.* (16–20)

18.95 With other words, used as adjectives.

18.951 Adverbs. NER 100 *A lo lejos.* (32–70)

18.955 Nouns. RAN 103 *Lo más siglo XIII de Santiago es el viaje.* (3–4)

18.97 *Lo* may be used with adverbial force, indicating degree. When followed by the relative *que* in this construction it becomes the equivalent of interrogative *qué* or *cuán*, in indirect questions. It may be so used with adjectives, past participles, nouns, and adverbial expressions.

18.971 With adjectives. PIN 141 *Cuanto dicen de la abundancia del dinero en América y de lo fácil que es ganarlo.* (20–29)

18.973 In the superlative. ARN 64 *Sin torcerse lo más mínimo.*   (4–4)

18.975 The adjective may be in agreement with a noun. MGR 30 *Se dan cuenta de lo estúpidos que han sido.*   (12–13)

18.976 Even after a preposition without a following relative. ORR 98 *Por lo franca no sabía ocultar las impresiones.*   (8–10)

18.977 With adjectival phrases. ARN 15 *¡ Hay que ver lo de mala fe que se ha puesto la caridá hoy en día!*   (4–4)

18.978 With adverbs. TIG 47 *Ya se corre por ahí la voz de lo requetebién que lo hace.*   (8–9)

18.979 In the superlative. REY 148 *Lo más lentamente posible.*   (5–7)

POSSESSIVE ADJECTIVES

19. The possessive adjectives are found in two forms: stressed and unstressed. The stressed forms are regularly used when they follow the noun modified, as attributives, or are used as complements. The unstressed forms regularly precede the noun modified.

19.1 Unstressed forms. (*mi, tu, su, nuestro, vuestro*).

19.11 Regular use. MAY 17 *¿ Cómo supiste la hora de mi llegada?*   (*)

19.111 If another adjective precedes the noun, it usually follows the possessive. MAY 69 *Su inmóvil pesadumbre.*   (60–441)

19.112 But in exclamations it sometimes precedes the possessive. SAS 82 *¡ Pobre mi hijo!*   (3–4)

19.114 Although the possessive usually follows the noun in direct address (see 19.551), it is sometimes used before the noun, with a connotation of intimacy. PAT 208 *Meg, mi alma, anda a buscarlo.*   (26–70)

19.115 If the antecedent is an inanimate thing, the possessive normally indicates something habitually associated with the antecedent. SON 17 *Era la campiña clásica de las vides y de los olivos, con sus acueductos ruinosos.*   (11–29)

19.117 With coordinated nouns, the possessive adjective is usually repeated with each noun. ROD 13 *Rige sus pensamientos y sus actos.*
(57–262)

19.118 But if the nouns form a unit, the adjective is not repeated. IDO 218 *Recontaban sus tristezas y angustias.*   (35–83)

19.2 With objective force. Since the possessive is the equivalent of a phrase with *de*, it may be used to indicate the object as well as the subject of an action. BEN 69 *Ya tendrá su castigo, ya lo tendrá.* (29–56)

19.21 With compound prepositions the possessive becomes the equivalent of *de* + a personal pronoun. REY 137 *A su alrededor se congregan los magos.*   (20–34)

19.31 Clarified by a phrase with *de* + a personal pronoun. The pronoun of the third person *su* has so many possible meanings that it is often necessary or desirable to indicate more exactly the particular possessor. This may be achieved by adding a prepositional phrase with *de* + a personal pronoun. ART 7 *Tampoco su ciudad de usted será como la ciudad en cuyas afueras vivimos.*   (20–41)

19.32 Replaced by the definite article and a phrase with *de* + a personal

pronoun. More frequently, however, the possessive is replaced by the definite article.

19.321 The antecedent is a person. URU 48 *Aprovechará la estadía de ustedes en Montevideo.* (34–78)

19.323 The antecedent is a thing. ALT 465 *El mismo secreto se observaba en la acusación; se comunicaba tan sólo al acusado los términos de ella, pero callando la persona.* (5–7)

19.324 Rarely a demonstrative pronoun is used instead of a personal pronoun in the prepositional phrase. IBA 25 *Ayudaban a la dueña de la casa en la rebusca del género, y además el carro de ésta le traía el saco al regresar de Madrid.* (3–3)

19.4 Reinforced by an intensive adjective.

19.41 *mismo.* Precedes the noun. FOM 98 *Él seguía su misma vida triunfante y alegre.* (15–20)

19.421 *propio.* Precedes the noun. JIM 56 *Herido por sus propios cristales.* (33–70)

19.422 Less frequently follows the noun. PEL 245 *Hay que ponerle en su medio propio.* Note the difference in meaning. (8–10)

19.43 With partitive force. The older usage of the unstressed possessives with partitive force, "of mine," etc. has almost disappeared in contemporary Spanish. The only situation in which it is still found with any frequency is after a demonstrative adjective. PAL 129 *Aquel su jardín rebosaba de fruta.* (8–8)

19.5 Stressed forms.

19.51 Attributive uses, following the noun modified.

19.52 The noun modified is also modified by the definite article. In this situation, the use of the determinative possessive is relatively rare. It is found chiefly in phrases in which there is some special reason for stressing the possessive, as in contrasts. JOA 66 *Porque los trajes tuyos vienen de París.* (11–21)

19.53 With partitive force.

19.531 The noun modified is indefinite and used as object of a verb. IGN 78 *¡Cuénteme cosas suyas, Papín Oca!* (3–3)

19.532 Used as subjective complement. IBA 362 *Es hijo tuyo.* (30–54)

19.535 Used in apposition with another noun. ZAM 131 *¿Y si ese don Pablo, amigo tuyo, vuelve?* (9–10)

19.536 Used after *como*. JES 36 *Se encariñaba en considerarla como obra suya.* (3–3)

19.54 The noun modified is also modified by a limiting adjective.

19.541 An indefinite article. PEQ 72 *Un convecino nuestro acaba de morirse.* **(25–42)**

19.542 An indefinite adjective. ORR 170 *Luego refirió varias anécdotas suyas.* (9–12)

19.544 A numeral. RAN 78 *Era por las niñas, dos hijas suyas.* (4–5)

19.545 A demonstrative adjective. SJQ 30 *Estos nietos míos tienen un pincho en cada pie.* (17–23)

19.55 The noun modified is used without a verb.

19.551 In direct address, in conversation. LIN 44 *Sí, hija mía.* **(44–194)**

19.552 In the heading of letters. STE 36 « *Adorados míos.* » (3–5)

19.555 In exclamations, oaths, etc. SEC 32 *¡¡ Dios mío ...!!* **(22–78)**

19.58 With objective force. Like the unstressed forms, the stressed forms of the possessive are frequently found indicating the object rather than the subject of the action. This use is most frequent with compound prepositions. DEB 44 *Éste paseó ante mí, acaso entristecido, a pesar suyo.* **(21–30)**

19.59 Replaced by a phrase with *de* + a personal pronoun. Like *su*, the form *suyo* often requires more exact identification. The most frequent method is to replace it with a phrase with *de* + a personal pronoun.

19.591 The antecedent is a person. DIV 12 *Quedo de usted afectísimo amigo y atento S. S.* (18–33)

19.593 The antecedent is a thing. PEL 228 *Y, finalmente, dos nuevos tipos, inventados al parecer por Santillana, puesto que no se ha señalado rastro de ellos en la versificación italiana.* (4–4)

19.6 As subjective complement. VIG 104 *No son míos.* This use of the adjective, to distinguish between a number of possible possessors, should be contrasted with that of the pronoun, to distinguish between a number of objects possessed; see 12.22. **(40–76)**

19.61 The stressed predicate adjective may be modified by an adverb. SIE 95 *El secreto de tu libro de caja ha sido inviolablemente tuyo.* (6–10)

19.65 The form for the third person may be replaced by a phrase with *de* + a personal pronoun. BYN 26 *¿ La casa no es de usted?* (3–4)

19.7 As objective complement.   UGA 25 *Todo lo que creía suyo, no era más que un reflejo.*   (5–5)

19.8 Without indication of function in exclamations.

19.81 Alone.   ZAM 134 *¡ Tuya! . . . ¡ Siempre!*   (7–9)

19.82 With another element of the sentence.   TRI 228 *¡ Bravo, suya una marquesa . . . obra al teatro!*   (4–6)

THE INDEFINITE ARTICLE

20. The indefinite article is a weakened form of the numeral *uno*.

20.1 Forms. The masculine form is regularly atonic and apocopated. LIN 8 *Un minuto.* The feminine form is *una.* There are also plural forms, *unos, unas,* which, although in a sense indefinite adjectives, may properly be called articles, since they serve as the equivalent of *un, una* with words which have only plural forms.   (*)

20.11 Before nouns beginning with stressed *a–, ha–,* the feminine article is usually elided into *un.*

20.111 Before *a–.*   MAY 15 *Un ánima.*   ([23]–40)

The commonest nouns are *alma, arma, arpa.*

20.113 Before *ha–.*   WAS 138 *Un hacha.*   (4–4)

20.2 Uses of the indefinite article. The chief use of the indefinite article is to indicate one, particular individual, person or thing, which has not thus far been identified or which the speaker identifies but does not wish to indicate to the hearer. It is more particularizing than the indefinite article in English. As was the case with the definite article, not only the character of the noun modified, but also the function of the noun modified bears a part in determining the use of the indefinite article.

20.21 Regular uses.   IBA 25 *Vivían en una especie de gallinero al extremo de un corral.*   (*)

20.22 Omission with special types of nouns.

20.221 With general and indefinite nouns. If the indefinite article is omitted with a singular noun, the noun ceases to be a particular, and becomes a random representative of its class. With mass nouns, this is regularly the case: *tiene dinero.* With common nouns in the plural, the noun without article indicates an indefinite number of random representatives of the class: PAL 13 *Alcánzame cerezas.*   (*)   With a singular noun, the article is omitted in certain stereotyped combinations of verb and noun, as *echar pie a tierra,* and also when the notion expressed is not literal but figurative or when the notion is not particular but universal. Figurative.   FAL 13 *Según un ritual que le imponía cuello de pajarita.* Universal.   ABC 38 *Dos líneas, formando ángulo agudo.*   (20–56)

20.23 In negative sentences. The use of the indefinite noun is most frequent in negative sentences. The negative may be expressed or implied. The indefinite article is regularly omitted.

20.231 The negative is expressed. ROD 86 *Leonardo no halla modo de figurar como quiere al Judas de* La Cena. **(46–256)**

20.233 The negative is implied by a question. OCC 194 *¿ Hay enajenación más absoluta que el trance en que el amor se consuma ?* (16–20)

20.234 The negative is implied by a condition. ZUN 15 *Si le daban contestación afirmativa, huía de allí.* (4–4)

20.235 By *buscar*. UGA 21 *Una hermana suya que busca novio.* (6–6)

20.236 By *sin*. TRI 231 *Su cadena sin reloj.* **(27–60)**

20.237 By other words. ABC 28 *Por falta de número reglamentario.* (8–11)

20.238 If *un* is used with a negative, it has the force of a numeral. PAT 23 *Yo no tengo un cuarto.* **(28–60)**

20.239 Similarly after *sin*. IBA 159 *He sido un mendigo, sin una peseta.* (12–18)

20.24 The indefinite article is not used with nouns modified by an indefinite adjective. MGR 18 *Acaso se le antoje excesivo semejante precio.*

The adjectives with which *un* is omitted are: *cierto* **(44–148)**, *igual* (7–12), *otro* **(58–402)**, *semejante* **(20–25)**, *tal* **(31–70)**.

20.241 Occasionally, however, the indefinite article is found with these adjectives. JES 28 *¿ Cómo podría justificarse de una tal crueldad ?*

The commonest cases are: *cierto* (5–7), *semejante* (only when the adjective follows the noun) (3–6), *tal* (4–5).

20.25 The indefinite article is not used before certain expressions of number and quantity.

20.251 Before *ciento* (*cien*). IDO 115 *Podemos vivir cien existencias.* **(31–51)**

20.252 Before *mil*. UGA 17 *En mil detalles.* (19–34)

20.253 Before *cuarto*. SIE 11 *Las nueve y cuarto.* (3–3)

20.254 Before *medio*. TRI 55 *Pagó medio mes a la patrona.* **(33–67)**

20.255 Before a noun followed by *y medio*. IGN 56 *Año y medio justo.* (7–13)

20.257 Before a noun modified by an adjective which is modified by *tan*. RUB 19 *De un país de cálculo brota imaginación tan estupenda.* **(21–42)**

20.259 Before indefinite expressions of quantity, space, or time. STE 36 *Lloraba largo rato.* **(27–53)**

20.261 Occasionally the article is found when *tan* modifies an adjective which follows a noun. ORT 131 *Una ley tan simple.* (18–24)

20.263 Also with indefinite expressions of quantity. DEB 4 *Después de una larga estancia en las capitales.* (4–4)

20.27 The indefinite article may at times itself have the force of "such a." SAS 67 *Lo dices de un modo que parece que estuvieras enojada conmigo.* (4–6)

20.3 With the proper names of persons. The indefinite article is used with proper names only when they become common nouns in force. ROD 214 *Un Rembrandt o un Velázquez nacidos en la comunión del Islam.* (19–36)

20.31 At times, it acquires the force of "a certain." STE 23 *Los otros que ella decía ser hijos de una Carmencita, y de un Alberto.* (3–12)

20.4 Uses of the indefinite article as influenced by the function of the noun modified. The remarks made concerning the use of the definite article apply with equal force to the use of the indefinite article. When it is used, the noun is presented as a particular individual; when it is omitted, the noun becomes an indication of class.

20.41 In adjectival phrases of characteristic. The article is not used. BEN 60 *Mis nervios de niña voluntariosa.* The *niña voluntariosa* is presented as a type. (38–188)

20.42 As subjective complement.

20.43 Without a preposition.

20.431 Unmodified. The article is used. OCC 263 *Él era un intelectual.* (54–458)

20.432 The article is not used. WAS 13 *El viejo era soltero.* (52–206)

20.435 Modified. The article is used. PIN 90 *Es una queja de unos hombres que envidian a los jabalíes.* (60–560)

20.436 The article is not used. PIN 52 *Es obra tuya la huelga.* (48–232)

20.44 With a preposition. The article is not used. VIG 60 *Esta narración sirvió de pretexto.* (24–60)

20.45 As objective complement.

20.451 Without a preposition. The article is used. URU 55 *¿Me crees un malvado?* (6–6)

20.453 The article is not used. UNA 99 *El que el penitenciario llama hijo del pecado.* (18–20)

20.455 With a preposition. The article is used. SEC 38 *Téngame por un servidor.* (5–6)

20.456 The article is not used. UNA 24 *No lo reconoce por hombre.* (16–18)

20.46 With a noun used in apposition with another substantive.

20.461 The article is used. SEC 26 *Don Ramón Cascales, un buen amigo de mi padre.* (41–114)

20.462 The article is not used. MAY 4 *Un solo hermano, militar como su padre.* (48–248)

20.465 The appositive may be introduced by a preposition or a subordinating conjunction: *de, desde, cuando, aunque,* etc. TRI 43 *Jugué mucho cuando niño.* ([24]–44)

20.47 The noun modified is used after an expression of comparison.

20.471 After *como.* The article is used. JIM 36 *Como un cuadro de Fra Angélico.* (56–332)

20.472 The phrase *como un* may have the force of "a sort of." JIM 57 *Hay por su enorme garganta como un pasar profuso de umbrías aguas de sangre.* (7–19)

20.475 The article is not used. BEN 34 *Dos personas que viven propiamente como matrimonio.* (52–140)

20.477 After *a modo de.* The article is not used. ROD 86. *A modo de pupila felina.* (5–5)

20.481 After *que.* The article is used. ARN 99 *Sois una familia más triste que un responso.* (18–32)

20.482 The article is not used. JIM 51 *Curros, padre más que poeta.* (10–10)

20.49 Use of the indefinite article with coordinated nouns. As with the definite article, the indefinite article is repeated with a second noun, if the two notions are distinct; it is not repeated, if the two notions form a unit.

20.491 Repeated. BRA 107 *Una copita y un consuelo.* (48–135)

20.492 Not repeated. OCC 147 *Una mágica solidaridad y unificación.* (9–12)

20.5 The plural form *unos*, is normally used to indicate a specific group of indefinite individuals, persons or things. It differs from the indefinite adjective *algunos* in that it does not convey by implication the quantitative value of "a few." In its use and omission it follows precisely the same practices as does the singular form.

20.51 Regular uses. ORT 80 *Quedan en el cielo unos restos de luna.*
(50–300)

20.52 Modifying a noun used as subjective complement. JAN 306 *Me parecen unos hipócritas.* English produces the same effect by saying "regular hypocrites." (14–18)

20.53 After *como*.

20.531 With *unos*. IBA 33 *Los chicos me siguen como unos bobos.* (6–7)

20.532 Without *unos*. UNA 95 *Se miraron como enemigos.* (26–42)

20.55 Special uses of *unos*.

20.551 Modifying a numeral, with the force of "about." ABC 34 *De unos cuatro o cinco días.* (15–24)

20.553 Used with plural nouns which indicate a pair. SIE 62 *Ante unos ojos claros.* (29–57)

20.557 With the force of "such." CAT 23 *Es una mano de gato, con unas uñazas que parecen de trigue.* (3–3)

20.56 With coordinated nouns. *Unos* is repeated in the only examples noted. PIN 11 *Unos tomates y unos mendrugos.* (4–5)

INDEFINITE ADJECTIVES

21. Indefinite adjectives are used to restrict the application of a noun in quantity, quality, or class. Most of the indefinite adjectives are also used substantivally as indefinite pronouns. As limiting adjectives, they normally precede the noun which they modify. In the following list of the most common indefinite adjectives a noun is expressed in parentheses with an adjective when necessary to illustrate its usage and also the position of the adjective. For the order of entry, see 13.1.

21.1 For the apocopation of certain indefinite adjectives (*alguno, cualquiera*), see 25.2. For the use of negative indefinites, see 40.61.

21.2 *ajeno* (*auxilio*) (3–3), (*boca*) *ajena* (9–10), *la* (*riqueza*) *ajena* (7–7); *alguno* (**60–435**), — Used instead of the indefinite article (9–18), — Modifying a singular noun, with plural force. ALT 14 *Ya en el siglo XII hubo algún ejemplo de lo mismo.* (19–26); *ambos* (**23–50**); *bastante* (*difusión*) (16–24), (*grandeza*) *bastante* (5–6); *cada* (**56–254**) — With a cardinal numeral (*cada dos versos*) (5–5), — With the force of " such a." RIC 266 *¡ Me hace pasar cada berrinche!* (4–4); *cien* (indefinite) (10–18); *cierto* (**48–222**), — *un cierto* (*Cimmino*) (5–7); *cualquiera* (**36–70**), — *cualquier otro* (*caballero*) (3–4), — *un* (*campero*) *cualquiera* (8–8); *cuatro* (" a few ") (9–12); *demás* (*frases*) (5–5) — *los demás* (*funcionarios*) (18–31); *demasiado* (6–7); *dos* — *los dos* (*hermanos*) (**30–76**); *entero* (3–4), — *el* (*cuerpo*) *entero* (10–13), — *un* (*día*) *entero* (4–4); *entrambos* (3–3); *igual* (6–13); *más* (**54–154**), — (*dos pesetas*) *más* (**54–150**); *medio* (**31–62**), — *el medio* (7–9); *menos* (**22–39**); *mil* (indefinite) (**24–39**), — *los mil* (4–4); *mismo* — *el mismo* (*día*) (" the same ") (**60–282**), — *el mismo* (*rey*) (" himself ") (**25–48**), — *el* (*rey*) *mismo* (" himself ") (**20–36**), — *este mismo* (*instante*) (" this same ") (**32–46**) — *este* (*instante*) *mismo* (" this very ") (4–4), *mi mismo* (*reloj*) (15–20); *muchísimo* (12–17); *mucho* (**57–381**), — *el mucho* (9–10); *no sé qué* (*menjurje*) (11–12); *nuevo* (" different ") (6–8), — *un nuevo* (4–5); *otro* (**60–699**), — *el otro* (**49–118**), — *este otro* (11–18), *mi otro* (3–4), — *otro tanto* (4–5), — *otros* (*dos*) (9–12), — *otros muchos* (4–8); *pleno* (**22–29**); *poco* (**36–66**), — *el poco* (19–27), — *pocos* (" few ") (**31–52**), — *pocos* (" a few ") (18–21); *poquísimo* (4–4); *propio* — (*dinero*) *propio* (9–13), — *el propio* (18–45), — *el* (*amor*) *propio* (11–11), — *mi propio* (**33–70**), — *mi* (*medio*) *propio* (8–10); *puro* (" sheer ") (12–15), — *un puro* (4–4); *semejante* (**21–37**), — *un* (*desatino*) *semejante* (11–14); *sendos* (" one apiece ") (9–10); *solo* (often predicate or appositive) (**41–144**), — *el solo* (6–6), *un solo* (**28–65**), — *un* (*peso*) *solo* (4–4), — *mi solo* (3–3), — *solo un* (*momento*) (3–3); *tal* (*caso*) (**52–170**), — (*caso*) *tal* (5–5), *tal como* (11–14), — *el tal* (*conde*) (" the said ") (11–15), — *un tal* (*libro*) (4–8), — *un* (*libro*) *tal* (4–4), *tal o cual* (*producción*) (6–6); **tanto** (**50–150**), — *tanto . . . como* (14–19), — *tanto . . . que*, see 42.79. — Modifying a singular noun with the force of a plural. SAS 58 *Tanta mala novela.* (6–7); **to** (for *todo*) (4–22), **todo** (*esfuerzo*) (**48–166**), — Modifying a proper noun of place. ROM 194 *Toda América.* (16–18), — *todos* (*modos*) (**48–102**). Used only in set phrases of which the commonest are: *a todas horas* (11–13), *a todas partes* (10–11), *de todas maneras* (5–5), *de todas suertes* (4–7), *de todos modos* (10–12), *en todas partes* (11–15), *por todas partes* (13–15), — *todo el* (**56–270**), *el* (*país*) *todo* (10–14), *todos los* (**60–482**), — *todo este* (**46–89**), *todo mi* (**50–188**), *mi* (*destino*) *todo* (5–7), *todo un* (16–21); **total** — *el* (*número*) *total* (4–4), **último** (*día*) (**21–30**), *el último* (*día*) (**43–119**), — *el* (*ocaso*) *último* (6–6), — *este último* (8–12), — *mi último* (19–27), *un último* (*desafío*) (5–6); **único** (*recurso*) (9–22), *el único* (*recurso*) (**28–49**), — *mi único* (9–14), *un* (*gesto*) *único* (3–6); **uno** — *un mismo* (" one and the same ") (15–27), — *uno* for *un mismo*. JIM 82 *Todo a un tiempo.* (6–7); **un . . . otro** BRA 15 *Corre de una parte a otra.* (**35–69**), — *un . . . el otro* (9–11), *uno y otro* (*lado*) (8–10), — *uno u otro* (3–3), — *unos y otros* (*elementos*) (3–3), — *unos cuantos* (" a few ") (19–33); **varios** (**38–98**).

INTERROGATIVE ADJECTIVES

22. Interrogative adjectives are either distinctive or quantitative, the older possessive interrogative having disappeared from use. Like other interrogatives, the adjectives are often used to introduce exclamations.

22.1 Distinctive adjectives.

22.2 In true questions.

22.21 Attributive.

22.211 *qué.* This is the normal interrogative in attributive position. MAY 125 ¿ *Qué flores son ésas?* **(60–273)**

22.212 *cuál.* Rarely used as attributive. SON 116 ¿ *Cuál arte cultiváis, señor Polonio?* (4–4)

22.219 *el . . . que.* Used only in indirect questions. URU 50 ¡ *Quién sabe el giro que pueden tomar las cosas!* (3–3)

22.22 Subjective complement.

22.221 *cuál.* ROD 213 ¿ *Cuáles serán los escogidos en el número de los llamados?* **(20–27)**

22.225 *qué.* Only after *parecer.* JES 39 ¿ *Qué te parecería un puesto de superintendente?* (3–4)

22.229 *cómo.* Used with adjectival force. FAL 216 ¿ *Cómo era el automóvil?* Limited to questions asking for a description of the subject. (6–6)

22.3 In exclamations.

22.31 Without another adjective. *qué.* REY 107 ¡ *Qué barbaridad!* **(44–352)**

22.311 *el . . . que.* IDO 118 ¡ *Este Mario! ¡ las cosas que tiene!* (3–4)

22.32 With another adjective.

22.321 *qué.* The adjective usually precedes the noun. JIM 64 ¡ *Qué mágico embeleso ver el paisaje!* (19–54)

22.325 *qué . . . más.* The adjective regularly follows the noun. RIC 270 ¡ *Qué casa más venerable tiene el buen señor!* (11–20)

22.327 *qué . . . tan.* The adjective regularly follows the noun. BEN 69 ¡ *Qué tristeza tan grande!* (15–23)

22.41 Instead of Old Spanish *cúyo,* modern usage has recourse to a

phrase, *de quién*, to express the possessive interrogative.   STE 22 *Dime,
Perla, ¿ de quién eres ?*   (5–6)

22.5 Quantitative.

22.51 *cuánto*.   PAT 16 *¿ Cuántas horas había estado durmiendo ?*   (**39**–**84**)

22.53 *qué*.   ORT 102 *¿ Qué tiempo llevan aquí ?*   (3–3)

22.54 *qué de*.   JIM 36 *Mira qué de rosas caen por todas partes.*   (3–4)

22.59 *el . . . que*.   In indirect questions and exclamations.   IBA 28 *¡ El
plomo que aquel hombre llevaba en el cuerpo !*   (4–4)

NUMERALS

23. It is almost impossible to secure information concerning the use of numerals from printed sources, since they are usually printed with Arabic or Roman characters, which in themselves offer no clue as to whether the form is a cardinal or an ordinal. In the scattered comments included below only forms which are actually written out are counted.

23.1 Numerals are divided into cardinals, ordinals, and collectives.

23.2 Cardinals. The cardinal numerals are invariable in form, except *uno*, *ciento*, which may form a plural, and the multiples of one hundred, which have both masculine and feminine forms. The cardinal numerals regularly precede the noun they modify, when they are used as limiting adjectives. occ 131 *Seis siglos.* (*)

23.21 The cardinal numerals are regularly used in expressing the date of the month, except the first. was 3 *En la madrugada del dos de abril.* (11–56)

23.22 They are also used to express the hours of the day. div 350 *A las seis de la mañana.* ([45]–158)

23.3 Ordinals. The ordinal numerals, when used as limiting adjectives, precede the noun modified. alt 8 *Los primeros años.* (*) But when used to give the number of a chapter, act, etc., they follow the noun. vig 35 *En el capítulo segundo.* (19–38)

23.31 The ordinal *primero* is used to express the first of a month. tri 226 *Un primero de mes.* (3–4)

23.32 The ordinals are used with *centuria*, in learned style, when it replaces *siglo*. pel 25 *La centuria décimasexta.* (4–4)
   With *siglo* the numeral is always written as a Roman character: *el siglo XIII.*

23.33 The ordinals are used to express the chapter, act, etc. in written works. vig 64 *Su monólogo del acto tercero.* (12–22)

23.41 Collectives. The word for "million" as a cardinal number is regularly a collective in Spanish, followed by *de*. arn 58 *Hay tantos millones de hombres peleando allí lejos.* (14–26)

23.42 The cardinal *mil* is also used in the plural as a collective. abc 36 *Los miles de propietarios satisfechos.* (9–14)

23.43 With other numerals, the collective is usually formed with the termination *–ena*. ART 38 *Tres docenas de ostras.* (21–34)

23.44 A few numerals, like *centar* and *millar*, form a collective with the termination *–ar*. PIN 145 *Unos centenares de fanegas.* (10–11)

23.45 For the use of numerals as indefinites, see Indefinite adjectives.

RELATIVE ADJECTIVES

24. The use of relatives as adjectives is to-day limited to *cual, cuanto,* and *cuyo.*

24.1 *cual.* The only construction in which *cual* is found as an adjective is in clauses correlative to *tal,* where *cual* is a predicate adjective with a form of *ser.*   IGN 92 *Hay que tomar la vida tal cual es.*   (3–3)

24.3 *cuanto.* As an adjective, *cuanto* is now the equivalent of *todo el . . . que (todos los . . . que).* It is used only as an attributive adjective preceding a noun.   PAT 18 *Desgarró cuantas reproducciones de cuadros famosos halló a mano.*   (15–17)

24.4 *cuyo.* *Cuyo* is a possessive relative adjective. It has the functions of other possessive adjectives.

24.41 With subjective force.

24.411 The antecedent is a person.   IDO 11 *Alberto conocía a las personas cuyos nombres acababa de escuchar.*   (**38–110**)

24.413 The antecedent is a thing.   PAL 12 *Frente a mí se alzaba una alta montaña, cuya crestería semejaba la de un castillo fantástico.*   (**37–128**)
As the figures show, Spanish has no such reluctance for the use of *cuyo* with things, as has English for "whose" in the same situation.

24.42 With objective force.

24.421 The antecedent is a person.   RET 124 *Llegaron de España seis monjas, cuyo envío fué solicitado por el obispo.*   (3–4)

24.423 The antecedent is a thing.   RUB 18 *La publicación de aquel libro cuya traducción hay que agradecer al señor Mayer, estaba destinada al grueso público.*   (6–8)

24.425 The antecedent is a general idea. In this case, *cuyo* is the equivalent of *de lo cual.*   NER 16 *Hecho esto, os matan, a menos que no estéis aún a punto, en cuyo caso os dejarán para más tarde.*   (5–7)

24.43 Introducing a noun which is logically in apposition and followed by a relative clause. An extension of the loose use of *cuyo* without a definite antecedent has lead to its employment in expressions where all possessive force is gone, and the relative becomes a device for introducing a noun which is logically in apposition.   ZUN 10 *Tomó Canuto asiento en el centro del palco, desde cuyo sitio podía exhibirnos perfectamente su*

flamante indumento. *Desde cuyo sitio* is the equivalent of *sitio desde el cual.* The construction appears to be old but careless. (4–5)

24.45 Replaced by a pronoun with *de*. At times *cuyo* is replaced by *de* and a relative pronoun. ALT 11 *Alcanzó grandes mercedes de Juan I, al lado de quien luchó bravamente.* (3–3)

QUALIFYING ADJECTIVES

25. Qualifying adjectives may be attributive, predicate (either as subjective or objective complement), appositive, or absolute. It should be noted that past participles are used in all of the functions of an adjective, while present participles are almost never used in any function except as appositives.

25.1 Attributive uses. An adjective is called attributive when it is closely connected with the noun which it modifies, being placed immediately before or immediately after the noun. Attributive adjectives have two main functions: to *distinguish* the noun, and to *describe* the noun. The function is revealed by the position of the adjective.

25.11 Position of adjectives. Since the same adjective may be used with either function, statistics do not illumine the problem of adjective position. But it will be well to state briefly the main principles.

25.111 An adjective which is used to distinguish a particular individual or individuals from other individuals of the same class is placed after the noun which it modifies: *una blusa blanca.* The adjectives which are most likely to be used as distinguishers are those which have commonly accepted objective value, such as those expressing physical qualities (size, color, form, etc.), those derived from proper nouns, and past participles used with verbal force.

25.112 An adjective which is used to add to a noun a description, which is not essential to our recognition of the individual or individuals, is placed before the noun: *santas reliquias.* The adjectives which are most likely to be placed before the noun are those which express subjective reactions, such as the speaker's interpretation of the value, appearance, character, etc. of the individual or individuals. If an individual is already identified or distinguished by a quality, either through actual statement or through habitual association, an adjective expressing that quality will be placed before the noun: *la blanca nieve.* Similarly any adjective which is transferred from its normal, objective meaning to a figurative, subjective meaning will be placed before the noun: *la pobre mujer.* Some of the commonest adjectives: *bueno, grande, malo, mayor, mejor,* usually precede the noun, because they serve to reveal the speaker's evaluation of the individual rather than to distinguish the individual from other individuals of its class.

25.113 In actual practice, the position of adjectives in general depends both on the subject matter and the style. Exposition and logical argument make natural the use of distinguishing adjectives placed after nouns. On the other hand, lyrical descriptions and emotional narratives will place adjectives before the nouns. Usage varies not only from author to author, according to their temperaments, but in the same author, from passage to passage, according to the emotional level of the discourse.

25.2 Apocopation of adjectives. A number of common adjectives, limiting and descriptive, which precede the noun modified, regularly drop the final *−o* of the masculine form. Another group loses the final syllable: *santo* in the masculine, when used as a title, *ciento* in both masculine and feminine, and *grande* in both masculine and feminine. With *grande*, however, the full forms are also used. In all cases, the final consonant of the apocopated adjective is *−l, −n,* or *−r.* For the apocopation of *uno* as article and as numeral, see 20.1.

25.21 Adjectives regularly apocopated. URU 33 *Mi buen nombre.*

The adjectives in this group are: *algún* (**49–137**), *buen* (**50–180**), *cien* (**26–43**), *mal* (**42–83**), *ningún* (**46–87**), *primer* (**50-135**), *San* (**32–134**), *tercer* (**7–8**).

25.211 *Cien* is occasionally apocopated even when used as a stressed pronoun. WAS 137 *Discutían si los novillos gordos, que se vendían a cuarenta pesos, volverían a valer cien.* (3–4)

25.22 Adjectives sometimes apocopated and sometimes used in the full form.

25.221 *cualquiera.* Apocopated, both masculine and feminine. RAN 22 *A cualquier hora.* (**33–73**)

25.223 Full form. More often feminine than masculine. DIV 17 *Cualquiera época o nacionalidad.* (4–5)

25.23 *grande.*

25.231 Before a consonant. Apocopated, both masculine and feminine. JES 27 *La gran nave.* (**54–336**)

25.233 Full form. RIC 26 *Con grande respeto.* (3–5)

25.235 Before a vowel. Apocopated, both masculine and feminine. PAT 204 *Del gran amor que le tenía.* (**38–84**)

25.237 Full form. PAX 21 *Un grande amigo.* (11–16)
The full form is far more common before vowels than before consonants.

25.24 Apocopation of *reciente,* **used adverbially.** The adjective *reciente* when used with the force of an adverb before a past participle is usually apocopated to *recién.* PAX 342 *Uniformes recién estrenados.* (**20–32**)

25.241 But the full form in *−mente* is also found. MGR 47 *Recientemente descubierto.* (4–4)

25.31 Predicate uses of adjectives.

25.32 As subjective complement. After *ser*, *estar*, and similar copulative verbs. IDO 214 *El cambio fué brusco.*
For further details, see 35.32 and 35.52.

25.321 After a preposition. An adjective is sometimes a logical subjective complement after a verb and a preposition. PIN 54 *Yo pienso llegar a viejo.* See also 2.734. (6–6)

25.33 As objective complement. BEN 43 *Al verme libre.*
The use of adjectives as objective complement, alone and with a preposition, is treated under Substantives, 2.74.

25.34 Appositive uses of adjectives. An adjective, like a noun, may be added to a noun, to give additional information; in this use it becomes the equivalent of a parenthetical relative clause. Adjectives are also sometimes added to a whole sentence, in which case they may be called predicate appositives, and their use in this case becomes almost adverbial. The participles are also used as appositives: the present participle regularly, and the past participle very frequently.

25.35 Adjectives. LIN 44 *Un marido de tu gusto, joven, rico y enamorado.*
Predicate appositive. IBA 8 *Saltaban ágiles sobre su asno.* (60–1752)

25.36 Participles.

25.361 Present. JIM 17 *Acaricia con su hocico, rozándolas apenas, las florecillas rosas.* For details, see 38.211.

25.363 Past. IBA 362 *La abuela, conmovida por el suceso, bajó a Madrid.*
See also 38.615. (57–1771)

25.37 Appositives introduced by a preposition. Adjectives and past participles used as appositives are frequently introduced by a preposition which serves to indicate the particular adverbial notion which the appositive conveys.

25.371 After *de*. Adjectives. FAL 25 *Siempre se las echaba de gracioso.*
Past participles. LLA 27 *En los primeros días de casada no sentí esto.*
De normally conveys the notion of "in the rôle of." (20–35)

25.372 It may at times have causal force. FAL 24 *Las luces no oscilaban de heladas que estaban.* For a similar use of nouns, see 3.53. (3–9)

25.373 After *desde*. MUJ 25 *No nos veíamos desde chiquitinas.* (5–8)

25.375 After *después de*. After participles only. See 38.616.

25.377 After *por.*   TIG 9 *Las mozas dejan de ser honestas, no por ino-
centes, sino por industria.*   (12–20)

25.39 Adjectives in descriptive absolute constructions. Adjectives and
participles are found in absolute constructions of two types. In the
first, which is found only with present and past participles, the absolute
construction takes the place of an adverbial clause; this type is discussed in 38.31 and 38.54. In the second, which is found with adjectives and past participles or with other adjectival expressions, the
absolute construction is the equivalent of a descriptive prepositional
phrase, by which it is often replaced. In such descriptive absolute
constructions, the adjective may precede or follow the noun modified.

25.391 Adjectives.   LUG 158 *Libre el pecho de la opresión que le angustiara,
deshizo Gerardo el camino.*   (23–68)

25.393 Past participles.   BRA 192 *Pasea por el escenario, la cabeza inclinada.*   (28–104)

25.395 Adverbs used adjectivally.   IGN 25 *Tenía yo que dormir boca
abajo.*   (9–14)

25.397 Adverbial phrases used adjectivally.   FAL 169 *La era antipático
aquel atrincheramiento, lejos los dos de todas las mujeres.*   (20–29)

25.399 Replaced by a phrase with *con.* The preposition *con* may be
used with any type of adjectival modifier and a noun to form the
descriptive phrase. ZUN 54 *Con la cabeza rodeada de vendas, me dijo:
— ¡ Aquí me tiene usted!*   (32–81)

25.4 Adjectives performing the function of other parts of speech.

25.41 As adverbs. Many adjectives are identical in form with adverbs,
as *bajo, quedo, temprano,* etc. Such cases are discussed under adverbs.
But any adjective when used appositively acquires something of an
adverbial function. As appositives, they agree with a noun in the sentence, usually the subject. The attempt to distinguish between a merely
appositive use and a truly adverbial use must be somewhat arbitrary and
subjective. PAL 305 *Ascendimos después todo lo más veloces que pudimos*
(if the unexpressed complement of *pudimos* is *ascender* or *hacerlo,* then
veloces must be an adverb).   (48–172)

25.42 As substantives. We have already remarked that many words
serve both in the substantival and adjectival function. It is therefore
natural that adjectives of all kinds should readily be used as substantives, either as nouns or pronouns. When a qualifying adjective is used
as a substantive, it may become a true noun: *los pobres,* or, if its application is limited to a particular individual or group belonging to a

class already indicated, it may become a pronoun: *las casas grandes y las pequeñas.* Limiting adjectives used as substantives are regularly pronominal. Used as a noun, an adjective may be modified like any noun and may perform in the sentence the functions which any noun performs.

25.43 Modified by an adjective.

25.431 Definite article. As a noun, generic. IBA 149 *Voy a los humildes.* As pronoun, specifically limited. LIN 76 *La gente se aparta por cosas graves. — Las pequeñas son más insoportables.* (Relatively rare) **(60–1056)**

25.432 The adjective may be modified by an adverb. NER 23 *Muchos de los allí presentes experimentamos gran sorpresa.* **(18–25)**

25.433 The adjective may be superlative; it is often pronominal in this case. FAL 24 *Era aquella noche una de las más fuertes del invierno.*
(45–127)

25.437 The adjective may be used in a partitive phrase with *de* modifying an indefinite noun, especially in the superlative. RIC 26 *Había sido un actor de los mejores de España.* **(8–9)**

25.438 The adjective may be followed by *de* and a noun. UGA 33 *Para vengarse se está haciendo cortejar por el imbécil de García.* **(5–5)**
For a similar construction with nouns, see 3.521

25.439 As an indefinite feminine, singular or plural, an adjective is found in adverbial phrases introduced by a preposition. TIG 27 *Tigre Juan vuelve a las andadas.* **([21]–35)**

The only common phrases are: *a la moderna* (4–4) and *a las andadas.* (4–4).

25.45 Demonstrative adjective. NER 78 *Este ciego considerábase feliz.*
(42–82)

25.458 Followed by *de* and a noun. JES 228 *Pero estos brutos de mozos, ¿ en qué piensan?* See 25.438. **(4–7)**

25.46 Possessive adjective. BEN 31 *Ése es Jesús y Cabrera y la Repelona, su morganática.* **(21–42)**

25.47 Indefinite article. RIC 254 *Tú eres un infeliz.* **(48–146)**

25.471 In the pronominal use, the article is usually replaced by the indefinite pronoun *uno.* ARN 38 *Sí, uno alto, con gorra, le conozco.* **(7–10)**

25.479 As an indefinite feminine. LIN 57 *Cállate, o tendremos una muy seria.* **(3–3)**

25.481 Indefinite adjective. IBA 29 *Fué saliendo de la parte delantera otro viejo.* (28–41)

25.483 Interrogative adjective. LLA 43 *¿ Qué muertos son esos que resucitan ?* (4–4)

25.49 Qualifying adjective. ROM 103 *El joven vienés me proporcionó dos de Bosnia.* (30–52)

25.5 Without modification. The adjective without modification is relatively rare as a substantive, except in those situations in which a noun is normally used without modification. RAN 96 *Se ven apenas más que viejos que ya han vuelto de América.* (9–13)

25.54 In prepositional phrases.

25.541 Adjectival. BEN 16 *Una compañía de cómicos.* (34–54)

25.543 Adverbial. ROM 9 *Se acudió desde antiguo a la literatura española.* Especially phrases of the type of *en serio, en general, por completo, por supuesto,* etc. It is possible that the adjective should in this case be considered neuter, see 25.585. (50–222)

25.55 In apposition. BRA 164 *Aparece don Lorenzo, joven.* (4–14)

25.56 In elliptical constructions.

25.561 After *como.* SJQ 70 *Estoy como chiquillo con zapatos nuevos.* (3–3)

25.57 In direct address and exclamations. IMP 81 *¡ Tonto, me has asustado!* (39–228)

25.578 Followed by *de* and a noun or pronoun. RUS 15 *¡ Pobre de mí!* See 25.438. (14–30)

25.58 Neuter uses. The use of limiting adjectives as neuter pronouns is treated under Pronouns; see 13.

25.583 In partitive expressions with *de.* URU 26 *¿ Qué tiene de malo ?* (32–45)

It should be remarked that when an adjective modifies a neuter pronoun it is, in effect, a neuter adjective. ART 15 *Tampoco tengo yo nada íntimo a la mano.*

25.585 In prepositional phrases, usually adverbial. JIM 18 *Los hombres del campo, vestidos de limpio, se quedan mirándolo.* For closely related phrases, see 25.543. (3–10)

25.59 Indefinite feminine uses, especially in the plural, in prepositional phrases. BRA 146 *Toda la casa ha quedado a obscuras.* ([39]–106)

The commonest phrases are: *a medias* (7–8), *a obscuras* (4–5) — Also written *a oscuras* (4–5), *a secas* (3–3), *a solas* (4–5), *de primera* (3–4), *de veras* (**26–50**).

26. Comparison of adjectives.

26.1 The degree of a given quality which is ascribed to a given individual or object may be indicated in three forms of comparison: equality, superiority, or inferiority.

26.11 Equality. Regularly expressed by *tan* and if the term of the comparison is also expressed, by the use of the correlative *como*.

26.111 The term is expressed. RET 125 *El virrey, tan celoso por la enseñanza como el obispo, fundó un asilo de niñas mestizas.* **(56–154)**

26.113 Without expressed term. The construction becomes merely a method of expressing a high degree. PIN 72 *Me duele que me esperéis, siendo tan puntuales.* **(58–456)**

26.2 Superiority. There are three degrees of comparison of superiority and inferiority: positive, comparative, and superlative. The regular method of forming the comparative in Spanish is by prefixing *más* to the positive adjective. There is no specific form for expressing a superlative in Spanish, but it is possible to indicate the highest degree in a group of more than two by using the definite article with the comparative form. As a result of this lack of specific form, Spanish uses the same form to express the higher degree of one of two individuals and the highest degree in one of more than two individuals.

26.21 Comparative degree. Comparatives are of two kinds: the degree of a given quality in one individual is indicated as greater than the degree of that quality in another individual in the same category, or one individual is indicated as possessing a greater quantity of a given attribute than another fixed quantity. The correlative used to express " than " is, in the first type, *que*, in the second type, *de*.

26.22 Comparatives derived from Latin comparatives. There are several common adjectives in which the Latin forms have survived. With most of them, however, the regular comparatives with *más* are sometimes used.

26.221 *bueno — mejor.* ARN 71 *El vino será mejor.* **(60–219)**

26.222 *— más bueno.* SIE 97 *¡ Eres la mujer más buena del mundo!* **(5–6)**

26.223 *grande — mayor.* MAY 8 *Soy mayor de edad.* **(56–218)**

26.224 *— más grande.* SJQ 31 *Me has dado el alegrón más grande de mi vida.* Usually with a distinction in meaning: *mayor* referring to values and to age, and *más grande* referring to physical size. **(18–25)**

26.225 *malo — peor.* DEB 93 *Estoy peor.* **(32–53)**

26.227 *mucho — más.* SJQ 14 *Otro día tendré más suerte.* (*)

26.231 *pequeño — menor.* ABU 210 *Mi dignidad por la menor cosa se ofende.* **(30–60)**

26.232 *— más pequeño.* SIE 13 *Parece una hermana mayor, y al mismo tiempo, más pequeña.* Like *más grande, más pequeño* is limited to expressions of size. **(7–10)**

26.233 *poco — menos.* IGN 42 *Yo tengo menos dinero que tú.* **(50–116)**

26.31 One concept is compared with another concept of the same category, as two nouns, two adverbs, two adjectives. The correlative is *que.* ORT 108 *La Naturaleza es más perfecta que la cultura.* **(60–498)**

All uses of *que* after a comparative are included in these figures; it involves the use of *que* after comparatives of inferiority and after comparative adverbs.

26.4 One quantity is compared with another fixed quantity of the same category. The fixed quantity is the point from which the comparison is measured. The correlative for " than " is *de.*

26.41 The point of comparison is fixed by a numeral. ZAM 48 *Ahorré más de cinco mil duros.* **(32–74)**

26.411 An expression implying number may replace the numeral. RET 135 *Más de la mitad se componía de turbas de analfabetos.* **(7–10)**

26.415 A numeral expression after "than" may be compared with another substantive. In this case the correlative is *que.* MGR 18 *Un marido así vale más que el millón de dólares. El millón* is compared with *un marido así.* **(4–4)**

26.42 The point of comparison is fixed by a neuter collective of quantity.

26.421 *lo que.* ABU 31 *Gastan más de lo que tienen.* **(15–24)**

26.425 *lo* + an adjective. SAS 132 *Voy a ganar más de lo lícito.* **(5–6)**

26.5 When the main clause is negative it may deny any alternative beyond that indicated in the second element and the correlative for "than" will be *de.* Of this construction, common down to the Golden Age, only one example remains: in the idiom *no poder menos de.* ORT 106 *No podemos menos de advertir el esfuerzo de la materia.* **(10–14)**

26.58 The comparative is used without term to the comparison. MAY 6 *Parecía más rubio.* **(57–432)**

26.581 With two coordinated adjectives, *más* may be repeated. JAN 312 *Había visto a su cuñada más trabajadora y más alegre.* **(17–25)**

26.582 Or *más* may be understood with the second adjective.   JAN 309
Estoy más sano y alegre ahora.   The difference is one of style.   **(22–36)**

26.585 The definite article may be used with the comparative to indicate the particular one of two which possesses the quality in the higher degree.   URU 66 *Yo se lo dije a Hilaria la mayor.*   Especially when the adjective is substantivated.   **(16–23)**

26.59 The comparative adjective may be modified.

26.591 *cada vez.*   *Cada vez* is used to indicate the cumulative character of the state.   SON 43 *Sus ojos cada vez más hundidos en las cuencas se nublaron.*   **(14–19)**

26.595 *a cual.*   *A cual* (probably in origin *a cuál*), is used to indicate that two or more individuals vie with each other in the quality involved.   FOM 236 *Joaquín y Rosendo corrieron a Caracas, a cual más furioso.*   **(4–5)**

26.6 Superlative of superiority.   Regularly *el más.*

26.61 Without indication of the class.   RUB 20 *Los que desfiguran la belleza de su rostro son dignos de la más justa censura.*   **(56–316)**

26.62 The class is indicated by a phrase with *de.*   TRI 53 *Su presencia es para mí el mayor embeleso del mundo.*   **(52–196)**

26.63 The class is indicated by a relative clause.   SEC 74 *Es la mujer más bella que he conocido.*   **(23–37)**

26.641 With two coordinated adjectives, *más* may be repeated.   SON 116 *La antigüedad más clásica y más remota.*   **(9–9)**

26.642 More frequently it is understood with the second adjective.   ROD 10 *Los más raros y asombrosos contrastes.*   **(29–59)**

26.65 When the adjective which is compared follows the noun, the article is not repeated after the noun.   RUB 91 *La poetización de las cosas más prosaicas.*   **(50–202)**

26.651 But a superlative adjective, in pronominal use, when used in apposition with a noun, will retain the article.   ZAM 71 *Esta noche, la más triste de todas las del año.*   **(7–8)**

26.66 The superlative degree is sometimes expressed without the use of the definite article.

26.661 When the noun modified is a subjective complement.   RAN 104 *Lo que me pareció más moderno fué la catedral.*   **(15–20)**

26.663 The noun modified is objective complement.   REY 110 *Van sacando lo que cada cual conceptúa como más útil.*   **(3–3)**

26.665 The noun modified is direct object. PEQ 168 *Las cosas que dejan más honda huella en nuestro espíritu, no son éstas.*   (9–9)

26.667 The noun modified is object of a preposition. RUB 21 *Pintan al desgraciado en sus días de mayor infortunio.*   (14–15)

26.69 The definite article may be replaced by another limiting adjective.

26.691 Possessive adjective. DIV 10 *Los salarios apenas alcanzan sus necesidades más imperiosas.*   (31–55)

26.695 Relative *cuyo.* PEL 239 *Estos versos cuyo mejor tipo fué la traducción del* Aminta.   (3–3)

26.7 Comparison of inferiority.

26.71 Comparative. Comparison of inferiority is expressed by *menos.*

26.711 With term expressed after *que.* SAS 48 *Siento la necesidad de otra voz menos bronca que la mía.*   (24–40)

26.715 Without expressed term. ART 18 *Menos pobre, pero pobre siempre.* Very frequently negative.   (35–68)

26.72 Superlative. The superlative is expressed by the definite article with *menos.* RAN 43 *La menos elegante de todas ellas ha hecho más que todos los profesores.*   (12–18)

26.73 Proportionate comparison. When the speaker desires to indicate that the comparative superiority of one quality is proportionate to the comparative superiority of another quality, he normally uses correlatives in the older period of Spanish. In contemporary usage, if the relative element precedes, the correlative is omitted with the second element.

26.74 The relative element precedes. The proportion is expressed by *cuanto* only. LLA 5 *Tú olvidas que estoy en plena luna de miel, y que cuanto más tiempo esté con mi mujer, mejor.*   (9–15)

26.75 The relative element follows. The only common combination now in use is *tanto . . . cuanto que.* DIV 176 *Todas estas cuestiones son tanto más difíciles de contestar cuanto que han aparecido últimamente nuevas manifestaciones, que agravan más la situación general.*   (4–4)

26.76 The " absolute " superlative. The so-called " absolute superlative " is superlative only in the sense that is derived from a Latin superlative. Its actual function is simply to express a high degree of a quality, without any element of comparison. The ending is regularly *–ísimo.* UNA 83 *El excelentísimo señor tenía horror a la luz del sol.*   (58–330)

26.78 Other methods of intensification of adjectives. In addition to the form in *–ísimo*, there are number of other devices for expressing a

high degree of a quality.   One of the most frequent is naturally the use
of adverbs of degree, such as *bien, muy, tan,* or adverbs in *–mente,* like
sumamente.   These are discussed under Adverbs, 39.22.

26.781   The prefix *re–.*   The prefix *re–* is used to express a high degree
in colloquial style.   JIM 99 *¡ Qué reguapo estás hoy!*   (3–3)

26.782   An adjective may be repeated for intensification.   IMP 13 *En los
días largos, largos, que pasé viéndole morir.*   (11–17)

26.783   The second expression of the adjective may be accompanied by
muy.   ART 13 *Estoy contenta ¡ muy contenta!*   (4–4)

26.784   The two expressions may be connected by *y.*   UNA 98 *Ha arrancado sangre, ¡ sangre azul! no, sino roja, y muy roja.*   (5–12)

26.787   The comparative form with *más* is not uncommon in conversational style as a mere intensive.   SIE 44 *¡ Cosa más dulce!*   The construction is comparable to the use of *más* + an adjective after exclamatory
qué, see 22.325.   (9–15)

26.789   *más que tonto.*   The use of *más que* before an adjective is another
device for intensifying the adjective.   It is chiefly used in affective expressions involving the emotions.   JOA 17 *¡ Idiota, más que idiota!* (6–7)

26.8 Agreement of adjectives.

26.81 Simple agreement.   An adjective of any type agrees with the
noun which it modifies in gender and in number.   IBA 34 *He ido muchas
veces al Observatorio a dar buenos consejos.*   (*)
      (2370 examples of simple adjective agreement were counted in one
unit).

26.82 Complex agreement.   When an adjective agrees with two or more
nouns, it may agree with the nearest noun or it may be masculine plural.
The differences depend upon the position of the adjective.

26.831   The adjective precedes nouns of different gender.   It normally
agrees with the first noun.   ROD 80 *Nuevas magias y prodigios.* **(28–67)**

26.835   The adjective precedes nouns of the same gender.   It usually
agrees with the first noun.   IMP 12 *¡ Cuánta mentecatez y engañosa salaci-
dad!*   (8–10)

26.836   At times, it agrees in gender and is plural, especially with proper
nouns.   PEL 7 *Los honrados Francisco Terré y Francisco Burgués.* (6–6)

26.841   The adjective follows singular nouns of different gender.   It is
usually masculine plural.   PAT 28 *Con voz y gesto lacrimosos.* (17–27)

26.845   The adjective follows plural nouns of different gender.   The adjective sometimes agrees with the nearest noun. MAY 7 *Modismos, tonos y formas características de la región.* (7–9)

26.846 But it also sometimes is masculine plural. FAL 26 *Tanto ellos como ellas muy abrigados.* (8–10)

26.847 The adjective follows nouns of different gender and number. The adjective is usually masculine plural. NER 71 *El lodo y las lágrimas del mundo, convertidos en substancia radiante.* (3–3)

26.851 The adjective follows singular nouns of the same gender. The adjective agrees in gender and is plural. JIM 64 *El paisaje y el cielo mismos.* (15–25)

26.853 The adjective follows plural nouns of the same gender. The adjective naturally agrees. ROD 205 *Las disposiciones y costumbres íntimas del alma.* (*)

26.89 Distributive agreement. Two or more adjectives are sometimes used to modify the same plural noun, indicating that each of the adjectives modifies the singular noun which is implied in the plural form. DIV 10 *Los gobiernos americano y francés.* (7–13)

26.9 Prepositional phrases used adjectivally. All prepositional phrases which modify a noun are in function adjectives.

26.91 Attributive modifier. IBA 26 *Los charcos de lluvia.* (*)

26.911 Coordinate with an adjective. ORT 117 *Es un ser fantástico o de la fantasía.* (29–75)

26.92 Predicate modifier.

26.921 Subjective complement. SJQ 85 *El caso no es de risa.* (28–81)

26.923 Objective complement. SIE 28 *Sabía que iba a encontrarte de mal humor.* (23–35)

26.93 In an absolute construction. MUJ 18 *Ha hincado la pierna en la silla, los codos en la mesa.* (8–10)

26.94 Like other adjectives, an adjectival phrase may be modified by an adverb. ROM 185 *El romance estaba más en voga.* (16–26)

26.95 Like other adjectives, an adjectival phrase may be used as a noun. BYN 90 *En el Círculo se reunen diariamente los sin familia.* (5–6)

26.99 Relative clauses, as adjectives. Relative clauses are usually adjectival modifiers. Their general use is discussed under Pronouns. Here, it may be remarked that they are sometimes found coordinated with adjectives or adjectival phrases modifying a noun. RUB 22 *Poe tenía un exterior notablemente agradable y que predisponía en su favor.* (19–39)

IV. VERBS

TYPES OF VERBS

27. According to their function in the sentence, verbs may be classified as transitive, intransitive, reflexive, reciprocal, copulative, and auxiliary.

27.1 Transitive verbs. A transitive verb is one whose action or state is exercised directly upon an object which is different from the subject of the verb. REY 148 *Hagamos nuestros preparativos.* (*)

27.2 Intransitive verbs. An intransitive verb is one whose action or state requires no direct object, but is complete in itself. MAY 70 *Iban casi a tientas.* (*)

27.3 Reflexive verbs. A reflexive verb is one whose action or state is exercised upon the subject. The reflexive object may be either a direct or an indirect object. Since it is impossible to distinguish in any other way, they are here studied according to the normal classification of the verb. A reflexive used alone after a transitive verb is considered a direct object; a reflexive used with a transitive verb which has another word as direct object and a reflexive used with an intransitive verb is considered an indirect object.

27.31 Transitive verbs with a direct reflexive object. In principle, almost any transitive verb may have a reflexive as a direct object. PAT 15 *Se contempló en la luna del armario.* **(54–302)**

27.311 Many verbs, however, when used reflexively, acquire an intransitive force. Thus *me siento* comes to mean "I am in the act of sitting down," "I sit down," or *se enamoró* means "he fell in love." Verbs of mental or emotional process, in particular, express the effective aspect, that is, they indicate the achievement of a state. So *se pierde* means "he gets lost." JES 235 *Al pasar, sonreía sin detenerse.* **([60]–6927)**

27.312 The number of transitive reflexives is very large; only those which were noted in at least ten texts are included in the following list.

abrirse	**(24–45)**	adelantarse	(16–25)	apagarse	(15–18)
aburrirse	(18–31)	agarrarse	(12–16)	apartarse	(15–21)
acabarse	(16–36)	ahogarse	(11–13)	apoyarse	(13–14)
acercarse	**(44–126)**	alegrarse	**(26–50)**	aproximarse	(14–24)
acordarse	**(40–94)**	alejarse	**(24–49)**	arreglarse	(15–20)
acostarse	(19–28)	alzarse	(16–25)	asomarse	**(22–35)**
acostumbrarse	(11–11)	animarse	(10–13)	asustarse	(17–25)

burlarse	(21–35)	encontrarse	(42–92)	negarse	(16–21)
calmarse	(12–17)	engañarse	(10–15)	ocuparse	(17–28)
cansarse	(18–30)	enterarse	(27–65)	olvidarse	(17–29)
casarse	(38–185)	entretenerse	(13–14)	oponerse	(13–18)
cerrarse	(11–14)	equivocarse	(18–32)	pararse	(20–28)
conformarse	(10–15)	erguirse	(10–14)	pasearse	(13–18)
contentarse	(10–16)	escaparse	(25–30)	perderse	(31–48)
convencerse	(14–17)	esconderse	(13–16)	ponerse	(50–212)
convertirse	(18–23)	estremecerse	(15–22)	preocuparse	(20–23)
cuidarse	(10–11)	explicarse	(15–18)	presentarse	(34–60)
decidirse	(19–27)	extenderse	(21–33)	referirse	(24–53)
dejarse	(13–17)	fiarse	(11–15)	refugiarse	(12–12)
desarrollarse	(11–13)	fijarse	(33–76)	resignarse	(10–13)
deslizarse	(12–18)	hacerse	(38–112)	resistirse	(10–13)
despedirse	(25–42)	hallarse	(26–80)	retirarse	(29–62)
despertarse	(14–19)	hundirse	(15–20)	reunirse	(19–26)
destacarse	(15–22)	inclinarse	(21–46)	sentarse	(38–125)
desvanecerse	(10–14)	incorporarse	(11–18)	sentirse	(35–83)
detenerse	(32–75)	instalarse	(12–17)	separarse	(19–32)
dirigirse	(29–67)	lanzarse	(12–17)	servirse	(10–21)
disponerse	(16–20)	levantarse	(35–104)	tranquilizarse	(11–17)
distraerse	(13–22)	llamarse	(40–98)	tratarse	(33–76)
divertirse	(23–56)	mantenerse	(11–14)	unirse	(10–10)
echarse	(18–29)	meterse	(30–55)	verse	(23–55)
empeñarse	(19–35)	molestarse	(14–16)	vestirse	(21–40)
enamorarse	(20–40)	mostrarse	(17–32)	volverse	(37–75)
encargarse	(12–18)	moverse	(27–41)		

27.32 As indirect object, closely related to the verb.

27.321 With transitive verbs. ZAM 78 *Anda, date prisa.*   ([53]–279)

The commonest verbs are: *dar* (**39–76**), *decir* (**21–36**), *explicar* (9–9), *guardar*, (6–9), *hacer* (**29–40**), *permitir* (11–18), *proponer* (13–18).

27.323 With intransitive verbs. The use of the reflexive pronoun with these verbs is strongly affective in character and indicates that the speaker has some special interest in relating the action or state to the subject of the sentence. SAS 69 *Dentro de ocho días nos vamos.* ([60]–1071)

The commonest verbs are: *caerse* (17–29), *callarse* (**22–39**), *dormirse* (11–12), *entrarse* (13–17), *estarse* (17–19), *irse* (**50–312**), *marcharse* (**31–127**), *morirse* (**32–113**), *parecerse* (**23–41**), *quedarse* (**48–196**), *reírse* (**31–87**), *salirse* (15–20), *subirse* (12–15), *venirse* (17–27), *volverse* (11–19).

27.33 Modifying the whole sentence.

27.331 Possession. SON 24 *Callaba enjugándose los ojos.*   (42–131)

27.332 Rarely a possessive adjective is used as well as the reflexive pronoun. RUB 83 *Se ciñó su corona de laureles en los bancos de la policía.*

(4–5)

27.333 Separation.   MAY 116 *Se quitó el chaquet.*   ([21]–36)

The only common verbs are: *preguntar* (10–13) and *quitar* (13–16).

27.335 Interest.   PEQ 95 *Un membrillo que yo voy partiendo poco a poco y comiéndomelo.*   ([58]–475)

The commonest verbs are: *abrir* (7–8), *beber* (9–10), *comer* (14–25), *comprar* (9–22), *creer* (15–19), *encontrar* (11–13), *figurar* (**31–114**), *ganar* (8–11), *gastar* (8–12), *imaginar* (9–17), *llevar* (**34–72**), *merecer* (8–11), *pasar* (13–20), *procurar* (5–7), *traer* (8–12).

27.336 The direct object of such verbs is often the indefinite pronoun *las.*   TRI 53 *Él tenía la culpa, quizás por echárselas de fino.*   (11–24)

27.337 Place.   BYN 74 *Algunos hasta nos ponemos corbata.*   ([18]–30)

The only common verb is *poner* (14–26).

27.34 Normally reflexive verbs.   A number of verbs have ceased to be used in simple forms and have become normally reflexive.   SIE 21 *Si no me quejo, es natural.*   ([52]–258)

The commonest verbs are: *acurrucarse* (5–5), *apoderarse* (14–21), *arrepentirse* (13–17), *atenerse* (5–8), *atreverse* (**46–104**), *dignarse* (7–9), *quejarse* (**24–40**), *suicidarse* (6–6).

27.35 Impersonal reflexives.   Other verbs are used as impersonal reflexives, the logical subject becoming a grammatical indirect object.   ABU 18 *¡ Ay, lo que se me ocurre!*   ([44]–151)

The common verbs are: *se me antoja* (16–19), *se me ocurre* (**25–44**), *se me olvida* (12–21), *se me va* (7–7).

27.36 Reflexive verbs used as intransitives.   Verbs which are usually reflexive are sometimes found as intransitives. This group does not include cases such as the varying use of verbs like *pasear* and *pasearse, despertar* and *despertarse.*

27.361 In the infinitive.   MAY 7 *Le obligaron a marchar, no sin que prometió volver muy pronto.*   (9–11)

27.363 Especially when a personal pronoun of identical form has already been expressed with the main verb.   ZAM 84 *Tú no me dejas divertir.*   (9–11)

27.364 In this situation, however, the reflexive pronoun may be expressed.   SON 187 *Me ordenaba presentarme en Roma.*   (7–7)

27.37 If two reflexive verbs are coordinated, the reflexive pronoun may not be repeated with the second verb.   BYN 116 *Se vierte o extiende en moldes bajos.*   (6–7)

THE REFLEXIVE USED AS AN INDEFINITE OR SUBSTITUTE
FOR THE PASSIVE

27.4 In addition to the reflexive uses with particular verbs which have thus far been discussed, the reflexive is also used, with both transitive and intransitive verbs, to express an indefinite subject, or, with transitive verbs, to express a passive. Its equivalence with an indefinite subject is assured by the fact that it is often followed by a direct object; its equivalence with a passive is evidenced by the fact that it is often followed by an agent. The construction must have arisen with transitive verbs which had a subject not referring to a person and this is still the most frequent use. But it has spread to transitive verbs with a personal subject and to intransitive verbs. Finally, it has become an indefinite transitive and is followed by a direct object.

27.41 Transitive verbs, with a definite subject, expressed or implied.

27.42 The subject is not a person.

27.421 Noun or pronoun. UNA 6 *Por las ventanas se veían las otras habitaciones del patio.* The position of the grammatical subject, normally after the verb, is evidence that it is felt as the psychological object.
(60–1653)

27.423 Infinitive. REY 160 ¿ *Se permite hacer una observación ?* **(30–76)**

27.425 Substantive clause. JIM 36 *Diríase que el cielo se deshace en rosas.* **(54–198)**

27.426 The clause may be an indirect question. PEQ 76 *No se sabe qué pueblos y qué razas vinieron.* **(4–5)**

27.43 The subject is a person. This use is rare, because it is open to the possibility of ambiguity; *se invita* may mean "he invites himself." It is normally replaced by the indefinite construction with expressed object: *se le invita.* RUS 77 *Creí que los hijos no se escogían.* **(7–9)**

27.44 Intransitive and transitive verbs, without expressed subject.

27.441 Intransitive verbs, alone or with adverbial modifier. FOM 93 *Por fin llegaron. Se comió; se tertulió un momento.* PAL 17 *Se hablaba de unas cosas espantosas.* **([51]–250)**

27.443 Rarely even with *estar* and *ser.* SIE 16 ¡ *Qué bien se está a tu lado!* **(4–5)**

27.445 Transitive verbs, alone. This construction is found only when the verb is modified or introduced by an adverb of manner (*así, como,* etc.) CAT 13 *No le registras los bolsillos, como debe hacerse con todo hombre casado.* (9–15)

27.45 Transitive verbs, with an expressed direct object.

27.46 The object is a person.

27.461 Expressed by a noun. DIV 170 *A fines de abril se podrá invitar a los delegados alemanes a venir.* (**24–46**)

27.463 Expressed by a personal pronoun. IBA 361 *Bien entrada la mañana se les veía por las calles más céntricas, discutiendo a voces.* (**42–91**)

27.465 By an indefinite pronoun. MUJ 34 *Di orden de que no se recibiera a nadie.* (3–3)

27.467 By a relative pronoun. IGN 30 *¿ Es que no se puede conocer más que a quien se trata ?* (7–8)

27.47 The object is a thing. This construction, which is quite as logical as the construction with persons, is not approved by grammatical purists. It is not uncommon.

27.471 Expressed by a noun. ORR 172 *Vomitaban chismes con la seriedad con que se comenta asuntos religiosos.* (9–11)

27.473 Expressed by a personal pronoun. ORT 87 *Los pueblos de esta tierra son súbitas apariciones. No se los ve hasta que se está muy próximo.* (10–13)

27.475 Even when the noun subject is expressed, the use of a present participle shows that the subject is felt to be indefinite. ALT 7 *De este modo se acumulaban propiedades, sustrayéndolas de la circulación.* It is probable that the participle is, grammatically, in an absolute construction, with unexpressed indefinite subject; but it is clear that, logically, the participle modifies the indefinite subject of the main verb. (16–45)

27.5 Other methods of expressing an indefinite subject. In addition to the reflexive, there are several other ways of indicating an indefinite subject. Of these, the most frequent is the use of the third person plural of the verb. Even this construction is much more frequent than the true passive with *ser*.

27.51 First person plural. BEN 17 *Ella dispone desde a qué hora ha de bañarse la gente, hasta la hora en que hemos de acostarnos.* (11–63)

27.52 Second person plural. PEQ 160 *Entonces os paseáis bajo los soportales; allá en el fondo se ve el resplandor de una lámpara.* (4–9)

27.53 Third person plural. URU 56 *¿ Qué le pasa, hija ? ¿ Qué le han hecho ?* (**52–451**)

27.531 It may be used even when the indefinite subject is singular, referring to one person. ZAM 41 *(Suena un timbre.) — Han llamado.*
(8–12)

27.54 An indefinite pronoun.

27.541 *gente.* SIE 11 *A las diez de seguro empieza a venir gente.*
(Not counted)

27.542 *la gente.* ART 68 *¡ Conque la gente cree que soy esclava suya !* Both *gente* and *la gente* have a collective value which is different from that of the other expressions discussed in this section. It is possible that they should not be considered indefinite pronouns. (Not counted)

27.545 *uno.* LIN 119 *De noche acaba uno siempre por dormirse.* *Uno* is especially common with reflexive verbs, where the indefinite reflexive is not possible, and with *tener.* **(33–73)**

27.546 *una.* RUS 123 *Aunque una no quiera, acaba por encariñarse con ella.* Regularly, when the indefinite is limited to feminine persons. For the use of *una* as a substitute for the first person, see 4.34. (15–27)

RECIPROCAL VERBS

27.7 A reciprocal verb is one whose action is exercised by two or more subjects directly upon each other or upon one another, or one whose action is indirectly of mutual concern to each of two or more subjects.

27.71 The reciprocal relation is direct. TIG 45 *Nosotros ya nos hemos visto.* **(49–188)**

27.72 The reciprocal relation is indirect. JAN 23 *Rehuyes las ocasiones en que podemos hablarnos.* **(33–56)**

27.73 The reciprocal character of the action may be reinforced by pronominal or adverbial expressions.

27.741 *uno a otro (unos a otros).* RAN 42 *Me quedé asombrado al ver que los hombres no se arrojaban unos a otros objetos de porcelana.* (5–5)

27.745 *el uno al otro (los unos a los otros).* ORR 170 *Estaban en el momento clásico de las confidencias, llamándose el uno al otro « hermanito. »* (5–5)

27.751 *mutuamente.* IGN 48 *¡ Qué poco proporcionados estarían los daños que mutuamente nos hemos hecho !* (3–3)

27.8 Copulative verbs. A copulative verb is one whose function is to connect the subject and a subjective complement, substantival or adjectival. The chief copulatives in Spanish are *ser* and *estar*. They, as well as other verbs used as copulatives, are discussed in 35.3.

27.9 Auxiliary verbs. An auxiliary verb is one whose function is to express, in combination with other verbs, tense, mood, voice, or aspect. Thus *haber* is an auxiliary verb used in the formation of the perfect tenses. *Ser* is an auxiliary used in the formation of the passive voice. *Ir* is an auxiliary used in the formation of the progressive aspect. *Poder* is an auxiliary used to express the potential mood. The use of auxiliary verbs is discussed in detail under the several headings of Auxiliaries, Tense, and Voice.

MOODS

THE INDICATIVE

28. The indicative is used to present an action or state objectively; it reports a fact. It is found in both main and subordinate clauses.

28.11 The indicative is used to state a fact, affirmatively and negatively, in statements, questions, and exclamations. ᴢᴜɴ 10 *Era noche de moda en el teatro Español.*   (*)

28.12 Similarly, it is used in parenthetical clauses. ғᴏᴍ 21 *Escenas como la del domingo, tú sabes, no son de muy buen gusto.*   **(38–116)**

28.15 If a statement in a main clause is made questionable by the use of *quizás, acaso,* or *tal vez,* the indicative is the normal mood when the action or state involved is present or past. ʀᴇʏ 162 *Algunos quizás comienzan a arrepentirse.*   **(40–96)**

For the use of the present indicative and the future indicative to express commands, see 32.18 and 32.628.

28.2 In substantive clauses, subject and object.

28.21 With verbs of declaring, knowing, perceiving, etc., affirmative, negative or interrogative, presenting the action or state as a fact.

28.211 Subject clauses. With logically impersonal expressions. ꜱᴇᴄ 10 *¿ No te consta que aquello fué una cosa de chiquillos ?*   **([28]–56)**

The commonest expressions are: *constar* (10–16), *ser cierto* (6–6), *ser verdad* (9–17).

28.213 With verbs used as indefinite reflexives. ɪᴅᴏ 116 *Se conoce que usted es artista.*   **(46–94)**

28.215 With negative verbs which themselves imply a negation (*no ignorar, no negar*), in subject or object clauses. ɪᴅᴏ 115 *No puede negarse que la escultura viene casi estacionaria desde los días de Grecia.*   **(7–8)**

28.217 Object clauses. ᴢᴀᴍ 26 *Te advierto que siento hacia Ricardo una pasión de madre.*   **([60]–1587)**

The commonest verbs in this class are: *advertir* (**27–45**), *afirmar* (12–18), *anunciar* (7–8), *añadir* (5–6), *asegurar* (**23–41**), *avisar* (5–6), *comprender* (**33–62**), *confesar* (**22–28**), *conocer* (9–11), *contar* (11–14), *contestar* (5–6), *decir* (**60–530**), *declarar* (7–9), *demostrar* (9–11), *encontrar* (5–6), *entender* (13–16), *explicar* (6–7), *ignorar* (5–5), *jurar* (17–27), *mirar* (10–16), *mostrar* (5–5), *notar* (9–13), *observar* (11–12), *oír* (16–18), *olvidar* (10–12), *probar* (9–10), *prometer* (12–14), *reconocer* (9–11), *recordar* (**22–36**), *repetir* (12–16), *saber* (**52–264**), *sentir* (**25–43**), *soñar* (6–7), *ver* (**44–110**).

28.219 After *he aquí* (*ahí*).   JES 25 *Pero he aquí que ahora no me quieren admitir a la convocatoria.*   (4–5)

28.22 With verbs of thinking, believing, imagining, etc.

28.221 Subject clauses, with logically impersonal expressions.   JIM 42 *Me parece que esta vez se han equivocado.*   ([57]–215)

The only common verb is *parecer* (**56–202**).

28.223 With verbs used as indefinite reflexives.   SJQ 45 *Se ha creído que vive en mi casa.*   (5–6)

28.225 Object clauses, after affirmative verbs.   SON 33 *Creo que además de sus labios me sonrieron sus ojos.*   ([58]–455)

The commonest verbs are: *adivinar* (5–7), *considerar* (7–14), *creer* (**50–224**), *figurarse* (19–36), *juzgar* (5–7), *pensar* (**37–75**), *presentir* (5–5), *sospechar* (9–10), *suponer* (**20–39**).

28.227 With interrogative verbs.   ORR 105 *¿ Crees tú que Balmaceda cederá ?*   (**28–71**)

28.229 With negative verbs.   IGN 48 *Nunca pensé que el duque había testado a su favor.*   The indicative is used to indicate that the fact of the action or state, not the speaker's attitude, is the important consideration.   (**20–31**)

28.235 With verbs and verbal locutions expressing doubt.   Examples are common only when the expression is negative or interrogative, implying a negative.   PAX 330 *No dudo que el país lo llamará a regir sus destinos.*
([12]–17)

The only common expression is *ser indudable* (7–7).

28.24 With verbs expressing occurrence, used as logically impersonal with a subject clause.   JES 227 *Resultaba que el joven tenía sus mismas aficiones literarias.*   ([12]–17)

The only common verbs are *resultar* (8–13) and *suceder* (6–6).

28.25 In indirect questions.   PEQ 11 *Lo mejor será que yo cuente dónde lo he escrito.*   (**60–417**)

28.261 With verbs expressing emotion.   UNA 158 *El conde tendió la mano a Julia, temiendo que se la rechazaría.*   (10–11)

The only common verb is *esperar*, in the sense of " hope " (8–9).

28.27 In clauses used as subjective complement after *ser*.

28.271 After expressions expressing a fact. JOA 39 *Una prueba de que tengo razón es que a mí me salen simpatías por todas partes.* **(36–86)**

28.273 Especially after *es que*. SIE 18 *No es eso; es que estás enfadado todavía por lo de antes.* **(46–203)**

28.275 Rarely after *ello es que*. PEQ 119 *Ello es que era una vieja menudita.* **(6–7)**

28.28 In clauses used in apposition with a noun or pronoun. URU 60 *¿ Verdad que me comprendes ?* **(6–12)**

28.29 In clauses used as object of a preposition. A special feature of Spanish is its use of substantive clauses after a preposition. They are found used in any case in which a noun or an infinitive is used after a preposition as a complement to a noun or a verb.

28.291 Adjectival phrases, modifying a noun and normally introduced by *de*. PAL 11 *Sólo me di cuenta de que había unas montañas muy altas.* **([39]–106)**

The commonest nouns thus followed by *de* and a clause are: *cuenta* (14–18), *idea* (5–5), *noticia* (6–7), *prueba* (6–6).

28.295 Adverbial phrases. Modifying a verb. ABC 41 *Confía en que la República española será clemente.* **([40]–113)**

The commonest expressions are: *apostar a* (9–9), *convencerse de* (8–8), *convenir en* (5–5), *enterarse de* (7–9), *pensar en* (5–8), *quedar en* (5–5).

28.296 Modifying a past participle. LUG 358 *El señor Roquer os lo dará, convencido de que nunca amaneció día más radiante que éste.* **([8]–11)**

The only common participle is *convencido de* (5–5).

28.297 Modifying an adjective. MGR 21 *Estad seguros de que en sus aguas hallaréis el calcio que necesitan los huesos.* **([12]–18)**

The only common adjective is *seguro de* (12–13).

28.299 Used independently, without a verb or adjective, but implying *apostar*. UGA 48 *Otros le desafiaron cómicamente: — ¿ A que no te atreves conmigo, fanfarrón ?* **(9–13)**

28.3 In adjective clauses (relative). The indicative is regularly used in relative clauses which qualify specific antecedents and report actual facts, particular or universal. RET 128 *Durante el siglo XVI no fueron escasos los hombres de superior cultura que visitaron a Méjico.* **(*)**

28.31 With a superlative antecedent, the indicative is regularly used to

state a fact which is limited in its application to the specific antecedent.
CAT 41 *Era el monstruo más grande que había producido la tierra.* (14–20)

28.4 In adverbial clauses. The indicative is used in a variety of adverbial clauses to qualify the meaning of a verb. In each case, the notion conveyed by the clause is presented as a fact, not as an unreality or an hypothesis. Under each group, the commonest subordinating conjunctions used to introduce the clause are arranged alphabetically.

28.41 Adversative clauses.

a pesar de que. ORR 100 *Me aburro en cama a pesar de que no me faltan amigos.* (5–8)

y eso que. SEC 90 *Me parece que le he gustado a la delgadita, y eso que el papel no me va.* (12–14)

28.42 Causal clauses.

como. SON 39 *Como ello era también mi deseo, me alejé.* (**54–226**)

por lo mismo que. SAS 130 *Por lo mismo que había estudiado, me convencí de que toda mi ciencia era cuentos de viejas.* (3–5)

porque. URU 27 *No pregunto por don Olegario, porque acabo de estar con él en el corral.* (**54–711**)

pues. URU 29 *Me felicito de que pueda continuar la conversación, pues nos interesa a todos.* (**36–92**)

pues que. RUB 91 *Y pues que vamos a esos paraísos, celebremos la blancura de las velas de seda.* (3–4)

puesto que. BEL 17 *Boscán era joven, puesto que Garcilaso le llama mancebo.* (**22–50**)

que. URU 40 *No dé esos gritos, que no está tratando con un niño.* There is no objective test for determining whether *que* in this usage is a subordinating conjunction meaning "because," or a coordinating conjunction meaning "for." (**40–146**)

ya que. LIN 128 *Por muchos años, ya que os satisface tanto.* (**26–39**)

28.43 Comparison, between realities, after *que*. NER 92 *Los ricos inteligentes más sufren que gozan.* Only after *más* meaning "rather." (*)

28.44 Concession.

aunque. PEQ 38 *He de decirlo, aunque no he pasado por este mal.* (**42–134**)

por más que. SIE 43 *Por más que hay ocasiones, la necesidad obliga a veces a la más cruel indelicadeza.* (7–8)

si bien. RET 33 *A ellos puede agregarse Silva, si bien la influencia de Silva comenzó a hacerse sentir después de su muerte.* (3–8)

28.45 Imaginative comparison.

como que. RIC 20 *Tan cierto es que las circunstancias parece como que cambian la naturaleza de las cosas.* The indicative used with *como que* stresses the reality of the imagined action or state, in contrast with the subjunctive which is used after *como si* to stress the unreality. (6–6)

28.46 Manner.

a lo que. NER 37 *La tierra defiende celosamente, a lo que parece, el bien que se le ha confiado.* (4–4)

a medida que. IDO 4 *A medida que se acercaba a la tierra, con más vigor el pasado revivía en su alma.* (11–17)

así como. RUS 73 *La mujer debe tener sentimientos religiosos, así como debe tener también ojos bonitos.* (13–13)

como. JIM 43 *Vuelan mudas, como andan las hormigas cuando un niño les pisotea el camino.* (60–426)

conforme. JES 224 *Josefina pasaba sus confidencias de unas amigas a otras, conforme la iban alcanzando.* (3–3)

que. CAT 18 *Este cristiano es el padre, que llaman, y yo mesma soy la madre.* Only in expressions such as *que dicen, que llaman.* (4–4)

según. RIC 254 *Nuestro padre las tuvo, según dice, a los treinta.* (32–71)

tal como. ROM 105 *Me limito a publicar los romances, tal como los hallo.* The *tal* must be adverbial. (4–8)

28.47 Place, without expressed antecedent for the adverb of place.

IBA 31 *Donde yo tuve mi primera barraca, hay ahora un gran café.* (*)

28.48 Result.

de modo que. IMP 201 *Estaba calzado de modo que podía andar subrepticiamente.* (4–6)

de suerte que. ALT 11 *Aprovechó su privanza para acumular honores, de suerte que llegó a ser el más poderoso de los señores castellanos.* (3–3)

de tal manera que. DIV 352 *Lo logró de tal manera que muchos concurrentes creyeron que la cantante era española.* (3–3)

que. After *tal, tan,* and *tanto.* BEN 43 *Me habían educado tan estrechamente que rompí todo freno al verme libre.* ([50]–216)

que. With the force of *de modo que.* RUS 27 *Aquello está montado que no hay oficina que le lleve ventaja.* (6–7)

28.49 Time, always in the present or past, never in the future.

a tiempo que. WAS 141 *Don Canuto y su compañero miraron hacia la puerta a tiempo que Midas se apeaba.* (4–4)

ahora que. UNA 157 *Y ahora que mi mujer está curada, no corre usted peligro alguno con venir acá.* (14–24)

al mismo tiempo que. IBA 27 — *Adiós, Isidro* — *dijo, al mismo tiempo que se enrojecían sus mejillas.* (5–5)

apenas. RUS 73 *Apenas me ve, me maltrata, me insulta.* (9–16)

apenas ... cuando. JAN 11 *Apenas había llegado a su puesto, cuando Irene se le presentó.* (4–4)

así que. UGA 9 *Así que se cerraba la Universidad, ambos amigos iban a reunirse con sus respectivas familias.* (7–10)

cada vez que. JAN 6 *Cada vez que la hablaba un hombre, se ponía como una guinda.* (9–10)

cuando. IBA 24 *Algo peor ocurría cuando los gritos eran acompañados de pedradas.* (**60–1062**)

desde que. PIN 27 *Desde que dejasteis de trabajar, no cobro un ochavo.* (**43–90**)

después que. ABU 17 *Después que le dejan en cueros los acreedores, le falla el negocio de América.* (8–8)

en cuanto. RUS 8 *En cuanto le cogemos nosotros, se para.* (**23–36**)

en tanto. PAT 26 *Jiménez, en tanto Alberto leía la gacetilla, había estado viendo tanto destrozo como yacía por tierra.* (5–6)

en tanto que. RUB 193 *En tanto que la literatura se deja arrastrar por el impulso científico, la medicina penetra al reino de las letras.* (8–13)

hasta que. REY 101 *Siguen nadando, hasta que Sipsom se pone de pie en el fondo.* (**37–78**)

mientras. ROD 13 *Mientras vivimos, nada hay en nosotros que no sufra retoque y complemento.* (**54–166**)

mientras que. ALT 8 *El nombre de fijodalgo se extiende, mientras que el de ricohombre se va perdiendo.* (8–9)

siempre que. PAT 208 *Meg los observaba atenta, como siempre que se besaban.* (10–13)

tan pronto como. VIG 68 *Tan pronto como Augusto ve pasar a la moza, ésta le descubre a las demás mujeres.* (4–4)

ya que. SEC 73 *Ya que estoy aquí, te confieso que estoy entusiasmado.* (3–4)

THE SUBJUNCTIVE

29. The subjunctive mood is used to present an action or state subjectively; that is to say, it does not report a fact, it serves merely to reflect the attitude of the speaker toward a given action or state. It is therefore primarily an instrument for expressing emotion, although it may rarely be used to reflect a merely intellectual attitude toward an experience. While it is not always possible to identify the exact emotion involved, the great majority of cases fall into two main classes, those that reflect some phase of desire, and those that reflect some phase of uncertainty.   In the first class belong such notions as will, command, causation, necessity, approval, permission, purpose, fear, joy and their likes and their opposites; in the second class are included such notions as doubt, possibility, permissibility, probability, and indefinite or hypothetical futurity.   The subjunctive is found in both main and subordinate clauses.   In each section, the basis classification into the two fundamental classes is maintained.

29.1 The subjunctive of desire.

29.11 Expressing a wish.   Wishes fall into two main groups: those which refer to the future, and are capable of fulfillment, and those which refer to the present or past and, not being capable of fulfillment, become a sort of expression of regret.   Wishes which refer to the future may be directly and vividly expressed (in the present subjunctive), or they may be expressed with a certain hesitancy or moderation (in the past subjunctive).

29.111 Future.   More vividly expressed, with the present subjunctive, in prayers or similar appeals for divine assistance.   FOM 224 *Cúmplase tu voluntad, Dios mío — pronunció el doctor.*   **(29–106)**

29.113 Contrariwise in curses.   PAL 305 *¡ Maldita sea mi suerte! — profirió don Eloy.*   **(12–20)**

29.117 In other expressions of wish.   RIC 254 *¡ Buen provecho te hagan!*   **(9–11)**

29.119 Especially in the exclamation *¡ viva!*   PIN 56 *¡ Viva la huelga!*   **(12–35)**

29.121 Future, less vividly expressed, with the past subjunctive in *–se.*   SON 202 *La niña se le colgó al cuello, hablándole con agasajo al oído: — Si le hicieses un vestido a mi muñeca.*   **(5–6)**

29.123 With the past subjunctive in *–ra.*   BEN 33 *Ya lo sé que un día nos darán un tiro; ¡ ojalá y fuera eso!*   **(4–7)**

29.131 Present, incapable of fulfillment, with the past subjunctive in *–ra.*   ZAM 134 *¡ Quien pudiera vivir contigo!*   **(20–31)**

29.133 With the past subjunctive in *–se.*   TRI 53 *¡ Ah, si pudiese afirmar lo mismo con respecto a ella!*   **(5–5)**

29.143 Past, incapable of fulfillment, with the pluperfect subjunctive in *hubiera.*   JES 238 *Sí, soy casado, y ojalá no lo hubiera sido nunca.* (7–9)

29.15 A wish is usually expressed without any introductory expression. But a number of conjunctions and adverbs are also used to intensify the expression.

29.151 Without introductory word.   IDO 222 *¡ Bien   venido   seas!*
(36–136)

29.153 With an introductory word.

así.   RUS 26 *¡ Por humilde que sea, es mi mujer! — ¡ Así lo fuese tanto la mía!*
(3–5)

ojalá.   JAN 315 *Ojalá les haga en la navegación un tiempo así.*   (11–12)

que.   STE 254 *Que Dios nos bendiga a todos — dijo Alejandra.*   (19–31)

quien (referring to the first person).   ART 42 *¡ Quien pudiera ser como usted!*
(3–3)

si.   RIC 259 *¡ Si vieras qué pena siento!*   (21–34)

29.157 The wish may be expressed by a parenthetical relative clause; this is the regular formula for expressing a pious hope concerning the eternal status of a dead person.   CAT 13 *Sanguijuela, que en gloria esté, era enemigo de convidar a nadie.*
(7–8)

29.16 Expressing a command.   The subjunctive may be used to express a command in any person, but is rare in the second person affirmative, since the imperative is here the common medium of expression. Its chief use is in the second person negative and in the third person, including forms in which *usted* (*ustedes*) are the forms of address. It is used without introductory word and also introduced by *que*.

29.161 First person singular.   LLA 53 *Insulta, fulmina.   ¡ Así!   ¡ Que reciba yo tu asco!*
(3–5)

29.163 First person plural (hortative).   PEQ 14 *Pasemos a la cocina.*
(54–219)

29.165 In the phrase *vamos a ver*, the auxiliary is the means of expressing the subjunctive.   MAY 61 *¿ Qué esperas? vamos a ver.*
(26–55)

29.167 If the verb is reflexive, the final *–s* of the verbal termination is lost before the reflexive pronoun *nos*.   URU 39 *Sentémonos y hablemos.*
(19–49)

29.171 Second person, affirmative, without introductory word.   IBA 35 *Tú, Isidrillo — dijo al joven — veas si puedes arreglarme esto.*   The subjunctive is much less blunt than the imperative; it has the form of a wish, rather than a command.
(4–5)

29.173 Introduced by *que*.   ABU 191 *Adiós, hijas; que os divirtáis mucho.*
(3–4)

29.175 Second person, negative. This is the regular form for expressing a negative command when the subject is *tú, vos,* or *vosotros.* IMP 17 *No lo dudes.* (40–396)

29.181 Third person. The subject is a noun, or a pronoun of the third person and the subjunctive is introduced by *que.* UNA 99 *Abrid esos balcones, que entre la luz.* (36–169)

29.182 The subjunctive is used without introductory word. RUS 8 *Ahí va el cronómetro y venga la papelita.* Especially common with *venga,* which has acquired almost the force of "give me." (32–87)

29.183 The subject is *usted* (*ustedes*) or other third person substitute for *tú* (*vosotros*). The subject is expressed. REY 90 *Vengan ustedes conmigo.* (48–611)

29.184 Somewhat less frequently the subject is understood. MAY 119 — *Suba, suba, ¡ por Dios! — suplica la dama.* (41–484)

29.185 Rarely, with *usted,* the subjunctive is introduced by *que.* SJQ 132 *¡ Que se calle usted, hombre!* As in other cases in which *que* is used, this form of expression tends to stress the feeling that a verb of ordering is or has been implied. (3–4)

29.187 The verb may be an indefinite reflexive; the command becomes general and is similar to the use of the infinitive. PEQ 93 *Véase lo que es mi vida.* Usually without *que.* (23–40)

29.188 The verb may be an indefinite third person plural. PAT 197 *Espero una carta importante — advirtió Alberto. — Pues que se la envíen a mi casa.* Usually with *que.* (14–25)

THE SUBJUNCTIVE OF UNCERTAINTY

29.21 After *acaso, quizás, tal vez.* When doubt is cast on the factual character of an action or state by the use of a word meaning "perhaps," the subjunctive may be used to indicate that the doubt is strong in the mind of the speaker. This situation is especially likely to occur when the time of the action or state is future, but the subjunctive is found as well referring to the present or past. WAS 5 *Tal vez pueda venderme un caracú.* (42–92)

29.22 In concessive clauses. The subjunctive is used in main clauses to express a concession of indifference, usually with some alternative indicated. It is probable that the original force of this subjunctive was one of command; the concessive value has been derived from the conventional groups established.

29.221 Followed by a relative clause. SAS 74 *Me tendrás aquí todos los días, suceda lo que suceda.* (12–20)

29.225 Followed by an alternative, usually introduced by *o.* ROM 207 *Tomaban el comienzo de un romance profano famoso, viniese o no viniese a cuento.* (7–8)

29.227 The most frequent combination of tenses is the present followed by the present. PIN 95 *Hará lo que usté quiera que haga, sea fácil o sea difícil.* (14–28)

For the use of the subjunctive in the conclusion of conditional sentences and for other potential uses of the subjunctive in main clauses, see 31.4, 32.83, and 33.64.

OTHER SUBJUNCTIVES OF ATTITUDE

29.25 The subjunctive is found in principal clauses in other cases to reflect an attitude on the part of the speaker toward an action or state. It is difficult to define the particular emotion involved; at times there seems to be no emotion, but only an approach toward the action or state as an assumption, rather than as a fact. They may be grouped according to the words by which they are introduced.

29.251 Introduced by *que.* SEC 88 (An actor has been playing a part extremely well) *¡ Que no tenga un teatro en Madrí este hombre!* (9–16)

29.253 By *de ahí que.* VIG 57 *De ahí que en el prólogo escribiera « no se escribe con las canas sino con el entendimiento. »* While the writing is a fact, the speaker does not present it as such, but only as a sort of abstract assumption. (4–4)

29.255 By *ni que.* LIN 52 *Andrés me dió la orden de no ir. — ¡ Ni que fueras un lacayo! — Lo mismo.* In this construction it is almost certain that the *que* was in origin a subordinating conjunction introducing a condition ("not even if you were a servant," [would he treat you any worse]), but it has become a conventional device for expressing indignation at someone's behavior. (7–10)

29.257 By *para que.* RAN 83 *¡ Y eso que le regalo de cuando en cuando unos huevos y unas manzanas! ¡ Para que digan que los hombres de iglesia son agradecidos!* While the origin must have been a clause of purpose, it is now merely a device for an exclamation indicating the speaker's feeling of incongruity in the action. (3–4)

THE SUBJUNCTIVE IN SUBORDINATE CLAUSES

29.3 The subjunctive in subordinate clauses expresses the same attitudes and emotions on the part of the speaker as does the subjunctive in main clauses. Since the subjunctive in subordinate clauses performs the functions of a substantive, an adjective, or an adverb, the various constructions in each of the groups will be arranged according to the function of the clause in the sentence.

THE SUBJUNCTIVE OF DESIRE

SUBSTANTIVE CLAUSES

29.31 As subject. The subjunctive is used as subject of a number of logically impersonal expressions, conveying notions of wish, opinion (involving approval or disapproval), emotion, necessity, and the like. The infinitive is also used as the subject of these verbs and is the regular construction when the subject of the subordinate verb is indefinite; see 37.211.

29.311 Subject of *ser* + a noun, usually abstract. SAS 118 *¡ Es una lástima que la alquilen!* ([14]–22)

The only commonly used noun is *lástima* (8–8).

29.317 Subject of *ser* + an adjective. DEB 52 *Es preciso que nos digas si te diviertes en ese pueblo.* ([39]–105)

The commonest adjectives are: *bueno* (7–8), *difícil* (5–5), *mejor* (6–13), *necesario* (8–9), *preciso* (11–20), *raro* (5–5).

29.321 Subject of *estar* + a complement. ABU 23 *¡ Estaría bueno que no se hicieran los honores debidos a la ilustre señora!* (7–8)

29.325 Subject of *parecer* + a complement. UGA 11 *Le parecía muy natural que las cosas fueran comunes.* (8–10)

29.331 Subject of logically impersonal verbs, transitive and intransitive. IGN 77 *Me gusta que cada cual conserve su rango.* ([40]–115)

The commonest verbs are: *bastar* (8–10), *convenir* (9–9), *dar* (*la gana*, etc.) (7–9), *gustar* (10–12), *importar* (9–10), *valer* (7–9).

29.335 Subject of verbs of wish, command, etc., used as indefinite reflexives. PAX 342 *Traía una resolución por la cual se ordenaba que cada soldado llevara en su morral « el libro de oro del soldado colombiano. »* (6–6)

29.34 As object. The subjunctive is used in object clauses after verbs expressing wish (command, approval, causation, request, etc.) and after verbs expressing emotion (fear, hope, pleasure, etc.). In both cases the subject of the subordinate verb is normally different from that of the main verb. After some of these verbs, the infinitive is also used; see 37.341.

29.341. After verbs of wish, command, etc.   UGA 27 *Déjame que me apoye sobre ti.*   ([60]–700)

The commonest verbs are: *aconsejar* (10–12), *conseguir* (6–9), *consentir* (7–8), *decir* (**29–77**), *dejar* (**24–43**), *desear* (17–20), *disponer* (5–9), *encargar* (6–8), *evitar* (6–8), *hacer* (**20–24**), *impedir* (9–13), *mandar* (7–10), *necesitar* (9–9), *ordenar* (10–19), *pedir* (18–31), *permitir* (18–24), *pretender* (7–17), *procurar* (13–15), *proponer* (10–12), *querer* (**40–200**), *rogar* (19–28), *suplicar* (8–9).

29.351 After verbs of emotion.   FAL 222 *Temía que saliese el mártir.*
                                                              ([32]–73)

The only common verbs are *esperar* (15–24) and *temer* (15–24).

The indicative is also found after verbs of emotion when the fact, rather than the speaker's feelings are stressed; see 28.261.

29.371 As subjective complement. The subjunctive is used in clauses which are subjective complements when the subject, noun or pronoun, expresses one of the notions which is regularly reflected by the subjunctive. They are differentiated from subject clauses used with *ser* + a noun by the fact that in the present group the subject is normally specific, while in the other type, the noun used after *ser* is normally generic. SJQ 30 *Lo que sí he procurado es que esté cargadito el café.*   (23–31)

29.381 In apposition with a noun.   WAS 141 *¡Qué lástima que no esté don Froilán!*   (15–17)

29.39 As object of a preposition. Like the indicative, the subjunctive is found in clauses used as object of a preposition, forming adjectival or adverbial phrases. In adjectival phrases the preposition is usually *de;* in adverbial phrases the preposition is the one which is normally used after a given verb to introduce a noun or an infinitive.

29.391 In adjectival phrases, modifying a noun and introduced by *de.* PAL 308 *Sentí un vago deseo de que la casa se derrumbase.*   ([28]–57)

Most frequently found after: *culpa* (4–5), *gana* (3–3), *miedo* (4–4), *orden* (4–4), *necesidad* (3–3), *temor* (3–4).

29.393 Introduced by other prepositions (*a, en*).   RIC 32 *Sin temor a que nadie pudiera reconocerle, recorría campo y playa.*   (5–6)

29.41 In adverbial phrases.

29.411 Modifying a verb.   CAT 35 *No se puede obligar a niños de distinta edad a que prefieran una misma cosa.*   ([36]–92)

The commonest verbs are: *alegrarse de* (5–5), *empeñarse en* (5–6), *esperar a* (12–13), *obligar a* (6–7).

29.415 Modifying a past participle. STE 22 *¿ Yo? . . . ¡ Soy la Perla! —*
contestó, como sorprendida de que alguien pudiera ignorarlo. ([11]–15)

29.417 Modifying an adjective. SIE 13 *¡ Poco orgullosa estaba yo de que*
fuera mi madre! (7–7)

29.45 Adjective Clauses (Relative). The only type of relative clause which
belongs under the subjunctive of desire is the relative clause of purpose.
IDO 231 *El joven insinuaba una respuesta ambigua que a todas satisfiziera.*
(4–6)

29.46 Adverbial Clauses. The only types of adverbial clauses which are
classified as related to desire are those of purpose, intended result, and
characteristic, correlative to *tal.*

29.461 Characteristic clauses. This construction includes only clauses
which are found after *tal*; the presence of *tal* implies an element of
choosing which makes them related to intended result and purpose.
ROD 15 *Una vida idealmente armoniosa sería tal que cada día significase*
un paso hacia adelante. (5–6)

29.463 Intended result. REY 171 *Allí se coloca la ametralladora de manera*
que sus tiros barran el frente. (5–5)

29.465 Purpose. ORT 100 *Lo aniquilaríamos, si pudiésemos, para que*
jamás volviera.

The commonest conjunctions expressing purpose are: *a fin de que* (5–7), *a que*
(especially after verbs of motion) (11–14), *pa que* (8–27), *para que* (**52–252**),
porque (8–10), *que* (especially after an imperative) (8–11).

THE SUBJUNCTIVE OF UNCERTAINTY

29.5 The subjunctive is used in subordinate clauses, as in main clauses,
to reflect a state of uncertainty in the mind of the speaker. This uncertainty is particularly likely to be found when the main clause is negative,
explicitly or by implication. It is also common after expressions of possibility or impossibility. It is frequent when the action or state involved
is in the indefinite future. In short, the subjunctive is found whenever
the action or state of the subordinate clause is considered, not as a
factual reality, but as something unreal, possible, or hypothetical.

SUBSTANTIVE CLAUSES

29.51 As subject.

29.511 Of negative expressions of declaring, believing, etc. ABU 424
No se dice que Jonás llevara periódicos que leer. (13–21)

The commonest expression in this group is *no es que* (7–11).

29.513 Of expressions implying a negative.

faltar. SEC 9 *Sólo faltaba que me tratases así.* (7–11)
parece mentira. ART 76 *¡ Parece mentira que por cosas tan insignifi-cantes se maten los hombres!* (8–10)

29.515 Of expressions of appearance implying unreality, as *parecer.*
MUJ 29 *Por toda su casa parece que se haya extendido la jaulita.* (9–15)

29.516 *No parece sino que* sometimes replaces *parece que.* SAS 134 *No parece sino que tener plata fuese una virtud.* (3–3)

29.517 Of expressions of probability (*es verosímil, es casi cierto*, etc.)
Obviously the subjunctive is used to reveal the margin of doubt which lingers in the mind of the speaker. IDO 107 *Es probable que se vaya pronto.* (6–9)

29.518 Of possibility. REY 113 *Es posible que cada uno quiera tirar por su lado.* (**34–62**)

The commonest expressions are: *es posible* (**21–29**), *parece imposible* (3–3), *puede que* (9–17), *puede ser que* (6–7).

29.519 The clause is modified by the definite article. When a sub-stantive clause is modified by the definite article, the article removes the notion expressed by the clause from the realm of concrete and par-ticular reality and presents it as an abstract generalization. The attitude of abstraction revealed by the article is also regularly revealed by the use of the subjunctive instead of the indicative. Such clauses usually are found at the beginning of the sentence, where they are presented as a sort of assumption, which may be verified or rejected. SIE 62 *El que yo haya perdido la razón no significa que usted no pueda estar tranquila a mi lado.* (7–9)

29.52 As object.

29.521 Of verbs of doubting, denying, etc., even when negative. DIV 11 *Dudo mucho que la censura permita que pasen.* (6–7)

29.525 Of affirmative verbs of believing. SJQ 85 *El caso no es de risa, pero comprendo que excite la hilaridad.* (8–12)

29.527 Of negative verbs of believing. ORT 98 *No creo que haya cuadro en el mundo tan optimista como éste.* (17–27)

Almost always *no creer* (16–24).

29.528 Of interrogative verbs of believing, implying a negative. PAX 10 *¿ Cree usted que sea pura galantería ?* (3–3)

29.531 Of negative verbs of declaring, knowing, perceiving, etc. SON 113 *¡ Yo no sabía que estuviese ciega!* ([19]–31)

The only common verb is *no saber* (5–5).

29.545 In indirect questions, after a negative verb. RIC 18 *No sabía qué clase de moneda fuese el ducado.* (9–11)

29.55 As subjective complement. After expressions of doubt, possibility, etc. LIN 126 *Lo que no es posible es que le respondan satisfactoriamente.* (6–7)

29.57 As object of a preposition, in adjectival and adverbial phrases.

29.571 In adjectival phrases, modifying a noun, with *de.* RUS 131 *¿ No hay modo de que usted me crea?* ([10]–13)

29.573 The noun modified may indicate no uncertainty, but the use of the subjunctive reveals that the action or state of the clause is considered not as an actual fact but as an abstract generalization. RET 135 *El hecho de que se presenten en cinco días doscientos poetas, demuestra que nuestros grupos de civilización eran esencialmente literarios.* (6–7)

29.575 In adverbial phrases, modifying a verb. TIG 43 *Dudo de que sea sincera la resignación.* (7–10)

29.6 Adjective Clauses (Relative). The subjunctive is used in relative clauses to indicate that the action or state expressed by the clause is one which is descriptive of an unreal or hypothetical antecedent. It therefore is regularly used when the antecedent is indefinite or negative or when the existence of the antecedent is denied. The relative pronoun in such a clause is always restrictive.

29.61 With an indefinite antecedent.

29.611 The antecedent is a noun or pronoun. The subjunctive is especially common when the action involved is in the future. TIG 23 *Será cosa que no admita pero.* Or when the antecedent is itself in a clause in the subjunctive and hence, hypothetical. BEN 41 *Siempre hemos de acabar por que sea usted el que me deba dinero.* **(57–269)**

29.613 When the antecedent is a superlative the subjunctive is used to indicate that the relative clause is felt as describing, not a particular individual or individuals whose action or state was a reality, but rather as characterizing a class, which is indefinite. ORR 172 *Pensando que la baba de aquellos deslenguados llegaba hasta una de las mujeres más puras que hubiese encontrado en su camino.* (10–10)

29.615 Similarly when the antecedent is an exclusive (*primero, único*). ABC 39 *Italia ha sido la primera gran potencia que reconociera a los Soviets.*

(not "the first power which recognized," but "the first power to recognize"). (6–8)

29.617 The relative may be an adverb of place, referring to an expressed antecedent. LIN 75 *¿ No comprendes que no habitamos una casa donde encaje esa figura?* (6–10)

29.618 Or a relative adverb of time. ARN 11 *No hay noche que no retire con sus tres pesetas corridas.* (5–7)

29.62 The antecedent is a substantive relative. ABC 48 *Los que se interesen, diríjanse a Weltfirma, Madrid.* ([53]–293)

The commonest relatives in this group are *cuanto* (13–14), *el que* (*los que*) (**37–70**), *lo que* (**44–126**), *quien* (**30–59**), *todo lo que* (16–18).

29.63 With a negative antecedent or antecedent whose existence is denied. In this class fall also sentences in which the unreality of the antecedent is implied rather than expressed.

29.631 The negation is expressed. NER 63 *Nada hay que evoque más imperiosamente la idea de la libertad que el mar.* (**43–100**)

29.633 The negation is implied by a question. PIN 145 *¿ Qué he prometido yo que no cumpliera?* (10–11)

29.635 The negation is implied by a condition. CAT 30 *Si hay alguna persona que más profundo respeto tenga por Ud., ésa soy yo.* (6–8)

29.637 The negation is implied by a single word (*buscar, faltar, necesitar,* etc.) ORT 118 *Necesitamos buscar un termino que exprese eso.* ([10]–14)

29.639 The antecedent follows *como* or other words of comparison and is presented as unreal. JIM 100 *Y Platero, lo mismo que un niño pobre que estrenara un traje, corre tímido.* (9–9)

29.64 The relative clause has concessive force. There are two types of relative clause which have concessive force; those introduced by *por*, and those involving *cualquiera*.

29.641 The clause is introduced by *por* + an adjective. It is probable that the relative is in this case neuter, summing up the notion of the adjective involved. BYN 31 *Una empresa, por vieja que sea, si no se perfecciona, al final muere.* See 15.25. (11–11)

29.643 By *por muy* + an adjective. SIE 87 *Parece imposible que, por muy villano que sea un hombre, se atreva a una infamia tan grande.* (4–4)

29.645 The clause is a generalizing indefinite, with *cualquiera*. The relative may be adjectival or adverbial. IMP 74 *De cualquier modo que fuese, el suceso le pinchaba como una espina.* (12–15)

29.66 *que yo sepa.* It is probable that the *que* in the phrase *que yo sepa,* used after negatives, is a relative, whether an adverb or a pronoun is not clear. ᴢᴜɴ 24 *¿ No le habían cortado una pierna ? — Que yo sepa, no se la han cortado.* (4–4)

29.7 Adverbial Clauses. In general, the adverbial clauses which are expressed in the subjunctive fall into two groups: those referring to indefinite future time (concession, manner, place, time), and those which are potential and which are unreal or contrary to fact in the present, or which though real, are presented as assumptions or hypotheses (concession, condition, proviso, supposition).

29.71 Cause.

> *como.* ᴘᴀᴛ 8 *Como nadie le respondiera, se retiró.* *Como* is the only conjunction of cause which is often followed by the subjunctive. Since the causal clause in this case normally precedes the main verb, it is probable that the subjunctive was, at least in origin, one of assumption. (10–14)

29.711 Negated cause. If the main clause denies that an action or state is the cause of another action or state, the action of the causal clause becomes unreal and the verb is in the subjunctive. ᴊᴏᴀ 12 *No creas que te lo digo porque me mortifiquen los celos.* (7–8)

29.713 The negation may be implied by a question or otherwise. ᴅᴇʙ 47 *¿ Crees, acaso, que porque yo calle han de ser de otra suerte las cosas ?* (3–3)

29.72 Concession. Three types of concessive clause are found in the subjunctive: those referring to an indefinite, hypothetical future, those referring to an action or state which is contrary to fact in the present or past, and those which present an actual fact, not as a fact but as an assumption or hypothesis which is to be rejected. This last type, which has been called " polemic", appears to be the most common.

> *aun cuando.* ᴘᴀᴛ 216 *Aun cuando el banquero me haya birlado todo lo que le confié, me quedan unas diez mil pesetas.* (5–10)
> *aunque.* Future, more vividly expressed. ɪᴅᴏ 222 *He de acompañarte, aunque no quieras.* Future, less vividly expressed. ʀᴇʏ 163 *No vendrán los de Bu-Tata, pero aunque vinieran, sólo con este aparato les haríamos retroceder.* Contrary-to-fact, present. ᴜɢᴀ 44 *No es posible que sea una coqueta, pero aunque lo fuera, no tendría fuerzas para olvidarla.* Contrary-to-fact, past. ᴘᴀʟ 129 *Pluguiese al cielo que ella hubiera sido, aunque me costase algunos coscorrones.* Polemic, present. ᴏᴄᴄ 267 *Aunque sea un financiero, es un financiero de estas costumbres.* Polemic, past. ᴡᴀꜱ 132 *Los ojos de aquellas*

mujeres no podían engañarse, aunque hubiera pasado casi un año desde que vieron el alazán.   **(50–116)**

por más que. JOA 54 *No me gusta por más que me lo quieran.* (3–3)

por mucho que. LUG 368 *Por mucho que quiera protegernos, nunca nos dará tanto como hemos tenido.*   (5–5)

29.73 Condition.

a no ser que. LIN 71 *Vendrá a darme las gracias, a no ser que su delicadeza se lo impida.*   (3–5)

como. ABU 32 *Como se entretenga en Polán, no vendrá hasta mañana.* Clauses of this type might with equal propriety be considered clauses of proviso.   (7–12)

como no. LIN 103 *Tu hermana no llora todavía, como no sea de rabia.* Normally in the set phrase *como no sea*, which becomes an equivalent of *sino*, " except."   (4–5)

que. PIN 69 *El mismo Veneno, que me pillase aquí, no se escamaría.* (3–5)

que, in the phrase *ni que.* UGA 51 *¡ Ni que fuera gobernador!* (7–10)

29.74 Imaginative comparison.

como si. ROD 88 *Surge la vocación tan clara y enérgica como si las dudas hubieran sido resueltas.*   **(57–444)**

cual si. JIM 23 *Alrededor, el campo enlutó su verde, cual si el morado del altar mayor lo cobijase.*   (3–8)

29.75 Negated attendant circumstance.

que ... no. LLA 81 *¿ Dónde iré yo, que no vayan conmigo mis tormentas?* The negative in the main clause may be implied, as here, by a question.   (3–4)

sin que. ARN 43 *Miramos cara a cara a la vida, sin que nos dé tristeza el bien de los demás.* Clauses with *sin que* sometimes carry implications of manner or of result. In every case, the subjunctive is due to the negative involved in *sin*.   **(38–74)**

29.76 Manner.

como. ZAM 78 *Como usted quiera.*   **(21–40)**

cuanto. With comparatives. BYN 57 *Esta adivinación resulta tanto más fácil cuanto más tímido sea el interesado.*   (4–5)

según. ARN 72 *Seguiré siendo unos días malo y otros bueno, según me arrime a unas cosas u a otras.*   (4–4)

Clauses of manner are regularly in the subjunctive when they refer to an indefinite future, in the indicative when they refer to a definite present or past.

29.77 Place, without expressed antecedent of the relative adverb, *donde,*
adonde, etc.   IDO 222 *A donde vayas, te seguiré.*   (22–31)

29.78 Proviso.

con tal de que.   RUS 71 *No importa, con tal de que se quede.*   (5–5)

mientras.   LLA 20 *¡ Un tiempo soberbio!   ¡ Lástima que pase! — No,*
mientras vuelva.   (3–3)

siempre que.   BEN 12 *Don Francisquito te lo traerá, siempre que tengas*
cuidado de no dejarlo luego por ahí.   (3–3)

29.79 Result, negated only, with *que.*   LUG 158 *Yo no soy tan egoísta que*
prive a mis amigos de sus placeres.   (3–3)

29.81 Supposition.

suponiendo que.   SIE 24 *Como caen con terror, apretan al caer. — Su-*
poniendo que caigan.   (4–4)

29.82 Time, always indefinite future, with relation to the time of the
main verb.

antes de que.   RIC 256 *Se fué rápidamente, antes de que Juliana le*
viese.   (19–26)

antes que.   SEC 25 *Tengo que suicidarme antes que amanezca.*   (9–12)

cuando.   REY 150 *¿ Queréis que intentemos huir, cuando lleguemos a*
ella ?   **(44–134)**

en cuanto.   ORR 183 *En cuanto concluya la comida, llame a Javier.*
                                                                     (12–17)

hasta que.   ZUN 43 *Y así estaremos hasta que nos vayamos con la*
música.   **(22–32)**

mientras.   LIN 73 *Mientras pueda, lo defenderé.*   **(24–36)**

29.9 The second of two coordinated verbs in subordinate clauses is
sometimes in the subjunctive, even when the first verb is in the indicative. The explanation for the phenomenon is probably to be found in the
predominance of an attitude of doubt or uncertainty in the mind of the
speaker as he develops an idea.   TRI 50 *Había perdido la noción de si le*
tocaría jugar a ella o si le hubiese tocado a él.   (3–3)

THE IMPERATIVE

30. The imperative is used to express an affirmative command when the
person to whom the command is directed is addressed as *tú* or *vos* in the
singular, and as *vosotros* in the plural. On the forms of address, see 4.4.

30.11 Singular. *tú.*   RUS 142 *¡ Márchate, quítate de mi vista!* **(53–1723)**

30.13 Singular. **vos.** STE 7 *Muschinga, bailá, — le ordenó la Perla.* In Uruguay and Argentina; also as an archaicism in Spain. (4–122)

30.2 Plural. **vosotros.** DEB 11 *Si queréis experimentar las emociones nuevas, volved a vuestros pueblos.* (31–133)

For the use of an expressed subject pronoun with the imperative, see 5.13.

30.3 dale. The imperative *dale* is used in idiomatic expressions to indicate that an action is irritatingly persistent. SJQ 128 (*La Trapitos vuelve a los pucheros.*) — ¡ *Y dale con el llanto!* (10–10)

30.53 quedaos, for *quedados.* When a reflexive object pronoun is attached to the plural imperative, the form is reduced from *quedados* to *quedaos.* ABU 195 *Sentaos ya y descansad aquí.* (12–19)

CONDITIONAL SENTENCES

31. Conditional sentences may be divided into three main groups, I. General conditions, in which the condition is assumed without any implications of uncertainty; II. Hypothetical future conditions, more vividly or less vividly expressed; and III. Contrary to fact conditions, either present or past. But these arbitrary divisions by no means cover all conditional sentences: within the future conditions there are many which combine more vivid and less vivid expression; in the contrary to fact conditions there are many which are part present and part past. There are still others which start with one type of condition and end with a conclusion proper to another type. And finally there is a very large number of incomplete conditional sentences. In some of these, another form of expression may be used to replace the lacking member; in others, and this is especially true in conversation, a condition may be left without conclusion or a conclusion may be drawn, though no condition has been expressed. Since it is usually possible to express a condition of a given type in several ways, "type" examples are used to indicate the mood and tense. Thus *si tiene, da* indicates a sentence in which both clauses are in the present indicative.

31.1 General conditions. While general conditions may be expressed in any combination of tenses, there are certain situations which occur with considerable regularity.

31.111 Present conditions, particular or universal. si tiene, da. UNA 91 *Si aun vivo, es porque me voy muriendo muy despacio.* FOM 98 *Si un amor se cura con otro, lo cuerdo es no dejarse dominar del corazón.* (50–132)

31.112 Present, iterative. JIM 104 *Si ve una flor, se ríe de pronto.* (11–30)

31.121 Past, particular or universal, usually a back-shifted present. *si tenía, daba.* IMP 198 *Si obraba mal, le importaba poco.* WAS 143 *Los serranos dijeron que era hora de partir, si querían llegar antes de la noche.*
(5–7)

31.122 Past, iterative. ALT 189 *Si procedían de villanos, heredaban una parte igual a los legítimos.* (11–30)

31.13 Other general conditions. RUB 88 *Si con sus cuadros urbanos de París ha realizado una obra única, con sus novelas ha llegado hasta las puertas del folletín.* **(30–57)**

31.2 Future Conditions.

31.21 More vividly expressed.

31.211 *si tiene, dará.* URU 33 *Si se va, lo acompañaré.* **(40–112)**

31.213 *si tiene, da* (or *dé*), command. IDO 222 *Si puedes, vuelve atrás los pasos.* **(31–64)**

31.214 *si tiene, da.* MAY 11 *¡ Mira que si no cumples, te condenas!* **(25–66)** Especially in conversational style. The present of the conclusion may be an auxiliary verb expressing future or, with modal verbs, a verb weak in time value. BEN 14 *Si sientes así, no vas a ser muy feliz.* (15–26) The present indicative may be used as a mild imperative. REY 116 *Una advertencia a las señoras. La bandera está aquí; si nos necesitan, la tremolan.* (7–7)

31.215 *si tiene, (que) dé,* the verb of the conclusion being a subjunctive in a dependent clause. SEC 57 *Dile que si lo que quiere es un bocao, que lo tire.* (4–4)

31.31 Less vividly expressed.

31.311 *si tuviera, daría.* PEQ 164 *Yo no sé lo que tiene esta pequeña ventana. Si hablara de dolores, no expresaría mi emoción con exactitud.* **(26–44)**

31.313 *si tuviese, daría.* SON 34 *Si todas mis hijas entrasen en un convento, yo las seguiría feliz.* (12–21)

31.315 *si tuviese, daba.* LIN 93 *Si ahora viniese un amor, os quedabais perdidas.* Primarily conversational. (5–5)

31.32 In back-shifted constructions, either expressed or implied.

31.321 *si tenía, daba* (for original *si tiene, da*). In conversational style. UGA 37 *Si prolongaba su maniobra, estaba perdido.* The verb of the conclusion is an auxiliary. DEB 53 *Si era tan débil, pensé, debía ser fácil convencerle.* RAN 39 *¿ Qué iba a ser de mí, si no me levantaba?* (6–6)

31.323 *si tenía, daría* (for original *si tiene, dará*). IMP 77 *Y si llegaba a conocer el alma de Celia, amaríala ciego.* (3–3)

31.34 Mixed future conditions.

31.35 The condition is more vividly, the conclusion less vividly expressed.

31.351 *si tiene, daría.* RUS 80 *Si te figuras que lo digo por ti, me haría un nudo en la lengua.* (5–5)

31.4 Contrary-to-fact conditions.

31.41 Present time.

31.411 *si tuviera, daría.* MGR 5 *Si no hubiera dolor, no habría acicate.* **(33–65)**

31.412 *si tuviese, daría.* ZAM 76 *Yo querría a los míos, si no se avergonzasen de que los quisiera.* **(22–33)**

31.413 *si tuviese, daba.* The verb is an auxiliary standing for the conditional. ART 76 *Si lo fuesen, ¡ qué de lutos íbamos a ver!* (3–3)

31.415 *si tuviera, diera.* LLA 63 *Si tuviera usted las vértebras torcidas, quizás fuera usted peor que yo.* (3–3)

31.43 Past time.

31.431 *si tiene, da.* ARN 15 *Me hizo a mí una ación que si no hay gente, la pego.* In conversational style, for vividness. (8–16)

31.433 *si hubiese tenido, hubiera dado.* FAL 159 *Si hubiese sido hombre, el sentido de su libertad hubiera sido más amplio.* (8–12)

31.434 *si hubiera tenido, habría dado.* ORR 171 *Si hubiera estado con su cabeza firme, habría visto que se trataba de una sarta de mentiras.* (4–7)

31.435 *si hubiera tenido, hubiese dado.* ABC 25 *Si hubiera nacido dos siglos atrás, hubiese sido fiscal de la Inquisición.* (4–5)

31.436 *si tuviera, hubiera dado.* SAS 23 *¡ Si no fuera por él, quién sabe lo que hubiera sido de mí!* (4–4)

31.437 *si tuviese, hubiera dado.* PAL 131 *Si le tocase la lotería, nos hubiera dado la noticia con acento desgarrador.* (3–3)

31.438 *si hubiera tenido, hubiera dado.* BRA 158 *Si hubiéramos realizado una ilusión, hubiéramos podido ser felices.* (3–3)

31.46 Mixed contrary-to-fact conditions.

31.47 The condition is present, the conclusion is past.

31.471 *si tuviese, habría dado.* RUS 14 *Si fuese por mí, antes me habría muerto.* (3–3)

31.473 *si tuviera, hubiera dado.* JES 27 *Si todas las razones que yo tuviera fueran ésas, ya la hubiera despachado.* (3–3)

31.48 The condition is past, the conclusion is present.

31.481 *si hubiera tenido, daría.* JOA 38 *Si no te lo hubiera dicho, sería mejor.* (11–11)

31.483 *si hubiese tenido, daría.* SIE 51 *¿ Qué sería esta casa, si yo no me hubiese reído tanto ?* (7–7)

31.5 Other mixed conditions. Combinations of any two types are possible. IGN 48 *Si eso fuera verdad, te has vengado.* (12–17)

31.6 Incomplete conditions.

31.62 The *si*-clause is omitted and replaced by some other element.

31.63 The *si*-clause is replaced by a coordinated clause, connected with the conclusion by *y*. SEC 20 *Ahí está loco por usté, que le ponen camisa de fuersa y la rompe.* (4–5)

31.631 The coordinated clause may be a command. PAX 10 *Repasa tu Génesis y encontrarás que esa costumbre nos viene desde el Paraíso.* (9–11)

31.64 The *si*-clause may be replaced by an adverbial clause of concession, condition (introduced by a conjunction other than *si*), exception, proviso, or supposition; for examples see 29.7.

31.65 The *si*-clause may be replaced by a substantive relative clause.

31.651 The subject of the relative clause may be identical with that of the main clause. SIE 96 *El que caiga siempre encontrará brazos que le recojan.* (4–6)

31.653 The subject may be different. UNA 16 *El que goza de una obra de arte, es porque la crea en sí.* (4–4)

31.66 The *si*-clause may be replaced by a subject clause. REY 146 *Sería terrible y cómico que tuviéramos que vivir aquí siempre.* (7–8)

31.7 The *si*-clause may be replaced by an adverbial phrase.

31.71 *a* + an infinitive. PAT 211 *No escribirá a no ser por fuerza.* (13–19)

31.72 *con* + an infinitive. MGR 9 *Expuso que con sólo preparar un poco el terreno, se comprometía a venir inmidiatamente con un trimotor.* (5–5)

31.73 *de* + an infinitive. VIG 65 *De no haber escrito* Del sentimiento trágico de la vida *ésta sería su mejor biografía espiritual.* (14–17)

31.74 *a* + a noun or pronoun. JOA 42 *A poco más, le doy una trompada.* (3–3)

31.75 *en* + a noun or pronoun. ABC 34 *En este caso, el martes próximo traería a las Cortes el proyecto.* (8–8)

31.76 *sin* + a noun or pronoun. UGA 40 *Sin aquel amor, hubiera roto con todos.* (10–12)

31.78 A phrase involving *otro.* RUB 85 *De otro modo, no se explicaría ese grupo de sonetos.* (3–3)

31.81 The verb of the *si*-clause may be omitted.

31.811 *si,* with another element of the sentence. ALT 190 *Muéstrase muy acentuado en la vida vecinal que, si común a todos los pueblos, aparece en Navarra notablemente favorecido por las leyes.* (5–5)

31.813 *si no,* with another element of the sentence. ART 41 *He sido, si no usted mismo, un reflejo de usted.* (5–7)

31.815 *si no,* alone. LIN 69 *No recibió las cartas; si no, hubiera pagado aquella deuda de honor.* (14–20)

31.83 The *si*-clause may be replaced by a participle.

31.831 Present. ARN 42 *¡Cómo va a tocarnos el premio, jugando de este modo!* (**21–31**)

31.833 Past. RUS 79 *Casada con ese angelito, tendrías suegros.* (3–3)

31.85 The *si*-clause may be replaced by a noun modified by a relative clause. SJQ 46 *Carta que llegue a nombre mío, no se la dé usted a nadie más que a mí.* (4–4)

31.86 The *si*-clause may be merely implied; for examples see 32.67.

31.87 The conclusion is omitted and replaced by another element.

31.871 A noun or pronoun. SIE 53 *¿Qué estás diciendo ahí? — Si te disgustas, nada.* (3–7)

31.872 An exclamation. URU 25 *Si se comprueban algunas cosas de su conducta, ¡pobre de él!* (15–27)

31.873 The verb of the conclusion may be a dependent infinitive. SON 46 *Si os negais, tengo orden de llevarle recado.* (6–6)

31.88 The conclusion may be omitted and not replaced in any way.

31.881 In exclamations, questions, or interrupted sentences in conversation. MAY 124 *¡ Si supieras! . . . quiere empezar Javier.* ZAM 77 *Si no le hago a la señorita mucha falta . . . — ¡ Ni poca ni mucha!* **(32–131)**

31.89 In comparisons, real or imaginative.

31.91 Real, after *que.* BEN 69 *Más vale que haya sido antes que si hubiera sido después.* **(3–3)**

31.92 Imaginative.

31.921 *como si.* IDO 110 *Alberto se enorgulleció, como si lo rindieran a él mismo.* **(52–352)**

31.923 *como que.* NER 61 *Parece como que una prisión a la orilla del mar debiera ser la mejor de las prisiones.* **(6–6)**

31.925 *el (lo) mismo que si.* PAL 311 *La levantó con la misma facilidad que si fuera una niña.* **(5–6)**

31.927 *cual si.* JIM 108 *Yo trato a Platero cual si fuese un niño.* **(3–8)**

31.93 The *si*-clause may be the object of a preposition.

31.931 *por.* OCC 196 *Y por si es tan amable que me los quiere pagar, siete pesetas van al rojo.* **(15–27)**

TENSES

32. Tenses are the linguistic device used to establish a temporal sequence of experience — in past, present, or future time. But the use of the tenses depends not only on the distinctions in time, but also on the attitude of the speaker toward his experience. Hence it is that in the past there are two different tenses of the indicative, and in past, present, and future, there are not only simple tenses, but also progressive tenses to make clear this difference in attitude. In addition to these tenses there is a special group of tenses which are used to indicate a completed action or state in past, present, or future; these tenses are called the perfect tenses. In general the tenses of the imperative and subjunctive may be said to correspond to the tenses of the indicative, but from the very nature of these moods, the future forms have almost disappeared.

Simple Tenses

THE INDICATIVE

32.11 Present. The present, in time, is not a point or a moment; it is an indefinite zone lying between past and future. Only one attitude toward the present is possible. We can never see the present as a unified whole; we can observe a present action or state only as a series, unbroken or intermittent, which began in an indefinite past and continues into an indefinite future. If the subject or our observation is an action, it may be unbroken, that is to say, progressive, or it may be intermittent, and in this case it may be merely repeated, that is to say, iterative, or the repetition may become involuntary, that is to say habitual. If the subject of our observation is a state, the state may be the background for a particular action, in the present, or the state may be indefinitely extended into the past and into the future and become a universal. In every case, the present overlaps the moment of speaking; in every case it is indefinite. A single tense, the present indicative is capable of expressing all these notions and attitudes. Because the present tense has so wide a variety of function, it has become necessary to create auxiliary devices to indicate which particular function is meant in a given case; these are discussed in detail under Auxiliary Verbs, 34. The commonest uses of the simple present are illustrated below.

32.111 Universal. ROD 9 *Reformarse es vivir.* This statement is valid from past infinity to future infinity.   (*)

32.113 Particular, progressive. PEQ 19 *Lector, yo emborrono estas páginas en la pequeña biblioteca del Collado de Salinas.*   (*)

32.115 Particular, iterative.   IBA 25 *Los chicos, cuando me ven, me hablan.*   (*)

32.117 Particular, habitual.   PAX 23 *Estos rumores caen siempre en los momentos de mayor alegría.*   (*)

32.12 The present is used to indicate that an action or state which began at a definite moment in the past is still in progress at the present. This construction, in which English uses the perfect or perfect progressive, is to be distinguished from that in which an action or state which began at an indefinite moment in the past is presented as continuing in the present through the use of *seguir* (*continuar*) and the present participle; see 34.91. To simplify the classification of the material, type sentences are used to indicate the forms and tenses used.

32.121 *hace mucho que os busco.*   IBA 369 *Hace días que quiero comprarla un ramo grande.*   (15–33)

32.125 *os busco hace mucho.*   BRA 158 *Lo estás pensando tú hace días.*
                                                                       (6–7)

32.127 *desde entonces os busco.*   UGA 19 ¿ *Desde cuándo la conoces?*
                                                                      (11–16)

32.129 *os busco desde hace mucho.*   SIE 53 *Estamos invitados desde hace tres semanas.* A fusion of the *hace*-construction and the *desde*-construction.   (10–12)

32.131 *llevo mucho buscándoos.*   SEC 11 *Es un criado que lleva diez años a mi servicio.*   (9–14)

32.135 *desde que os conozco, os busco.*   VIG 69 *Desde que conoce a Eugenia, gusta de todas las mujeres.*   (5–5)

32.14 If the speaker wishes to indicate the period which has elapsed since a past event or the duration of a period up to the present, he uses the preterite or perfect, even after *hace.*

32.141 *Hace mucho que os busqué.*   SON 24 *Aún no hace un año que falleció.* *Que* has the force of " since."   (12–18)

32.145 *os busco desde que llegué.*   ART 40 *Estoy buscándolo desde que me leyó usted el drama.*   (5–5)

32.151 *hace mucho que no os he buscado.*   RUS 89 *Hace tiempo que no la hemos visto.* Usually with negative verbs of action.   (5–5)

32.16 The present used for the future. The present is the tense of vivid immediate experience. Therefore any action, past or future, can be transferred in imagination from its actual time to the present and the speaker may present it as though it were in progress in the present. This practice is particularly common in vivid narration. It has become the regular form in many conditional sentences; see 31.214; 31.431. In the future, the tendency toward the use of the present is strong in conversation, and particularly when some other element in the sentence makes clear that the time is future.

32.161 Vividly presented. SEC 84 *No te pongas fino o te mato.* (**25–113**)

32.163 An adverb or conjunction of time indicates futurity. ART 44 *Vuelvo en seguida.* (**24–81**)

32.165 In questions of all types, the answer to which involves the future. URU 31 *¡ Ay, se ha escapado el tordo! ¿ Pero cómo lo agarro ?* ([**23**]**–40**)

32.171 The present used for the past, in vivid narration (historical present). This use of the present is found not only in colloquial style but very frequently as a literary device. MAY 15 *Salta Javier y mira el reloj. Son las cinco y media.* (**34–1666**)

32.18 The present used to express a command. This is a considerate form of expression, used when the speaker has no accepted authority to issue orders. REY 116 *Ustedes se dedican a secar los fusiles.* (**23–62**)

32.19 The present used instead of the conditional perfect. This is another of the vivid uses of the present. It is found after *por poco, de poco, a poco más,* etc., which replace the condition of a contrary-to-fact past conditional sentence. PAL 304 *Una ola de placer invadió mi cuerpo y por poco me hace dar con él en el suelo.* The phrase *por poco* has now become the practical equivalent of " almost " and the verb seems to have a past force; its original force must have been: " if there had been a little more, I would have." (4–6)

For the exactly parallel use of the present indicative in contrary-to-fact past conditions, see 31.431.

32.2 The past tenses. There are two possible attitudes which the speaker may adopt in reporting past experience. He may, from the point of view of the present, consider a past action or state as a definite, unified whole, through a process of reflective memory. He may also transfer himself in imagination to the past and there observe the action or state, in precisely the same way in which he always observes a present action or state. In this case, as in the present, the action or state will appear as an indefinite series, unbroken or intermittent, without definite beginning or definite ending. And it will be susceptible of all the minor variations to which the present is susceptible. Spanish and the other Romance languages have two separate tenses to indicate these two attitudes. The preterite tense is used to present past experience as a series of definite units. It is the regular tense in narration. The imperfect tense is used to present the past as an indefinite series of progressive or intermittent parts. It is the regular tense in description, both the description of states (the background of actions) and of actions themselves when they are observed rather than recollected. If we add to these two methods of presenting the past, the even more vivid method of using the present tense (see 32.171), Spanish has three devices for reporting past experience.

32.21 Imperfect. We have said that the imperfect is the indefinite past; its uses correspond precisely to the uses of the present, which is also indefinite, and again as in the present, if it becomes necessary to distinguish which particular function it is to perform in a given situation, it may be replaced by a progressive or other auxiliary construction; see 34. In the discussion of the past tenses it is desirable to distinguish between the expression of actions and of states.

32.22 Actions.

32.221 Progressive, and presented as in progress at a definite moment in the past which is indicated by another verb in the preterite. PAT 21 *Fumaba aún Alberto de la pipa, cuando Manolo le anunció la visita.* The time of the imperfect overlaps that of the preterite indefinitely. (**54–777**)

32.223 Progressive, and concomitant with another indefinite past action or state which is indicated by another verb in the imperfect. RIC 252 *En tanto lloraba estériles soledades, Silda rezaba por él.* The beginning and end of both actions is indefinite. (**60–1782**)

32.23 In narrative style, the imperfect is often introduced among preterite tenses to reflect a more intense emotion on the part of the speaker which makes him transfer his point of view and report the action as observed in actual progress; the action thus becomes visualized rather than recollected. FOM 8 *El suave lamento cambióse de súbito en grito. Adolfo se levantó a inquirir la causa del grito; y los tres, ambas mujeres y Adolfo, tocaban a la misma puerta. Nadie respondía; pero oyóse dentro el gemir de un hombre.* The imperfect appears to be especially common after adverbial expressions which fix the temporal sequence. UNA 153 *Pocos días después, recibía el conde una invitación.* (**34–235**)

In Spanish, as in French, this usage has been a mannerism of modern realists, but it is by no means limited to them.

32.235 The use of the imperfect of verbs which introduce a quotation has become very common; it is possible that the construction has been influenced by the similar construction found in quotations from written documents; see 32.245. LIN 133 *Tú no puedes autorizarlo, me decía.*

(21–73)

32.24 Repeated (iterative). JIM 46 *En sus ojos rojeaba a veces un fuego vivo.* (60–1047)

32.243 With verbs of perception, the reflexive form of the imperfect acquires the force of possibility. WAS 147 *Llegaron a la cresta de la loma desde la cual se veía el caserío de la villa* ("you could see"). (28–88)

32.245 In citations from written works, books, journals, letters, etc. the imperfect is regularly used, since written works convey their message to each reader. IMP 86 *Compró el Blanco y negro y empezó a hojearlo. Hasta que, de pronto, una plana en color le causó gran sobresalto. Decía: «La ensoñada, por Alverdi.»* (25–54)

32.25 Habitual (customary). IDO 4 *Antes, esos mismos pormenores no le llamaban la atención o le causaban hastío.* (57–1854)

32.26 States. Verbs indicating state fall into two main groups, those which present the physical circumstances, the external background in which an action took place; and those which report the mental and emotional states of the actors in the scene.

32.27 Physical circumstances. This is the most frequent use of the imperfect. It is the descriptive use which provides a setting for actions. It is especially common in relative clauses. RIC 265 *La estancia decía bien a las claras el desorden en que vivía su dueño. El suelo estaba sembrado de libros; en un rincón había un baúl abierto.* UNA 161 *Alejandro miró al crucifijo que estaba a la cabecera de la cama.* (60–6129)

32.28 Emotions, moods, thoughts. In this group fall not only verbs of thinking and feeling but also modal auxiliaries. PAT 16 *Deseaba morirse.*

(54–585)

32.3 Uses of the imperfect which are common to verbs of action and verbs of state. Certain uses of the imperfect are general and do not depend upon the type of verb involved.

32.31 The imperfect, like the present, is used to indicate that an action which began at a definite point in the past was still in progress at a subsequent time. English uses the pluperfect or pluperfect progressive.

hacia mucho que os buscaba. PEQ 144 *Hacía dos meses que permanecía inactiva.* (8–9)

desde entonces os buscaba. MUJ 25 *No nos veíamos desde chiquitinas.* (7–8)

os buscaba desde hacía mucho. ORR 177 *Era una de sus caracterís-*
ticas desde hacía tiempo.   (7–9)

llevaba mucho buscándoos. IMP 73 *Llevaban ya una hora callejeando.*
                                                                        (5–6)

32.32 The imperfect is used in modest or guarded statements instead of
the present. The transfer of the tense from present to past makes the
statement less abrupt, because it leaves room for the possibility that the
action or state is no longer true. RUS 90 *Ésa es una excepción. — Pues de*
ella quería yo hablar a usted.   (13–16)

32.331 In indirect discourse, introduced by a verb in the past, the
imperfect is always used to report a present indicative of direct discourse. PAL 13 *Me preguntó si quería hacerle el honor de acompañarle* (the
original question in direct discourse was present: *¿ Quieres hacerme el*
honor . . . ?). The preterite is never used in this situation.   **(57–555)**

32.335 The original present indicative may have been used instead of
the future; the imperfect in this case will have the force of a conditional.
ABU 205 *Dijo que volvía pronto y no volvió* (the original: *Vuelvo pronto*
was used for: *Volveré pronto;* hence *volvía* has the force of *volvería.*)
                                                                        (18–24)

32.341 The indirect statement may be implied, rather than expressed.
A mannerism of modern Spanish (as of modern French), is the frequent
use of the imperfect to report the thoughts, soliloquies, and the like, of
a character, without the introduction of any word to indicate that the
actions or states are reported as indirect discourse. This informal
indirect discourse, or "free" indirect style, appears to have been adopted in
Spain in imitation of French realists and naturalists. TRI 219 *Claro es que*
quedaron en suspenso la comedia y los cuentos. ¡ No importaba! Lo
esencial era cultivar las relaciones (beginning with *¡ No importaba!* the
imperfects represent the original present tenses in which the character
thought, or expressed to himself, the notions involved).   **(22–267)**

32.345 As in actual indirect discourse, the original thought may have
been a present which stood for a future. LUG 12 *El tenía su plan. Su*
padre le acompañaba hasta Venta de Baños, en donde tomaría el expreso
(the original *acompaña* stood for *acompañará*).   **(6–7)**

32.35 The imperfect is used instead of the conditional in direct state-
ments. The origin of the use of the imperfect for a conditional must be
sought in its use as a vivid tense in the conclusion of conditional sentences; see 31.315.

32.351 Similarly the imperfect is found in sentences in which the condition is replaced by another form of expression or in which the condition

is merely implied in the context.   CAT 25 *Yo en tu lugar no le aguantaba semejante grosería.*   (6–7)

32.355 *no faltaba más.* Especially common in this use is the idiom *no faltaba más* and kindred expressions.   ZAM 69 *Si viene alguien, le recibiré . . . ¡No faltaba más!*   (9–13)

32.4 Preterite. The preterite is the definite past; it reports past actions and states as unified wholes, seen from the point of view of the present. In addition to this central function, the preterite is also used with verbs expressing state to stress the beginning or end of the state; in stressing the beginning of the state, it serves as an effective, that is to say it reports the achievement of the state; in stressing the end of the state, it is a terminative, that is to say, it indicates that the state has ceased to exist.

32.41 Actions.

32.421 Single actions or units of connected actions. Any attempt to distinguish between a single action and a connected series of actions would be purely arbitrary, for even so simple an act as opening a door is, in fact, made up of a series of connected actions. Looked at from the point of view of the present, any action, however complex, may be considered a unified whole. This integrating attitude is expressed by the preterite. REY 89 *La noche pasada un golpe de mar arrancó del puente al capitán Jenkins y lo hizo desaparecer entre las olas.* JAN 119 *Irene hizo esfuerzos por aparecer amable.* This is the most frequent tense use in Spanish, outside of the use of the present indicative.   **(60–9030)**

32.425 Progressive actions. A special variant of this unit usage is that in which the action is presented as progressive, through the use of an auxiliary verb and the present participle. In this situation, the preterite is used only when the duration of the progressive action is definite, either by explicit statement or by implication of the context.

32.426 The duration is defined.   ALT 186 *El Consejo real se fué organizando en los siglos XIV y XV.*   (Not separately counted)

32.428 The duration is implied.   URU 70 *Después se le fué pasando.*
(Not separately counted)

32.43 Repeated actions. As in the case of progressive actions, the preterite is used to express repeated actions in the past only when the duration of the repeated series is made definite.

32.431 The duration is defined.   PEL 460 *El cancionero fué varias veces impreso desde 1573 hasta 1681.*   **(21–51)**

32.435 The duration is implied. occ 194 *Volvió ya todos los días al Clib.* (54–270)

32.44 Verbs of transition. Between verbs of action and verbs of state fall a group of verbs which may be said to indicate transition from one state to another; such are *nacer, morir, quedar, quedarse, hacerse, volverse, tornarse.* Closely related are reflexive verbs like *dormirse* or *asustarse* which are used with effective force, to express the achievement of a state. With all these verbs the preterite is used to express the moment of effective transition in the past. PEQ 30 *Luego se hizo clérigo.*

(Not separately counted)

32.45 States. Past states are expressed in the preterite when the duration of the state is definite. The preterite is also used to stress the achievement of the state and the termination of the state.

32.451 Definite duration.

32.453 The duration is defined by an adverb, or adverbial expression of time. ARN 42 *Y así estuvimos dos años.* (51–252)

32.454 The duration is defined by a conjunction. PAL 12 *Mientras vivió, nunca pudo consolarse.* (10–11)

32.455 The duration is defined by some other temporal word in the sentence. SAS 36 *Tuve un día atareadísimo.* (12–15)

32.456 *Nunca*, in spite of its apparently indefinite meaning, appears to have defining value, for it is normally accompanied by the preterite. DEB 11 *Nunca creí que retornar al pueblo fuera tan doloroso.* (40–132)

32.457 The duration is implied by the context. In the course of any given narrative account, states which are contemporaneous with the actions reported are regularly expressed in the preterite; they are considered as units of the same kind as the units of action. MGR 15 (News report of a bullfight) Niño del Barrio, *si no tuvo una actuación brillante, supo salir del paso decorosamente. Estuvo sereno y fué el que oyó más aplausos.* All the verbs of state are in the preterite because all of them cover the definite period within which the bullfight took place. (50–408)

32.459 Copulative verbs and modal auxiliaries, which in themselves have slight temporal value, regularly reflect the tense of the accompanying action. If that tense is preterite, they are found in the preterite. IDO 9 *Entonces no fué la voz de su hermano que rompió su éxtasis.* The common verbs in this group are *ser*, impersonal *haber, deber, poder,* and *querer.* (56–358)

32.47 The beginning or achievement of the state is stressed. With a number of verbs of state, the preterite, rather than indicating the definite duration of the state, stresses the achievement of the state. In most cases in this group English uses a different verb to express this aspect of the verb. DIV 15 *Hoy en un lunch conocí a Ramiro de Maeztu.* The common preterites in this group are: *conocí,* " I met," *supe,* " I learned," *tuve,* " I got *or* received."   (Counted figures not valid)

32.48 The ending or termination of the state is stressed. PAT 217 *Éste era cuñado de una muchacha que fué novia mía.* The distinction between *era* and *fué* is obvious: the imperfect is used to express the family relationship because that relationship was indefinite and not subject to termination; the preterite, on the other hand, shows that the relationship of *novio* and *novia* has ceased. The common verbs in this group are *creer, pensar,* and *ser.*   (Counted figures not valid)

32.49 The preterite is used to indicate that a state was expressed in a definite action. JES 235 *Sobre el cielo sereno cayó hacia el norte una exhalación como una gota de luz. Ambos tuvieron un ¡ ah! de admiración.* The common verbs in this group are: *pude,* " I succeeded in," *quise,* " I tried," *no quise,* " I refused," *supe,* " I managed to."   (Counted figures not valid)

32.5 Common to both action and state. In a number of constructions the preterite is used under conditions which are not related to the type of verbal action involved.

32.51 The preterite has the force of a perfect. In conversational style the preterite is frequently used to express an action or state which, in its effects, reaches the present and which would be normally expressed by the perfect. The use of the narrative past in this case adds a note of finality to the occurrence. SIE 45 *¡ Adiós, burgués feliz! Llegó el momento fatal.*   ([40]–117)

32.515 *ya se acabó.* When the preterite is accompanied by *ya,* as in the phrase *ya se acabó* and similar expressions, the time involved becomes in effect a present, rather than a perfect. SJQ 39 *En Madrid tiene un novio. — ¡ Ja, ja, ja! Ya pareció el defecto grande.*   (16–28)

32.52 The preterite has the force of a pluperfect. When a preterite is used in a temporal clause in narrative, and the action or state expressed in the temporal clause is followed by another action or state, the events of the temporal clause are completed at the time of the events of the main clause and, in strict logic, should be expressed by a compound tense, pluperfect or preterite perfect. But Spanish rarely uses this type of expression; the mere sequence of expression makes clear the order of events. DEB 98 *Cuando todo terminó y salimos de la iglesia, vimos a Pau-*

lina acercarse a nosotros. Similarly with other subordinate clauses. LUG 159 *Deshizo Gerardo el camino que cierta noche, dos meses antes, anduvo desesperado.* ([40]–117)

32.525 An analogous usage is found when an original preterite of direct discourse is retained as a preterite, instead of becoming a pluperfect, in indirect discourse, expressed or implied. DIV 20 *Recordé que esta pretensión quedó manifiesta en el* meeting *de los miembros de la Asociación de Petroleros.* (5–7)

32.6 Future. The future can be considered as a definite whole or as an indefinite series of parts, unbroken or intermittent, but both lie in the realm of the imagination. A single tense is used to express both attitudes, although the progressive character of an action may be stressed by the use of the progressive auxiliaries. In addition to its use as a tense, the future has a number of modal functions, expressing intention (determination), inference, and command.

32.61 Expressing future time. The future is used to express actions or states which the speaker assumes or deduces will take place at a future time. WAS 6 *Hemos de toparnos algún día. Entonces se acordará bien de mí.* (60–1410)

32.621 Expressing present intention or determination. SON 98 *Pues yo escribiré hoy mismo a Roma.* In the first person, this is the usual value of the future. (44–288)

32.624 Expressing present inference. The future is frequently used to express the inference which the speaker draws from attendant circumstances. This use is sometimes called the "future of probability," but it should be remembered that the construction covers the whole range from mere supposition to almost certainty. It is almost the equivalent of the use of *debo* (*debo de*) with the infinitive; but the latter construction carries with it an implication that the inference is inevitable, while the future suggests that the inference is a personal variable. JIM 82 *¿Es un burro perdido? ¿Qué querrá?* ("What do you suppose he wants?") (47–303)

32.628 Expressing a command. The future is used to express a command when the speaker assumes that his instructions will be carried out. It implies authority on the part of the speaker. Hence it is used in laws and similar expressions of authority. In conversation it has a similar force: it is less blunt than an imperative, but it is more inexorable. ART 11 *Ustedes se quedarán a la lectura. — Como usted disponga.* (20–48)

32.65 Conditional. In origin, the conditional is a past of the future and this usage survives in indirect discourse, expressed or implied, covering the uses of the future as a tense and as a modal form expressing inference. But from its use in the conclusion of contrary-to-fact conditions, the conditional is also used as a mood, expressing possibility or unreality; this use of the conditional is called its use as a potential.

32.651 As a past of an original future in indirect discourse after a past verb. FOM 97 *Pensaba que alejarse de su tierra sería tontuna.* **(40–156)**

32.653 The original future may have been a future of inference. IBA 26 *Los guardas preguntábanse por qué lado del bosque trabajaría aquel bandido.* (7–12)

32.655 The indirect discourse may be implied. MAY 7 *Le obligaron a marchar, no sin que prometiese volver muy pronto. En el mes de octubre estaría allí de fijo: lo juraba.* (15–82)

32.657 Again, the original future may have been a future of inference. TRI 119 *Le preocupó un momento su frase de aclaración. ¿Cómo diablos sabría el nombre de tal danza?* (7–47)

32.66 A special use of the conditional is that of expressing past inference in direct discourse. BEN 13 *Anoche cuando llegamos me pareció de peor color; sería la luz* ("it must have been the light"). **(24–60)**

32.67 Potential uses of the conditional. The use of the conditional in the conclusion of less vivid future and contrary-to-fact present conditional sentences is discussed in detail under conditional sentences; see 31.31 and 31.41. We are here concerned only with those cases in which the condition is not expressed.

32.671 The potential has present force. The condition may be replaced by another form of expression or merely implied. VIG 64 *Unamuno no trata de disimular este influjo; sería inútil.* This is now the most frequent usage of the conditional form. **(57–528)**

32.675 The potential has past force. Very rarely the conditional has the force of a past contrary-to-fact; in this case it is the equivalent of a conditional perfect. IMP 191 *Se odiaban; cada uno desearía velar solícito la agonía del otro.* (3–3)

THE IMPERATIVE

32.70 The imperative has only one tense, which is called a present, although the time indicated by the command is always future. RUS 142 *¡Márchate!* For a full discussion of the uses, see 30.

THE SUBJUNCTIVE

32.71 Like the indicative, the subjunctive has tenses which refer to past, present, and future. But the subjunctive is an emotional mood and often overlaps the field of time realities. Hence the present subjunctive has come to refer not only to the present time but also to the future. The two past subjunctives are differentiated in ways quite at variance with those which differentiate the two past indicatives. And finally the future subjunctive has almost disappeared from usage. The various types of clause in which the subjunctive is used are discussed elsewhere. The present section is limited to a summary of special uses of the tenses.

32.72 Present. The present subjunctive refers both to the present and to an indefinite, hypothetical future. BYN 3 *Pida Vd. folleto y demostración gratis.* The present subjunctive is the most frequent of the tenses, after the present, imperfect, and preterite indicative. **(60–2730)**

32.73 Past. Spanish has two forms for the past subjunctive: ending in *–se* and in *–ra*. The first of these was a subjunctive in origin; the second was an indicative (pluperfect) in origin and is still used at times in its original sense. In main clauses the *–ra* form predominates; it is the only form normally used as a potential. In subordinate clauses, the *–ra* form and the *–se* forms are of approximately equal frequency, except in conditional clauses, where the *–ra* form predominates. In Spanish America, the *–ra* form is the more frequent. In some American writers it is the only form used; other American writers of more cosmopolitan contacts use both forms.

32.74 The *–se* form.

32.75 In main clauses. The only situation in which the *–se* form is normally found in main clauses is in expressions of wish, less vivid future and contrary to fact present. TRI 53 *¡ Ah, si pudiese afirmar lo mismo!* For details, see 29.1.   **([8]–11)**

32.76 In subordinate clauses.

32.761 Conditional clauses. PAT 215 *Y si fuese verdad, alégrese usted.* For details, see **31.31** ff.   **([34]–79)**

32.765 In other subordinate clauses, including clauses which replace a condition. UGA 31 *¿ No le había dicho ella misma que no dejase de venir ?* PIN 124 *Emigra el pueblo como si ésta fuese una tierra maldita.* **([59]–517)**

32.81 The *–ra* form.

32.82 In main clauses.

32.821 In expressions of wish, contrary to fact present and less vivid future.   SIE 94 *¡ Si vieras qué a destiempo has venido a echarme en cara mi frivolidad!*   For details, see 29.1.   ([22]–38)

32.83 As a potential.

32.831 Present, in the conclusion of a conditional sentence.   LLA 63 *Si tuviera usted las vértebras torcidas, quizás fuera usted peor que yo.*   The construction is rare.   See also 31.   ([5]–6)

32.835 The condition may be implied.   JIM 36 *De las siete galerías del Paraíso se creyera que tiran rosas a la tierra.*   The construction is common only with a few verbs: *creyera, dijera, fuera, valiera.*   (30–50)

32.84 Past.   As a past potential the *–ra* form is found rarely in sentences implying a contrary-to-fact past condition.   URU 24 *Más valiera que se quedara allá* ("it would have been better . . .")   (4–4)

32.87 In subordinate clauses.

32.871 In conditional clauses.   SJQ 30 *Si el hablar fuera pecado, al infierno iba ésa.*   For details, see **31.31** ff.   ([43]–143)

32.875 In other subordinate clauses, including clauses which replace a condition.   LIN 22 *No creía que fueras tan instruida.*   SEC 54 *Le vamos a pasear en hombros, como si fuera el patrón de Navas de San Juan.*

([60]–579)

32.88 As a present potential.   RAN 90 *Es posible que tengan razón y que más valiera el que las cosas siguiesen así.*   (9–12)

32.89 The past subjunctive form in *–ra*, used with its original force as a pluperfect indicative.   This usage is limited to subordinate clauses, relative, adverbial, and indirect discourse.   It is found most frequently in writers from the North of Spain (Asturias, Galicia) and in some Spanish American writers.   DEB 91 *Unos días después de aquel en que Agustín cantara su primera misa, estaba yo al balcón del comedor.*   (11–35)

32.9 Future.   The future subjunctive has practically disappeared in contemporary Spanish.   It survives in laws, and in fixed phrases, some of them proverbial in character.   Rarely it is used to give a sort of archaic dignity or elegance to speech.   The most interesting phenomenon in its use is its appearance in past clauses, where it could not have been used when it was still a living instrument of expression.   A majority of the cases noted fall in this group.   The future subjunctive has never been used except in subordinate clauses, conditional, relative, temporal, etc., referring to a hypothetical future.   DIV 12 *Si hiciere algunos gastos extraordinarios, puede usted avisarme* (the President of Mexico, writing to an ambassador).   In a past sequence.   ALT 471 *Todo el que saliese del reino*

*tenía que presentarse al corregidor. Los que sacaren cosas vedadas debían
ser denunciados* (summarizing a medieval law).   (6–6)

PERFECT TENSES

33. The perfect tenses, or compound tenses, indicate an action or state
as completed at the time expressed by the auxiliary verb of the tense.
They are regularly formed, in all types of verbs, by the use of the proper
tense of *haber* and the past participle. In rare cases, with intransitive
verbs, the auxiliary is still *ser*.

THE INDICATIVE

33.11 Perfect. The perfect tense is used to indicate that an action or
state is completed in the present. It must be remembered that the
present is indefinite and therefore it may be conceived as extending
into the past as well as into the future. This wide conception of the
present makes it possible for the Spanish speaker to use the perfect in
any case in which the action or state appears to him to have relationships
which are still effective in the present. There is a tendency in contemporary usage toward the use of the perfect as a narrative past, instead of the preterite; the usage has perhaps been influenced by French.

33.12 Expressing actions or states which are completed in the present.
SIE 20 *He hecho mi media horita de gimnasia; he leído el periódico.* If
a narrative is expressed in the vivid historical present, completed actions
and states will be found in the perfect. MAY 16 *El pasado retorna sobre el
alma de este hombre: ha encontrado a su novia esperándole allí.* **(60–2538)**

33.13 Used instead of a preterite. It is often difficult to determine
whether a given perfect indicates a completed present or a definite past.
The only criterion which appears to be fairly safe is that of the sequence
of tenses; if a perfect tense is followed by a past sequence, in the indicative or the subjunctive, it is probable that it should be considered a true
past. ZAM 63 *La he dicho que aquí vivía mi abogado.* **(23–96)**

33.21 Pluperfect. The pluperfect is used to indicate that a given action
or state was completed at a given moment or period in the past. It is
also regularly used to represent an original perfect indicative in indirect
discourse, expressed or implied, after a verb in the past.

33.22 Expressing actions or state which were completed in the past.
IBA 365 *Había transcurrido muy poco tiempo.* **(60–1017)**

33.231 Representing an original perfect, in indirect discourse. ABC 21
Se dijo que el señor Azaña había pretendido eludir de este modo. **(43–125)**

33.233 The indirect discourse may be implied. JES 155 *Ella comenzó a hacerle reflexiones. ¿Había sufrido algún quebranto en los negocios?*

(12–46)

33.24 In temporal clauses. The pluperfect is used in temporal clauses to indicate that an indefinite state or indefinitely repeated action was completed at the time of the main verb. JAN 111 *Durante todo el almuerzo Rigoberto respondía apenas cuando Irene le había dirigido la palabra.* (8–9)

33.31 Preterite perfect. This tense is normally found only in temporal clauses to indicate that a definite past action was completed at the time of the action of the main verb. It is rare in Spanish, being regularly replaced by the simple preterite. ORR 180 *Cuando hubieron quedado solos, Sandoval ofreció el brazo a Elisa.* This is the least frequent of all Spanish tenses. (5–6)

33.41 Future perfect. In origin, the perfect indicated that an action or state will have been completed at a given future time. In this use the tense is now rare. But it is still frequent as a means of expressing the inference that an action or state has been completed in the present.

33.42 Expressing an action or state completed in the future. NER 54 *El sol calentará menos. Su luz habrá pasado ya del amarillo al rojo.* (6–9)

33.43 Expressing the inference that an action or state has been completed in the present. UNA 24 *¿ De dónde habrá sacado este autor esto?*

(42–108)

33.51 Conditional perfect. In origin, the conditional perfect was a past of the future perfect. Of this usage the only trace which is still in any common use is that of expressing inference in indirect discourse after a past verb. But like the conditional, the conditional perfect has also become a mood, of potential character, which is used in the conclusion of conditions and in other sentences in which a condition is implied.

33.525 Expressing inference after a past verb in indirect discourse. MUJ 31 *De él imaginaba yo que habrías sacado aquella virtud.* (3–4)

33.53 As a potential, past.

33.531 In the conclusion of conditional sentences. ROM 201 *Si la venganza de Bernal Francés fuese histórica, ¿ el romance castellano habría inspirado el francés y el italiano?* ([11]–16)

33.535 The condition may be implied. IDO 7 *Cualquiera otro se habría rendido al cansancio.* (11–15)

THE SUBJUNCTIVE

33.6 The subjunctive has now only three perfect forms, the perfect and two pluperfects, formed in *hubiese* and *hubiera*, the older future perfect having practically disappeared from usage.

33.61 Perfect. The perfect subjunctive is used in subordinate clauses to express an action or state that is completed in the present or in a hypothetical future. ORT 78 *Amar el pasado es congratularse de que efectivamente haya pasado.*   (44 88)

33.64 Pluperfect. Of the two forms of the pluperfect subjunctive, that in *hubiera* is the more common in all situations, both in main clauses and in subordinate clauses. In contrast with the use of the simple past subjunctives, the use of the pluperfect subjunctive in *hubiese* as a potential appears to be becoming established.

33.65 The *hubiese* form.

33.651 In main clauses, as a potential, past, in the conclusion of a conditional sentence. ABC 25 *Si hubiera nacido dos siglos atrás, hubiese sido fiscal de la Inquisición.*   (5–6)

33.655 The condition may be implied. IMP 206 *¡ Hubiese preferido que allí mismo la tirantez de sus nervios se rompiese!*   (7–8)

33.66 In subordinate clauses.

33.661 Clauses expressing a condition. FAL 159 *Si hubiese sido hombre, el sentido de su libertad hubiera sido más amplio.*   ([14]–22)

33.665 Other subordinate clauses, including clauses used to replace a condition. UNA 92 *Yo creí que tú me hubiese traído sol y libertad.* ([27]–54)

33.7 The *hubiera* form.

33.71 In main clauses.

33.711 Expressing a wish, impossible of fulfillment, in the past. PEL 454 *¡ Ojalá se hubieran trocado los papeles!*   (5–6)

33.713 Potential, past, in the conclusion of a conditional sentence. PAL 131 *Si le tocase la lotería, nos hubiera dado la noticia con acento desgarrador.*   ([14]–21)

33.715 The condition may be implied. ZUN 16 *De haber querido casarse, lo hubiera hecho inmediatamente.*   ([30]–65)

33.72 In subordinate clauses.

33.721 In clauses expressing a condition. BRA 40 *Si no se hubiera muerto, no tendrían ustedes los millones que van a tener.* For details, see 31.

([16]–26)

33.725 In other subordinate clauses, including clauses used to replace a condition. LLA 27 *Parece como si todo hubiera cambiado para mí.*

([26]–50)

33.727 As a potential, past. CAT 27 *Voy a referirte un caso que hubiera preferido mantener en reserva.* (14–19)

AUXILIARIES USED IN FORMING THE PERFECT TENSES

33.8 The regular auxiliary used in the formation of the perfect tenses is *haber*. It is found with all types of verbs. Transitive. SAS 26 *No ha leído El primo Basilio de Eça de Queiroz.* Intransitive. RET 13 *Tamayo y Baus había enmudecido desde 1870.* Reflexive. LIN 34 *¿Os habéis olvidado del paño?* (*)

33.81 Other auxiliaries, used with transitive verbs. Certain other verbs are found with the past participle of transitive verbs, forming a sort of tense. But it should be noted that the verbal locution thus formed is very rarely a true perfect tense; it is a device for expressing the attainment of a present state as a result of the action. The verbs which are commonly found in this construction are:

> *tener.* ARN 11 *Tengo oído que es una alhaja* (this is almost a true perfect.) **(35–71)**
> *llevar.* IBA 151 *Más de una parte de rosario le llevo dedicada.* (5–8)
> *traer.* SIE 13 *A todas nos traía vuelto el juicio.* (5–5)

33.82 *ser* used as an auxiliary with intransitive verbs. The older method of forming the perfect tenses of intransitive verbs with *ser* as the auxiliary still finds sporadic expression. SON 196 *Era llegado el momento supremo.* The participle in this construction has active force. (4–4)

33.85 When two perfect tenses are coordinate, the auxiliary verb may be omitted with the second participle. PAX 12 *He rezado la Novena del Niño y bailado después.* (15–18)

AGREEMENT OF THE PAST PARTICIPLE IN PERFECT TENSES

33.86 Formed with *haber*. The past participle of perfect tenses formed with *haber* is invariable. WAS 19 *Te has cortado la barba.* (*)

33.87 With *tener, llevar, traer,* etc. The past participle of tenses formed with *tener, llevar, traer,* etc. agrees with the direct object in gender and in number. MGR 8 *El Estado tiene realizadas las explanaciones del aeródromo.* ([35]–84)

33.88 With *ser.* The past participle of perfect tenses of intransitive verbs formed with *ser* agrees with the subject in gender and in number. PEQ 41 *Yo me ponía más triste que nunca porque sabía era llegada la hora de ir al colegio.* (4–4)

STRUCTURE OF THE PERFECT TENSES

33.91 The perfect forms with *haber* have become an almost inseparable unit, in which the auxiliary *haber* regularly precedes the past participle. ZUN 24 *¿ No le han cortado una pierna ?* (*)

33.93 Occasionally, however, other elements of the sentence are placed between the auxiliary and the participle.

33.931 If a personal object pronoun follows the verb, it is regularly attached to the auxiliary. PAT 209 *Habíanse acomodado ya todos a la mesa.* (7–14)

33.935 A subject pronoun is sometimes found in the same position. STE 33 *Habían ellos pagado ya anticipadamente.* (7–12)

33.937 Similarly a short adverb. JIM 45 *Platero me había ya saludado con un rebuzno.* (5–6)

33.939 Or even an adverbial phrase. FOM 100 *De ahí el que hubiese, durante meses, visitado la casa sin toparse con María.* In this, as in other cases of interpolation of forms between auxiliary and participle, the usage is more common with longer forms of the auxiliary than with monosyllabic forms. (3–3)

SEQUENCE OF TENSES

33.94 Like the other Romance languages, Spanish reflects in subordinate clauses the tense of the main verb. This reflection is found primarily in two types of expression: in indirect discourse, in the indicative, and in subordinate clauses in the subjunctive. In other cases involving the indicative in subordinate clauses, the tense of the verb may express any time, present, past, or future.

33.95 The use of the tenses of the indicative in indirect discourse has been discussed in detail under each of the tenses. It will suffice here to summarize the situation by saying that after past tenses (imperfect, preterite, conditional, pluperfect and conditional perfect), the present tenses are transferred into the past according to definite rules: the present becomes imperfect, the future becomes conditional, the perfect becomes pluperfect, and the future perfect becomes conditional perfect.

33.96 In subordinate clauses in the subjunctive, there is also a normal pattern of sequence: the present tenses are followed by the present (or perfect) subjunctive, the past tenses are followed by the past (or pluperfect) subjunctive. The usage is illustrated below.

33.961 Present sequence.

Present indicative. SIE 9 *¿ Quiere el señor que vaya a ver ?*
Imperative. SJQ 73 *Pregunta lo que quieras.*
Present subjunctive. RUS 11 *Diga usted el que quiera.*
Future. SJQ 38 *Cualquiera que lo oiga pensará que estamos en un desierto.*
Perfect. SIE 30 *Ha llegado el momento de que se acabe de volverse loco por usted.*

33.963 Past sequence.

Imperfect. ABU 195 *No quería que viniésemos.*
Preterite. UNA 100 *Hizo que su marido lo reconociera como suyo.*
Conditional. RUS 35 *A nadie le consentiría que me dijese las cosas que me dices tú.*
Pluperfect. IMP 199 *Había dejado un balcón abierto, para que la despertase el día.*
Conditional perfect. ORR 179 *Le habría agradado que Mario le dirigiera cumplidos.*

33.97 These rules of sequence are not inflexible. If it is necessary, it is possible to use past subjunctives after present verbs, or present subjunctives after past verbs.

33.98 A present is followed by a past subjunctive.

33.981 When the time of the action or state of the subjunctive clause is actually past. PEL 6 *Es muy verosímil que este armador y el jurado fuesen la misma persona.*   (16–36)

33.983 When the past subjunctive has the force of a less vivid future. RUS 81 *Yo necesito muchas más cosas para hacer feliz a una mujer que fuese sola mía.*   (6–6)

33.985 When the past subjunctive has the force of a contrary-to-fact present. JIM 69 *Parece que estuviéramos dentro de un gran panal de luz.* Common after *parece.*   (8–12)

33.989 The perfect is sometimes used as a past tense and followed by a past tense.　DEB 94 *Ha habido que buscar quien la sustituyese.*　(16–22)

33.99 A past is followed by a present subjunctive.

33.991 When the notion expressed in the subordinate clause continues in force in the present.　JAN 304 *Yo propuse al Inspector que hiciera una combinación para que Ud. quede en Santiago.*　(6–7)

AUXILIARY VERBS

34. Auxiliary verbs fall into three classes, of I. Aspect, II. Mood, and III. Tense. Auxiliaries of aspect are used to indicate some phase of an action or state, as Effective (*llegar a*), Inceptive (*empezar a*), Progressive (*estar* + present participle), Continuative (*seguir* + present participle), Iterative (*ir* + present participle), Single repetition (*volver a*), Customary (*soler*), Perfective (*acabar de*), Terminative (*cesar de*). Auxiliaries of mood (modal auxiliaries) are used to express the speaker's interpretation of an action or state, involving notions such as necessity, obligation, inference, ability, possibility, and the like. Auxiliaries of tense are used instead of the regular tenses to express the time of an action or state, as *acaba de* + infinitive, immediate present perfect, or *ha de* (*va a*) + infinitive, future. Some of these auxiliaries are used with the infinitive, others with the present participle. Since several of the auxiliaries have more than one function, it will be desirable to arrange them alphabetically in each group.

34.1 Auxiliaries used with the infinitive.

34.21 *acabar de.*

34.211 Aspect — Perfective. RIC 276 *Acabó Silda de leer los versos.* **(21–33)** Almost never in the present or imperfect indicative.

34.22 Tense.

34.221 *acaba de.* — Immediate present perfect. LUG 11 *Acabo de remediar este daño.* **(31–47)**

34.222 *acababa de.* — Immediate past perfect. FOM 91 *María acababa de despertarse.* **(17–34)**

34.23 *cesar de.* Aspect — Terminative. ALT 13 *Los procuradores no cesaron de reclamar.* **(11–14)**

34.25 *comenzar a.* Aspect — Inceptive. PEQ 84 *Comencé a leerlo.* **(31–85)**

34.3 *deber.* Like most modal auxiliaries, *deber* is used in a number of different functions. Its chief use is to express obligation of different kinds, as determined by moral considerations, by circumstances, custom, or social sanctions, by destiny, and by commitment; it is also used to express necessity and inference. In all fields except that of moral obligation, it competes with *haber de* and it is probably due to this identity that *deber* is often accompanied by *de*, especially to indicate affirmative inference. Like other modals in Spanish and in English, *deber* is weak in time value; past and present of such notions as obligation or necessity are not easily distinguished, with the result that when distinction is required, it is necessary to devise new methods. Moreover, from their very nature, modal verbs are readily presented as potential and hence are found in the conditional or the past subjunctive in *–ra*. In the following outline of usage, present time and past time are used as a basis under the main headings.

34.31 Moral obligation.

34.32 Present time, "ought," "should."

34.321 *debo.* REY 98 *Debemos intentar coger el bote.* (50–220)

34.322 *debo de.* ARN 104 *Conoce uno que no se debe de reír del mal de otro.* (3–3)

34.323 *debía.* TIG 20 *Tuya es la culpa. Desollarte debía.* (20–41)

34.324 *debiera.* BYN 56 *No nos encontramos más que un órgano, por lo que debiera decirse la nariz.* (11–15)

34.33 Past time, "ought to have," "should have."

34.331 *debía.* IMP 192 *Eduardo debía querer mal a aquel por quien Celia estuvo a punto de dejarle.* (11–17)

34.332 *debí.* IGN 87 *Esto es consecuencia de tus amistades con el padre a quien nunca debiste tratar.* (10–12)

34.333 *he debido.* SIE 93 *¡Tú dirás qué he debido yo hacer por ti y no he hecho!* (3–4)

34.334 Back-shifted present, expressed or implied. "ought," "should."

34.335 *debía.* FOM 221 *A Ramón se le convenció de que debía permanecer con la familia.* (11–12)

34.34 Circumstantial or social obligation, derived from a consideration of external experience in circumstances, traditions, custom, or social patterns, "is to," "was to," "is supposed to," etc. ART 21 *Casi siempre da a sus estatuas proporciones justas al sitio que deben ocupar en la vida.* SON 117 *Traía puesto el blanco hábito que debía llevar durante toda la vida.* ABU 24 *Su Excelencia debió llegar a Laín anoche.* (11–14)

34.35 Destiny. RET 31 *En el rostro llevaba « la honda tristeza de los seres que deben morir temprano. »* (3–3)

34.36 Inference, representing the speaker's evaluation of circumstances and by extension indicating various degrees of probability which approach certainty. This use of *deber* and *deber de* overlaps that of the future and conditional. See 32.624.

34.37 Affirmative.

34.371 Present time, "must."

34.372 *debo.* MUJ 30 *Por las muestras debe ser bribona.* (24–53)

34.373 *debo de.* ZUN 21 *Aquellos cimientos deben de ser de guayaba.* (17–30)

34.375 Past time, "must have."

34.376 *debía.* FAL 25 *Ayer debía llegar; ayer entró en el puerto el vapor.* (7–11)

34.377 *debía de.* RAN 103 *Ya en el siglo XIII, se debía de comentar en Santiago la guerra europea.* (7–12)

34.378 *debí.* NER 81 *Yo debí ser uno de ellos por el señorío con que porto el acero y la pluma.* (8–8)

34.379 *debí de.* PAT 27 *Desperté hará cosa de dos horas, vestido y en la cama. Rosina debió de llevarme allí.* (4–8)

34.38 Negative.

34.381 Present time, "cannot," "can't."

34.382 *no debo.* URU 31 *Se ha escapado el tordo. No debe estar muy lejos.* (3–3)

34.39 Necessity, implying a sort of acquiescence on the part of the speaker, like *haber de* and in contrast to *tener que.* MGR 6 *Como resulta que el año anterior ya tuvo el mismo conflicto, este asunto deben resolverlo las Comisiones arbitrales.* (10–12)

34.41 *dejar de.* Aspect — Terminative. PAL 138 *Juanito dejó de hacer muecas.* (10–15)

34.42 *empezar a.* Aspect — Inceptive. SON 33 *Empezó a hablarme en voz baja.* (46–162)

34.43 *haber de.* *Haber de* is used as an auxiliary of mood and as an auxiliary of tense. In the first function, it overlaps all the uses of *deber* except those of moral obligation and inference. In the second, it is an equivalent of the future and conditional, which were in origin composed of the infinitive and the present (and imperfect) of *haber.*

34.44 As auxiliary of mood. Its chief use here is to indicate necessity, implying, like *deber*, acquiescence on the part of the speaker in the justice or propriety of the necessity.

34.45 Necessity. VIG 103 *La vida no tiene que justificarse ante los hombres, en tanto los novelistas han de justificarla ante sus personajes.* (35–125)

34.451 An adverbial expression is sometimes used to identify necessity as the force of the auxiliary. PAT 198 *En esa carta me dirán que a prima tarde he de estar por necesidad en Madrid.* (3–3)

34.46 Circumstantial or social obligation. MUJ 31 *Yo sé que usted me quiere . . . pero cuando me trajo usted aquí, no pensó bien. Con usted yo era feliz . . . Y ahora . . . ¿Qué he de hacer?* BYN 26 *El arquitecto habrá de* (future necessity) *tener en cuenta que la casa es nuestra vida, que ha de* (present necessity) *estar a la medida de las necesidades y los gustos de quienes la hayan de* (social obligation) *habitar.* **(25–58)**

34.461 Especially in exclamations and questions, to express an impatient protest against a preceding question or statement and to imply that an affirmative reply is the only answer possible. ABU 204 *¿Os acordáis de él? — ¿Pues no hemos de acordarnos?* SIE 28 *Ya sabía yo que había de* (for conditional) *encontrarle en buena compañía. — ¿Dónde había de estar?* **(20–32)**

34.47 Destiny. SON 213 *Se abrió la ventana con ese silencio de las cosas que están determinadas en lo invisible y han de suceder por un destino fatal.* (18–31)

34.48 As auxiliary of tense.

34.481 *he de,* for future. MAY 8 *Te escribiré todos los días. — ¿De verdad? — Lo has de ver.* **(36–123)**

34.482 *había de,* for conditional. JES 141 *Había de ser uno de esos paseos clásicos al canal. En todo caso se harían las cosas con reserva.* (11–18)

34.49 *hay que.* — Mood — Necessity, impersonal. URU 22 *Hay que cuidar los intereses.* **(50–226)**

34.491 In the negative *no hay que* occasionally takes on the force of impossibility or futility. PAL 130 *Subir por la pared, no había que pensarlo.* (3–3)

34.51 *hacer.* Vicarious verb, replacing another verb, like English "do."

34.511 With *lo* as direct object. JAN 6 *Si tenía que hablarle, lo hacía en tono altanero.* (12–20)

34.513 After *como.* FOM 14 *Quería casarse con un hombre a quien amase, como hizo Rosalia.* (4–4)

34.6 *ir a.* *Ir a* is primarily an auxiliary of tense, but it has a few modal functions.

34.61 As auxiliary of tense. It has so far become the equivalent of the future (and conditional) that it is used to convey all shades of future usage. It is also used, with special force, to indicate a proximate futurity.

34.611 *voy a,* for future. MUJ 7 *Si tú te enamoras algún día, va a pasarte igual.* (48–512)

34.612 Expressing intention. BRA 152 *¿ Vas a estar leyendo toda la noche ?* (30–100)

34.615 Expressing a mild command. ZUN 57 *Vas a llamar en el cuarto de mi prima.* (5–6)

34.616 *iba a,* for conditional. IGN 139 *Lo que iba a pasar ya lo sabía yo.* (30–64)

34.618 Expression past intention. LLA 28 *¡ Papá! Iba a verte mañana.* (8–14)

34.621 *va a,* proximate futurity, " is about to." JIM 57 *Se dijera, a cada instante, que vamos a descubrir un palacio abandonado.* (35–124)

34.623 *iba a,* past proximate futurity, " was about to." TIG 37 *¿ Por qué lloras? ¡ Yo que iba a darte la enhorabuena!* (12–20)

34.63 As auxiliary of mood. *Ir a* is penetrating the field of *haber de* in the function of circumstantial obligation. RAN 27 *¿ Para qué se va a hablar de mujeres? Mejor es hablar con ellas.* Expressing impatience in questions and exclamations and implying that an affirmative answer is inevitable. IGN 20 *¿ Es aquél? — ¡ Qué va a ser aquél!* (9–11)

34.64 As auxiliary of aspect. *Ir a* is sometimes used in the preterite and in direct or indirect commands merely to stress the unitary character of an action. MAY 15 *Fué a añadir con bárbara sinceridad: Creía que estabas en América.* (11–15)

34.65 *ir y.* Aspect — Unitary. Used only in familiar conversational style, in the preterite, vivid present, or commands. ARN 12 *¡ Ella que va y me da dos pesetas pa traer aceite, y voy y las pierdo.* (6–31)

34.66 *llegar a.* Aspect — Effective. To indicate the beginning of an action or state as the goal of a preceding series of actions or states. FAL 224 *Todos esos jóvenes que han nacido para príncipes de Gales, pero no han llegado a serlo.* (43–94)

34.67 *osar.* Mood — Daring. CAT 11 *¿ Osarías ofenderme con alguna falsa suposición?* (6–8)

34.7 *poder.* *Poder* is an auxiliary of mood, expressing various shades of possibility. Like *deber*, it is weak in tense values and is often found in potential forms. The chief functions are to express ability or power, mental or physical, resting in the subject; possibility, resting in exterior circumstances; and permissibility, resting in another individual. But it should be remarked that the lines between these functions are often shadowy, particularly in potential forms (*podría, pudiera*), and that it is often difficult or impossible to determine whether a given past is a simple past or a potential past.

34.71 Ability.

34.711 Present, "am able," "can." ***puedo.***   PAL 14 *No puedo recordarlo.*
(10–792)

34.712 Perfect, "have been able." ***he podido.***   PEL 30 *No he podido encontrar todavía su poema sobre Carlomagno.*   (17–25)

34.713 Past, "was able," "could."

34.715 ***podía.***   ABC 38 *Los socialistas no podían tragarlo ni en pintura.*
(**40–103**)

34.716 ***pude.***   SAS 130 *En Madrid no pude hacer nada con mi Medicina.*
(**32–74**)

34.719 Other tenses.   BEN 63 *Con él, podrá trabajar.*   (9–18)

34.72 Potential forms.

34.73 Present, "would be able," "could."

34.731 ***podría.***   PAX 13 *Entonces es Irving quien consigue el éxito. — Nada podría hacer sin el tema grandioso.*   (**34–70**)

34.733 ***podía.***   LLA 59 *Con nadie podía entenderme yo más ni mejor que con usted. ¡Y a usted lo odio!*   (5–7)

34.735 ***pudiera.***   ROD 91 *No sé de hombre verdaderamente grande que no pudiera ser toda manera de hombre.*   (8–9)

34.74 Past, "would have been able," "could have."

34.741 ***podría.***   DEB 14 *En mi alma revivían sentimientos que podría creer muertos.*   (5–6)

34.743 ***podía,*** as back-shifted present.   MUJ 12 *Y así podía usted seguir al lado de Carmina.*   (5–5)

34.745 ***pudiera.***   IMP 203 *Unos instantes después salía la diosa. No pudiera decir Guillermo cómo era la maravillosa.*   (4–5)

34.747 ***hubiera podido.***   ZUN 16 *Ella y el favorecido no hubieran podido estar acordes jamás.*   (5–6)

34.749 ***hubiese podido.***   SIE 80 *Si tú hubieras mirado la cuestión con un*

criterio un poco más . . . aristocrático, yo hubiese podido aceptar la respon-
sabilidad del hecho. (3–4)

34.75 Possibility.

34.751 Present, " may," " can." ***puede.*** RUS 139 *Me da miedo lo que puede*
pasar. (**41–109**)

34.752 Perfect, " may have," " can have." ***puede haber.*** BEN 62 *Dice que*
tiene dinero: ¿ de dónde puede haberlo sacado honradamente? (4–4)

34.76 Past, "might have," "could have."

34.761 ***podía.*** FAL 217 *Se podía decir que estaba pasmada.* (11–18) As
back-shifted present. ZUN 52 *Caí en sospechar de que algo malo podía*
pasarle. (3–5)

34.762 ***pudo.*** MGR 15 *El toro se metió por la puerta del patio de caballos y*
pudo cometer un desaguisado serio. (6–9)

34.765 ***pudo haber.*** TIG 6 *¿ Y por eso la mata? ¿ Pues qué se te ocurre que*
pudo haber hecho? (3–3)

34.77 Potential.

34.771 Present, "might," "could."

34.772 ***podría.*** RET 139 *Son monumentos que podrían figurar muy bien en*
las mejores calles de París. (**25–37**)

34.773 ***podía.*** RAN 104 *La catedral de Santiago podía estar perfectamente en*
Francia. (6–7)

34.774 ***pudiera.*** RAN 27 *Los españoles hablan de mujeres como pudieran*
hablar de viajes. (13–17)

34.775 Past, "might have," "could have."

34.776 ***pudiera.*** MAY 5 *Cuanto le pudiera ser gustoso tuvo en las niñas de*
Morano una realización. (4–6)

34.777 ***habría podido.*** ORR 93 *Sentía la dolorosa melancolía de las cosas*
que habrían podido ser y que no fueron. (3–3)

34.778 ***hubiera podido.*** STE 242 *Ella hubiera podido aspirar a la luna.*
(7–8)

34.779 ***podía haber.*** ZAM 69 *¿ Que no puedes venir? Ya podías habérmelo*
dicho antes. (3–3)

34.78 Permissibility. JES 30 *Dispensa, chico; delante de ti no se puede*
hablar de estas cosas. — No; puedes continuar. (**22–56**)

34.79 Without a dependent infinitive.

34.791 *Poder* is frequently used with ellipsis of the infinitive. CAT 3 *Hijo mío, tú has hecho cuanto has podido.*   **(27–72)**

34.792 With a substantive clause, *puede* becomes a device for expressing possibility. LIN 89 *Puede que no llegue.*   (5–9)

34.793 With an indefinite pronoun as direct object, *poder* indicates power. FOM 227 *Crispín ya no podía más.*   (10–11)

34.794 A special use of this type is the expression *no poder menos de.* TRI 50 *Usted y yo no podemos menos de ser amigos.*   (10–14)

34.797 *Poder* may even be followed by an adverbial phrase. ABU 421 *Dame la mano; no puedo ya con mis huesos.*   (5–5)

34.81 querer. — Mood — Wish. FOM 229 *No quería confesarse.* **(57–627)**

34.811 Potential forms, used to express a modest wish.

34.812 Present.

34.813 querría. RUS 32 *No querría usted empeñármelos.*   (3–4)

34.814 quisiera. First person. DEB 85 *Javier — me dijo — quisiera ir contigo.* **(20–36).** Other persons. MAY 127 *No sabe qué decir; quisiera darle un poco de felicidad.*   (6–18)

34.819 *Querer* is often used elliptically without an infinitive. SIE 96 *¿ Que ni ellos ni yo somos perfectos, como tú quisieras ?*   (9–1.2)

34.82 saber. Mood — Ability, in the sense of skill; it overlaps *poder.* JIM 34 *Adela apenas sabía correr.*   **(51–150)**

34.821 Potential, present. **sabría.** IMP 196 *Me encuentro tan suya que no sabría más tiempo mandar en mí.*   (6–8)

34.83 soler. — Aspect — Customary action. REY 140 *En muchas ocasiones suele llover toda la noche.*   **(40–108)**

34.84 tener que. Mood — Necessity, arising from exterior compulsion and often implying that the justice or propriety of the compulsion is not accepted by the speaker. WAS 20 *Tengo que seguir mi camino.* **(54–346)**

34.85 terminar de. Aspect — Perfective, like *acabar de.* SON 46 *Está terminando de oír misa.*   (4–4)

34.86 tornar a. Aspect — Single repetition. JES 152 *Creyendo enternecerla, tornó a tratar de embobarla.*   (5–5)

34.87 venir a. Aspect — Effective, like *llegar a.* ROM 15 *Son simplemente obras que han venido a ser anónimas.*   (15–24)

34.88 *volver a.* Aspect — Single repetition. URU 32 *Si vuelves a saltar, tomo la escopeta y . . .* (**56–210**)

34.9 Auxiliaries used with the present participle.

34.901 Of the several auxiliary verbs used with the present participle only the colorless *estar*, with progressive force, may be said to be merely an intensifier of the present or imperfect tenses. The other verbs retain something of their basic meaning, even though they are used to indicate a special aspect of the verbal action or state.

34.91 *andar.* Iterative, but since *andar* involves no specific goal, with an added force of effort, confusion, or futility. JIM 73 *Diana, temerosa, andaba escondiéndose de uno en otro.* (**23–31**)

34.92 *continuar.* Continuative, indicating that the action or state began at an indefinite prior moment. DIV 177 *La Comisión continúa preocupándose por los preliminares de paz.* (**26–37**)

34.93 *estar.* Progressive, indicating that the action or state is considered as an uninterrupted series of parts. PIN 12 *Paco, que están alzando a Dios. Destócate siquiera.* (**52–304**)

34.94 *hallarse.* Progressive, but with an added note of fortuitiveness. SON 129 *Recuerdo que me hallaba hablando con aquella devota Marquesa.* (**6–6**)

34.951 *ir.* Iterative, but with an added feeling for some kind of goal. ART 7 *He ido siguiéndoles a ustedes palabra tras palabra.*

34.953 Progressive. OCC 259 *Allí en su celdita, va escribiendo el* Teatro crítico.

34.954 Especially when the subject of the verb is actually in motion. SEC 41 *Ibamos en la diligencia. Y en aquel momento iba yo hablando con Agripina de negocios.*

34.955 Cumulative, especially with reflexive verbs which have effective value. IBA 31 *He visto cómo la villa ha ido poco a poco ensanchándose.* (Total: **56–374**)

34.96 *quedar.* Progressive, but implying a failure to move on the part of the subject. UNA 90 *Incorporóse en la cama y quedó mirando hacia la puerta.* (**9–13**)

34.97 *quedarse.* Progressive, but like *quedar.* TRI 117 *Se quedó mirándola al través de la limpia lente.* (**9–13**)

34.98 *seguir.* Continuative. ARN 71 *El pueblo seguirá creyendo que aquí lo que faltan son políticos.* (**48–138**)

34.99 *venir.* Progressive, but with the added force of motion toward the position of the speaker. MUJ 13 *Carmina me ha visto y viene siguién-dome.*   (29–46)

34.991 It is also used, in the present and imperfect, as a substitute for the simple tense to indicate that an action or state which began at a definite prior moment is (or was) still in progress at the moment in question. RAN 15 *Desde hace medio siglo vienen anunciando esta trans-formación.*   (4–6)

34.999 In the case of other verbs of motion, such as *irse* (BRA 99 *Me voy corriendo*), (5–5), or *salir* (ORT 115 *¿ Qué salimos ganando con eso ?*), (12–14), the force of the verb of motion is so clearly the dominant idea that they cannot be considered as auxiliary verbs, but are rather main verbs, with a participle used as an appositive modifier of the subject.

VOICE

35. A statement which represents the subject of the sentence as performing an action or being in a state is called "active." A statement which represents the subject of the sentence as acted upon is called "passive." Only a transitive verb can be used in the passive. The person by whom the action is performed in the passive type of expression is called the "agent."

35.1 Active voice. The active form of expression is by far the most frequent in Spanish. RET 125 *Antonio de Mendoza fundó un asilo de niñas.* (*)

35.2 Passive voice. The passive is expressed in Spanish by the use of the auxiliary *ser* and the past participle. It always expresses an action. But Spanish can also express, through the use of *estar* and the past participle, the state which results from an action. It is possible therefore to distinguish between passive action and passive state.

35.21 Passive action, with *ser*. The passive of action is far more limited in Spanish than in English. For Spanish never expresses a progressive passive action with *ser* and the participle; in this situation it uses the active construction with an indefinite subject. The chief uses in Spanish are to express a definite, unified action (infinitive, present participle, preterite, future, perfect, pluperfect) or an iterative, habitual, or universal action (any tense, including present and imperfect indicative). The use of the different tenses is illustrated below. It will be noted that the forms most frequently used in the passive are the infinitive, the preterite and the present indicative.

Present indicative. ROM 15 *Para muchos modernos la poesía popular no es hecho por el pueblo.* (**32–61**)

Present subjunctive. BEN 59 *Y la verdad sea dicho, hace mucho tiempo que no ha dado ningún escándalo.* (5–6)

Imperfect indicative. IBA 24 *Algo peor ocurría cuando los gritos eran acompañados de pedradas.* (13–24)

Preterite. FAL 134 *El mundo fué sacado por Dios de la nada.* (**27–72**)

Future. RIC 263 *¿Quién no será consolado?* (9–18)

Perfect. SON 24 *¿Monseñor ha sido trasladado al Colegio?* (15–35)

Pluperfect. ROM 14 *Las canciones habían sido escritas por la clase noble.* (11–15)

Infinitive. IDO 115 *Para ser interpretada la vida necesita todas las formas de arte.* (**30–72**)

Present participle. BYN 76 *Carnicerito tuvo que despachar los seis toros, siendo ovacionado por el público.* (3–3)

Perfect infinitive. DEB 15 *Recorrí nuestras antiguas posesiones, ya muy subdividas por haber sido repartidas entre todos los de la familia.*
(4–4)

Other forms. WAS 8 *No se advertían señales de que el pasto hubiera sido hollado por jinetes.*   ([7]–9)

35.22 The passive is far more frequently expressed in Spanish by the use of the reflexive construction or by an indefinite third person plural; see 27.4; 27.53.   The infinitive alone also is used with passive force; 37.80.

35.23 Passive state, with *estar*.   When *estar* is used with a past participle, the statement stresses, not the action itself but the state or condition in which the subject is found as a result of the action expressed by the participle. URU 33 *El asunto está arreglado.*   **(60–540)**

35.24 The agent of passive action or state. The agent is regularly introduced either by *por* or *de*.   In general it may be said that *por* is used when the action is specific and the agent is specific; *de* is used when the action or state is universal or iterative and when the agent is indefinite or collective.   When *ser* or *estar* are expressed, *por* is the only form in common usage.

35.25 Passive action.

35.251 With *ser*.   Only *por* is common.   ART 16 *¿ Y teme usted ser vencida por ella ?*   (17–45)

35.253 With a reflexive substitute for the passive.

> *de.* UGA 8 *Los jardines se poblaban de grupos que desbordaban hasta la acera.*   (4–4)
> *por.* BYN 1 *Representábase por la compañía que dirigía Molière una obra basada en el* Quijote.   (4–4)

35.257 With an infinitive used with passive force.

> *de.* RUS 125 *¿ No ves que te has hecho aborrecer de todo el mundo ?* (5–5)
> *por.* FOM 236 *Yo no estoy dispuesto a dejarme estafar por un gandul.*
> (10–10)

35.26 Passive state.

35.261 With *estar*.   Only *por* is common.   ALT 191 *El elemento popular estaba representado por los labradores.*   (5–7)

35.264 With other verbs (*ir, quedar,* etc.) **por.**   REY 143 *Las tres canoas van dirigidas por el jefe.*   (6–6)

35.267 With a past participle used appositively.

de.   BYN 74 *Unos músicos recorren las calles, seguidos de numerosos chiquillos. De* is common after *acompañado, rodeado,* and *seguido.*
(11–17)

por.   VIG 64 *Es la primera salida del hidalgo al nuevo campo de aventuras inventado por él.*
(32–106)

35.29 Agreement of the past participle in the passive. The past participle regularly agrees with the subject.   ROM 14 *Las canciones habían sido escritas por la clase noble.*
(*)

OTHER USES OF *estar* AND *ser*

35.3 In addition to their use in the expression of passive actions and states, *estar* and *ser* are the chief copulative verbs in Spanish, performing between them the functions of English "to be." Their functions are sharply different: *estar* is used to express the notion of position or place, and with adjectival expressions to express state; *ser* is used to express identity between two substantives, and with adjectival expressions to express qualities characteristic of a class. In addition to these fundamental functions, *ser* is occasionally found in constructions which have survived from an older period of the language.

35.31 *estar.* Expressing position or place, literal or figurative.   BEN 6 *La señora Marquesa no estaba aquí.*
(60–672)

36.311 The word expressing place may be understood, so that the verb acquires the meaning of "be here," "be there," "be at home," etc. SIE 17 *Lleváis los pájaros a la estufa . . . no, a la estufa, no, que está la mona.*
(10–15)

36.313 With adverbial expressions expressing duration of time, it may be used instead of *estarse,* "to stay."   ABU 18 *Nunca está más de dos días.*
(4–5)

35.32 Expressing state with adjectival expressions. In this usage, *estar* indicates that the quality expressed by the adjective is accidental, that the quality is subject to change under other conditions.

35.321 With adjectives.   PAT 27 *El rostro de Alberto estaba sereno.*
(57–387)

35.322 With past participles, see 35.23.

35.324 With adverbs used adjectivally.   JIM 69 *¿Cómo está la mañana?*
(44–116)

35.326 With adverbial phrases used adjectivally.   PAL 16 *Aquellos carneros estaban a mis órdenes.*
(40–110)

35.328 With a noun introduced by *como*, forming an adjectival phrase. LIN 47 *Estarías como tu hermana.* (5–5)

35.33 The adjectival expression may be replaced by the personal pronoun *lo*. DEB 54 *Las campanillas de mi ventana, abiertas a la aurora, todavía lo estaban.* (9–12)

35.34 Without an adjective, the verb acquires the meaning of "to be ready." RUS 124 *Dice el tío que si está la merienda.* (9–14)

35.39 *Estar* replaced by other copulative verbs before an adjectival expression. A number of other verbs are used as copulatives before an adjective indicating state. Each of these verbs retains its own basic meaning. It will be observed that some of these verbs are also used as auxiliary verbs with the present participle; see 34.9. The commonest are indicated below in alphabetical order.

andar. MAY 12 *Anduvo ciego por ella varios meses.* (18–26)

aparecer. IDO 5 *Ahora aparecía transformado.* (11–16)

caer. FOM 230 *Cayó enferma.* (3–5)

continuar. TRI 46 *Continuaba sentada en el diván.* (9–11)

encontrarse. PEL 459 *Sanciones cortesanas se encuentran mezcladas con las castellanas.* (30–50)

hallarse. ALT 190 *Los vecinos se hallan sujetos unos a otros.* (27–73)

ir. UGA 41 *Iba acompañado de otras señoras.* (32–52)

mantenerse. UNA 85 *Se mantenía rígida.* (4–4)

mostrarse. IBA 363 *Por fin se mostró resuelto.* (11–20)

parecer. WAS 11 *Los matorrales parecían espolvoreados con azúcar.* (16–30)

permanecer. REY 103 *Permanecen sentados en la arena.* (20–51)

ponerse. PEQ 41 *Yo me ponía más triste que nunca.* (31–64)

presentarse. OCC 133 *Todo ello se presenta borroso.* (3–4)

quedar. VIG 111 *El tenorismo del conde queda vencido.* (42–122)

quedarse. BYN 90 *El grupo se queda reducido a su más mínima expresión.* (38–78)

salir. PEQ 30 *La criada salía vestida bizarramente.* With *salir* it is possible that the adjectival expression should be considered an appositive modifier of the subject. (6–7)

seguir. ART 76 *¿Qué tal sigue?* (11–19)

sentirse. DIV 343 *Todos se sienten obligados a hacer algo.* (32–76)

venir. IMP 194 *Venía muy contento.* (19–27)

verse. ROM 21 *El marinero hace votos porque su galera se vea libre de las tormentas.* (26–46)

vivir. MUJ 31 *Piénsalo, Pilar, y vive alerta.* (15–16)

volverse. RUB 199 *Desgraciadamente se volvió loco.* (10–14)

yacer. MAY 124 *El cuerpo helado yace indolente.* (4–4)

35.4 The chief function of *ser* is to establish an identity between the subject and the subjective complement; it is the linguistic version of the mathematical sign of equality (a = b). Hence its most important usage is before a substantive. It also serves to identify the subject according to its class; in this case the subjective complement, whether a noun or an adjective, is felt as adjectival and is therefore used without the article.

35.41 Expressing identity, before substantives.

35.411 Nouns. MGR 18 *Para algunas mujeres el marido es su salvador.*
(60–2982)

35.412 Pronouns. FOM 238 *Soy yo quien sostiene la casa.* (60–807)

35.413 Adjectives used as nouns. IDO 117 *Será usted siempre el bien-venido.*
(19–39)

35.415 Infinitives. JIM 53 *La mayor diversión de Anilla era vestirse de fantasma.*
(52–194)

35.417 Clauses. PAL 309 *El caso es que me voy a presentar para el grado de bachiller.*
(48–198)

35.419 The substantive may be introduced by *como.* PIN 104 *Es como el que mata a su prójimo.*
(27–67)

35.42 Similarly, *ser* is used to establish the identity of two adverbial elements, expressing cause, manner, place, time, etc.

35.421 Both elements are expressed. PAX 13 *Es ahí donde debe juz-gársele.*
(31–55)

35.423 One element may be implied in a noun or other element of the sentence. Cause. ART 8 *¿ Por qué es la pregunta ?* (7–10) Place. WAS 136 *Allí es el apeadero.* (4–4) Time. TRI 229 *La cita fué a las siete.* (5–5)

35.43 Only one element is expressed. In this case the element of identity is so slight that the verb has almost the force of "to happen."

35.431 Cause. LIN 119 *Siento que por mí retraséis la hora. — No es por mí, es por Andrés.*
(15–18)

35.432 Especially before *porque.* REY 154 *Si el rey manda en nosotros, es porque Dios le ha conferido ese poder.*
(17–25)

35.433 And in the phrase *si no (es) por.* RUS 10 *Si no fuera por nosotros, la llevarían debajo del ala.*
(8–14)

35.435 Place. With an adverb. SAS 124 *Incendio es. — ¿ Dónde será ?* (3–5) With an adverbial phrase. RAN 37 *Le conté al amigo mi experiencia. Fué en Barcelona hará cosa de unos dos años.*
(9–9)

35.437 Purpose. Adverbial phrase. UNA 154 *No es que me duelan las tripas; es para estar más a tono.* (6–6) Adverbial clause. SJQ 75 *Yo le explicaré a usted lo que hay.* — *¡ Si no lo necesito! — Es para que no se figure que se trata de nada feo.* (4–4)

35.439 Time. Adverb. NER 14 *Todas las noches nos preguntamos — ¿ Será hoy ?* (5–5) Adverbial phrase. TRI 230 *¡ Si es a las siete !* (3–3) Adverbial clause. JAN 20 *Es cuando conviene dormir juntos.* (3–3)

35.441 Other adverbial expressions. ZAM 85 *Si voy, será con el vestido que yo quiera.* In this as in other examples before an adverbial expression, *ser* is almost a vicarious verb, equivalent in this case to *iré.* (8–11)

35.45 In the same way, *ser* is used to establish identity between two objects of the verb, direct or indirect. RAN 43 *A estas mujeres es a las que se debe esta transformación.* (6–8)

35.5 Expressing class, before nouns and adjectives. In this case the adjective regularly expresses an inherent quality of the subject. It is often the equivalent of a noun in English.

35.51 Nouns. REY 93 *Yo he sido marinero.* (60–516)

35.52 Adjectives.

35.521 Logically impersonal expressions, with an infinitive or clause as the grammatical subject. PAL 307 *No me era posible prepararme bien.* For details, see 37.241, 28.211, and 29.317. ([53]–292)

35.523 With a neuter subject, summing up a previous idea. ORT 80 *Habéis leído este cantar, ¿ no es cierto ?* (20–40)

35.525 With a person or thing as subject. BEN 15 *Tú has sido muy bueno conmigo.* (60–1608)

35.53 Adjectival phrases.

35.531 Characteristic. RUB 195 *Había mil versos que eran de una completa belleza.* (48–120)

35.532 Origin or source. LUG 8 *¿ Estas botellas son también de allí ?* (20–34)

35.535 Partitive. MGR 9 *El campo es de lo mejor que se conoce.* (20–30)

35.537 Possessive. NER 63 *¡ El mar es libre ! ¡ El mar es de todos !* (30–62)

35.54 Adverbial expressions used adjectivally.

35.541 Adverbs. SJQ 83 *Yo soy así.* Especially *así, bien, cómo.* (31–84)

35.543 Adverbial expressions introduced by *para*. BEN 58 *Aquí tienes una carta. No, ésta es para mí; ésta es la tuya.* (21–30)

35.545 Other adverbial expressions. RAN 35 *Todo era en vano.* (3–3)

35.55 A substantive or adjectival expression may be replaced by the personal pronoun *lo.* ARN 43 *Somos felices, lo que cabe en el mundo, — claro está, — pero lo somos.* ([46]–170)

35.56 *Ser* **is replaced by other copulative verbs before a substantive or adjectival expression.** As with *estar*, verbs which are used to take the place of *ser* as a copulative always retain their original meaning. The commonest verbs are listed below.

> **antojársele.** SEC 10 *Eres capaz de pelearte con las que se te antojan tus rivales.* (4–4)
> **aparecer.** OCC 139 *Cada objeto aparece corpóreo, tangible.* (3–5)
> **hacerse.** JES 142 *La conversación se hizo de pronto general.* (**25–59**)
> **mostrarse.** RET 127 *Se había mostrado ingenioso moralista.* (8–8)
> **nacer.** STE 31 *La niña nació débil.* (3–3)
> **parecer.** UNA 83 *La casona parecía un arca de silenciosos recuerdos.* (**52–220**)
> **quedar.** ABC 42 *El debate quedó interrumpido por lo avanzado de la hora.* (14–18)
> **quedarse.** UNA 92 *Poco después se quedó viudo.* (5–5)
> **resultar.** SEC 62 *Una de ellas me ha resultado un poco rara.* (**24–40**)
> **salir.** ARN 28 *A lo mejor el hijo le sale a uno calandria.* (6–7)
> **semejar.** RIC 266 *El búcaro semejaba una ofrenda de cementerio.* (9–11)
> **tornarse.** VIG 65 *Lo que fué delirio atormentado se tornó tema apasionado de creador.* (3–4)
> **volverse.** SON 122 *Ahora todo se vuelven parabienes.* (13–19)

35.6 Special uses of *ser*.

35.61 To express existence, in the abstract sense. CAT 20 *Ahora puede decirse que somos y no somos.* (8–15)

35.611 To this group belong expressions in which *ser* is used without any subjective complement. IGN 50 *Te has puesto de acuerdo con éste para robarme. ¡ Pero no será!* (3–4)

35.613 Especially in the phrase *puede ser que*. MUJ 30 *Puede ser que sea vieja.* (6–7)

35.615 And *no puede ser*. RUS 70 *No le eche usted. — No puede ser.* (4–7)

35.62 In impersonal expressions of time. MAY 120 *Ya es de noche.* (**23–43**)

35.63 Followed by *de* and a noun or pronoun, with the meaning of "to become." TIG 18 *Sin mí ¿qué hubiera sido de ti?*   (20–24)

35.7 Expressing position or place, instead of *estar*. This construction is an archaicism. It has survived in the phrase from the *Ave Maria*. All the examples noted seem to be derived from this usage, for all are followed by the preposition *con*. URU 63 *El Señor es contigo.* TIG 29 *Los caramelos son conmigo.*   (6–7)

AGREEMENT OF VERBS

NUMBER

36.1 Simple. A finite verb agrees with the subject in number. JIM 80
Los niños saltaban; Diana los seguía.   (*)

36.2 Complex.

36.21 The subject is a collective noun.

36.211 Alone. The verb is normally singular. ABC 21 *Ayer se reunió la
minoría agraria.*   (43–97)

36.213 The verb may be plural, when the individuals which form the
collective are considered, rather than the group. RUS 80 *La gente de
orden no saben en qué casilla meterme.*   (7–9)

36.22 The collective is modified by a phrase with *de.*

36.221 With a singular noun. The verb is regularly singular. ORR 92
Una compañía de infantería cruzaba.   (4–4)

36.225 With a plural noun. If the verb precedes the complex subject,
it is usually singular; if it follows the subject, it is usually plural.

36.226 The verb precedes and is singular. PEL 28 *Poco a poco había ido
desapareciendo aquella generación de humanistas.*   (20–29)

36.227 The verb precedes and is plural. LUG 360 *Formaban esta milicia
la mayoría de los estudiantes.*   (5–6)

36.228 The verb follows and is singular. DIV 24 *La gran mayoría de las
acciones ha sido acaparado por las cinco grandes potencias.*   (9–12)

36.229 The verb follows and is plural. ROM 109 *Multitud de romances se
ofrecen en un estado lastimoso.*   (15–22)

36.23 If the subject is *más de* followed by a numeral, the verb is normally plural. ARN 14 *Quisieran más de cuatro sus modales.*   (4–5)

36.24 If the subject is an indefinite pronoun modified by a phrase with
de and a plural noun, the verb is normally singular. NER 45 *Uno de los
atacados poníase a cantar.*   (8–13)

36.25 Rarely a noun, not a collective, which is modified by a plural
noun will be followed by a plural verb. JAN 23 *La fuerza de las circunstancias lo obligaban a adoptar este procedimiento.*   (4–4)

36.26 Singular subject with plural predicate. If a singular subject is followed by a plural predicate noun or pronoun, the verb is normally plural. RET 12 *Lo demás son cuentos.* (21–29)

36.3 Compound subject.

36.31 Without connective. If the individual elements are considered as an integrated unit, the verb is singular. RUB 16 *El repiqueteo de los cascos, el vuelo sonoro de las ruedas parece aumentarse.* (12–16)

36.311 Especially when a series of nouns is summed up by *todo.* OCC 136 *Un árbol, un castillo, una serranía, todo adquiere un aspecto irreal.* (7–9)

36.315 If the individual elements are considered separately, the verb is plural. STE 249 *Una alegría inmensa, una suprema dicha aparecieron en el rostro de la niña.* (20–42)

36.32 Connected by *y* (*e*). The verb is normally plural, but when it precedes the subject, the singular is not uncommon.

36.321 The verb precedes and is singular. BEN 66 *¿ Dónde está tu madre y esas señoras ?* In this case, the verb may be said to agree with the first of the two subjects; the second subject is independent. (11–18)

36.322 If the verb in this position is an indefinite reflexive, it is regularly in the singular. OCC 143 *Se ha exagerado su modernidad y su cercanía a Velázquez.* (10–14)

36.323 The verb precedes and is plural. UNA 17 *De aquí surgen la tragedia y la comedia.* (50–138)

36.325 The verb follows and is singular. DEB 12 *El movimiento del vehículo y el son de los cascabeles nos sacó de aquel mutismo.* In this case, as in 36.31, the individual elements are considered as forming a unit. (3–3)

36.327 The verb follows and is plural. JES 142 *Otra joven y su hermano acudieron sin invitación.* (57–254)

36.33 Connected by *ni* (*ni* ... *ni* ...). The choice of number reflects the attitude of the speaker: the singular represents the subjects as alternatives; the plural adds them together.

36.331 The verb precedes and is singular. JIM 103 *No le queda muela ni diente.* (6–6)

36.333 The verb precedes and is plural. SEC 74 *No son conocidas ni la doblez ni el engaño.* (6–6)

36.335 The verb follows and is singular. OCC 95 *Ni usted ni nadie ha ganado el juego.* (4–4)

36.337 The verb follows and is plural. FOM 236 *Ni usted ni Ramón tenían derecho para disponer de lo ajeno.*   (8–8)

36.34 Connected by *o*. The subjects are usually considered as alternatives and the verb is in the singular; less frequently it is found in the plural.

36.341 The verb precedes and is singular. ROD 10 *No son menester bruscas rupturas que cause la pasión o el hado violento.*   (6–6)

36.345 The verb follows and is singular. MGR 42 *Su marido o su novio no se fijará más que en usted.*   (7–9)

36.347 The verb follows and is plural. IMP 23 *¿ Qué gran sacrificio o qué gran crimen le estaban reservados ?*   (4–5)

36.4 Plural subject with singular predicate. If a plural subject is followed by a singular predicate noun or pronoun, the verb is normally plural, but it is occasionally found in the singular.

36.41 The verb is singular. RUS 85 *Esperanzas no es lo mismo.*   (5–5)

36.42 The verb is plural. SIE 58 *Las cuentas son artículo de primera necesidad.*   **(40–93)**

36.5 Agreement in relative clauses. The verb of a relative clause follows the general principles of agreement; a relative pronoun used as subject retains the number of its antecedent. NER 64 *Hay músicas, y fiestas, y mujeres que pasan.*   (*)

36.51 With a complex antecedent. If the antecedent is complex, involving both a singular and a plural, the relative may agree with either antecedent. In practice, it is usually plural.

36.511 The antecedent is a collective noun modified by a phrase with a plural noun; the verb is plural. ROD 213 *Esa otra multitud de almas que quedan fuera.*   (8–8)

36.515 The antecedent is an indefinite pronoun modified by a phrase with a plural noun; the verb is plural. ZAM 111 *Es una de las manos más bonitas que han pasado por la mía.*   (7–7)

36.52 With a compound antecedent. The verb is usually plural, less frequently singular.

36.521 The verb is singular. ORT 88 *El aliento de optimismo y la impresión de rápido mejoramiento que comienza a ganar las clases superiores.* Cf. 36.325.   (5–5)

36.523 The verb is plural. PEL 249 *La ingeniosidad y la soltura de mano que contrastan con el penoso esfuerzo.*   (12–14)

PERSON

36.6 A finite verb agrees with the subject in person. IGN 40 *Tú no sabes las cosas que ha hecho esa mujer.* (*)

36.61 If the subject is *usted* (*ustedes*), or other substitute for the pronoun of the second person, the verb is regularly in the third person. RAN 29 *¿ Qué dice usted, señora ?* (*)

36.62 Compound subject. If one of two or more subjects is of the first person, the verb is first person plural. Combinations of the second and third person are rare.

36.621 First and second person. LLA 63 *Seamos amigos tú y yo.* (9–9)

36.625 First and third person. SAS 41 *Mi mujer y yo nos adoramos.* (10–26)

36.629 Second and third person. Connected by *ni*, the verb is in the third singular. JOA 16 *Yo no necesito que tú ni nadie toque mis cosas.* (3–3)

36.63 Complex subject. If a personal pronoun is used in a phrase with *de* to modify an indefinite pronoun, the verb normally agrees with the indefinite pronoun. REY 148 *Por la noche uno de nosotros las echa a pique.* (4–4)

36.7 Agreement with a personal pronoun in the predicate. When a personal pronoun is used as subjective complement of the verb *ser* (Eng. ' it is I (me),' Fr. ' c'est moi '), the verb agrees with the pronoun, and is not used impersonally. ZAM 69 *¡ Ah, eres tú!* (25–67)

36.71 If a personal pronoun used as subject of the verb *ser* has a numeral as a subjective complement, the verb agrees with the pronoun and is not replaced by a phrase with *hay* (Eng. ' there were three of us '). TIG 5 *Agora que sois dos.* (3–3)

36.8 When an unexpressed pronoun of the first or second person is modified by a noun or pronoun, the regular agreement is preserved.

36.81 With a noun in apposition. ART 18 *Los artistas somos francamente insoportables.* (22–39)

36.82 With an indefinite pronoun.

　　ambos. PAL 304 *Ambos disparamos.* (3–4)
　　los dos. LIN 121 *No estará demás que os corrijáis las dos.* (14–23)
　　todos. UGA 49 *Todos sabemos dónde están las moscas.* (29–53)

36.85 Agreement in relative clauses. A relative pronoun used as subject retains the person of its antecedent and the verb agrees with the antecedent in person.

36.851 In attributive clauses.   RIC 272 *Léelos tú, que los entiendes mejor.*
(28–78)

36.855 The antecedent may be implied in a word used in apostrophe.
PAL 135 *Padre nuestro, que estás en los cielos.* (3–5)

36.86 In appositional clauses, with a substantive relative.   ORT 138
Todos los que escribimos nos damos clara cuenta de eso. (8–10)

36.87 In predicate clauses, with a substantive relative. In this situation, agreement with the relative pronoun is somewhat more frequent than agreement with the personal pronoun.

36.871 The verb agrees with the personal pronoun.   LIN 62 *Soy el que te enojo.* (11–14)

36.875 The verb agrees with the relative.   TIG 8 *Eres tú quien habla.* Especially common when the main verb is negative. (14–24)

36.88 If a relative clause modifies a noun which is the subjective complement of a personal pronoun, the verb is normally in agreement with the personal pronoun.   IBA 33 *Somos peregrinos que vamos caminando.*
(7–10)

IMPERSONAL VERBS

36.9 An impersonal verb, sometimes called a "unipersonal verb," is a verb which has no subject, either expressed or implied. Its finite forms are always third person singular. A number of verbs which are logically impersonal, such as *convenir, ser preciso*, etc., are grammatically personal since they have an infinitive or a clause as subject; they are therefore not included here but will be found in the discussion of the infinite and the subjunctive.

36.91 Expressions of time.

36.911 *haber.*   NER 45 *A Francia fué llevado no ha mucho un grupo de negros.* (4–4)

36.913 *hacer.*

36.914 Present.   DEB 53 *Hace una semana resbaló en la acera.* (**43–106**)

36.915 Imperfect.   JES 230 *Se habló de un cofrecillo llegado hacía tres días.*
(4–6)

36.916 Future. PAX 331 *Mañana, hará un año justo, les manifesté lo que iba a hacer.* (3–4)

For the use of *hacer* with the present and imperfect indicative, see also 32.12; 32.31.

36.919 *ser.* WAS 20 *Ya es tarde.* (23–43)

36.92 Expressions of weather and other natural phenomena. ART 6 *Hace calor.* ([23]–41)

The commonest verbs in this class are: *amanecer* (6–7), *hacer* (13–17), and *llover* (7–11).

36.93 Other impersonal verbs.

36.931 *bastar.* OCC 130 *Bastaría con colocar los cuadros en orden.* (5–7)

36.933 *dar.* ZAM 101 *Le da por reñir.* (6–7)

36.935 *haber.* VIG 63 *En esta obra hay una nota muy original.* (60–930)

36.937 *ir.* TRI 220 *Hola, Pepe, ¿ cómo va?* (5–5)

36.938 *tratarse.* IDO 107 *No se trata de bailar.* (33–74)

36.94 If an impersonal verb is used with an auxiliary verb, the auxiliary is in the third person singular.

36.941 Infinitive. ORT 123 *No puede haber otra situación.* (20–26)

THE INFINITIVE

37.1 The infinitive is a verbal substantive, preserving the functions of both substantive and verb. It may lose its verbal force and become a common noun: *el deber, el poder,* etc. We are here concerned only with those uses which reveal its dual function.

THE INFINITIVE USED AS A VERBAL NOUN, WITH ADJECTIVAL MODIFIERS

37.11 The infinitive may be used as an abstract verbal noun and be modified like other nouns. The adjectival modifier may be:

37.111 The definite article. REY 107 *Se oye a lo lejos el sonar de los truenos.* **(50–198)**

37.112 The indefinite article. PAT 15 *Fué un despertar lento y doloroso.* (19–33)

37.113 An indefinite adjective. JOA 54 *Con tanto charlar y dar vueltas me has mareado.* (10–12)

37.114 A demonstrative adjective. VIG 62 *Pero no es en ese prestarse frases en lo que estriba.* **(24–60)**

37.115 A possessive adjective. ORT 119 *Nada es tan diferente de mi ver como lo visto; de mi oír, como lo oído.* (19–37)

37.116 An interrogative adjective. PAL 113 *Y con esto ¡qué reír, qué gritar, qué bromear!* (5–8)

37.117 A qualifying adjective. PEQ 38 *A ella le debo esta preocupación por el interminable sucederse de las cosas.* **(35–84)**

37.118 An adjectival phrase.

    (a) Subjective. JIM 117 *Se oía el duro herir de los cascos en la piedra.* **(31–79)**
    (b) Objective. UNA 19 *Siente ese querer desesperado de la unión.* (3–3)

37.119 Relative clause. VIG 40 *Preguntándose si la guerra es aquel incesante andar que le obligan a llevar.* (3–3)

37.12 The infinitive thus modified by an adjective may at the same time reveal its verbal function by the use of objects, complements, or adverbial modifiers.

37.121 With an object, direct or indirect. URU 64 *¿ Qué saben los do-tores ? . . . Mucho tomar el pulso.* (40–100)

37.123 With a subjective complement. ARN 50 *Le tengo un cariño más infinito que a mi tía, a la que debo el ser zapatero.* (6–6)

37.125 With an adverb. FOM 230 *Se reprochaba a menudo el no querer bastante a su hijo.* (13–19)

37.127 With an adverbial phrase. IDO 107 *Creía humillante el ir en busca de una reconciliación.* (24–44)

37.13 The infinitive thus used as a noun may be used in any function in the sentence in which a substantive is used: as subject, object, or subjective complement of a verb, in apposition with a noun or pronoun, and in elliptical expressions after *que, como,* etc. UGA 42 *Nada era más encantador que aquel rodar de vehículos.* (*)

37.135 Similarly after prepositions. MAY 113 *Se afana en volver a su loco discurrir.* (37–110)

37.136 Especially frequent is its use after *a,* in phrases with temporal value. BEN 12 *Al volver a Moraleda, me encontraré en casa con cuatro pequeños.* (57–516)

For the use of *al* + infinitive with expressed subject, see 37.945.

WITHOUT ADJECTIVAL MODIFIERS

37.2 The infinitive, without adjectival modification, is used in a variety of constructions in which it has the force of a complement to a verb or verbal locution. It may be used alone or may be introduced by a preposition.

WITHOUT A PREPOSITION

37.21 As subject of a verb. The infinitive is used as grammatical subject of a number of verbs and verbal locutions which are logically impersonal and which in English are introduced by " it." These verbs fall into two groups: copulative verbs (*ser, estar, parecer*) used with a subjective complement, and other verbs, transitive, intransitive, and reflexive, used as logically impersonal. In the second group, the infinitive is sometimes strongly verbal, almost a complement of the verb of which it is the subject; in other cases it is merely a verbal substantive and might be replaced by a verbal noun or postverbal noun. But the distinction between the two uses is so difficult to establish on objective grounds that it has seemed preferable to group all such verbs together, with the exception of the reflexive verbs.

37.211 With most of the verbal expressions in this class, the infinitive may be replaced by an annunciative clause in the subjunctive. If the subordinate verb has a noun subject, the subjunctive construction is the regular one; if it has a pronoun subject, both infinitive and subjunctive are found, the subject appearing as an indirect object with the main verb. This latter construction is particularly common with *ser* + an adjective. If the subject of the subordinate verb is indefinite, the infinitive is the regular construction.

37.22 Subject of *ser* + a complement.

37.221 The complement is a noun, usually abstract. LIN 46 *Es mérito no comprenderlo.*   ([39]–111)

The most frequent noun is *menester* (8–12).

37.225 The complement is an infinitive. UNA 18 *Creer es crear.* (18–29)

37.231 The complement is the personal object pronoun, *lo*, replacing a noun. ART 77 *¿ Qué crimen ha cometido usted ? ¿ Lo es admitir una invitación ?*   (3–3)

37.235 The complement is a relative pronoun. BEN 15 *Tú no sabes lo que es pasar de los mimos de nuestros padres a la indiferencia de los extraños.*
(6–8)

37.241 The complement is an adjective. PAL 307 *No me era posible prepararme bien.*   ([46]–172)

The commonest adjectives are: *difícil* (15–19), *fácil* (12–16), *imposible* (18–20), *inútil* (5–5), *mejor* (7–8), *necesario* (8–10), *posible* (12–18), *preciso* (18–23).

37.243 The complement is a past participle and the construction is a true passive. SON 41 *Pensé que algún día seríame dado regir a la Cristiandad.*   (4–6)

37.245 The complement is an adjectival phrase. LLA 39 *De sabios es mudar de consejo* (a *refrán*).   (3–3)

37.25 Subject of *estar* + a complement.

37.257 The complement is an adjectival phrase. RUB 196 *De más está decir que las ideas son de una estética singular.*   (3–3)

37.26 Subject of *parecer* + a complement.

37.261 The complement is an adjective. URU 67 *¿ Te parece más lindo quedarte soltera ?*   (7–9)

37.265 The complement is an adverb, used adjectivally. TRI 216 *Le parecía mejor debutar con una comedia.*   (3–3)

37.27 Subject of intransitive and transitive verbs. PEQ 33 *Le gustaba plantar muchos árboles.* ([52]–261)

The commonest verbs are: *bastar* (12–18), *caber* (6–6), *convenir* (18–25), *costar* (*trabajo,* etc.) (18–25), *dar* (*pena,* etc.) (10–13), *faltar* (5–5), *gustar* (**23–45**), *hacer* (*daño,* etc.) (8–12), *importar* (5–8), *parecer* (" to seem best, etc.") (12–17), *sorprender* (5–5), *tocar* (6–11), *valer* (5–7).

37.28 Subject of reflexive verbs.

37.281 The reflexive is a substitute for the passive. SJQ 132 *Soy la esposa de este pendón de viejo. — Se prohibe insultar.* (16–26)

37.285 The reflexive is indefinite. CAT 22 *Se le permitió regresar a sus lares.* (16–27)

37.31 As object of a verb. The most frequent use of the infinitive as object of a verb is as a complement to another verb. The subject of the infinitive may be identical with that of the main verb, or different from that of the main verb. Less frequently it is found as object of another verb, without complementary force.

37.32 The subject of the infinitive is identical with the subject of the main verb. Most of the verbs which are followed by a complementary verb, without a preposition, are transitive verbs and in these cases the infinitive is both grammatically and logically the direct object of the main verb. The frequency of this construction has attracted to the same use other verbs which are intransitive and in this case the infinitive cannot properly be called an object. Both classes are, however, included in this section, since it is impossible to establish any logical distinction between them. SIE 19 *No necesitas darme cuentas.* ([60]–835)

The commonest verbs in this class are: *acostumbrar* (5–6), *anhelar* (5–5), *ansiar* (5–6), *conseguir* (18–24), *creer* (**30–54**), *decidir* (12–12), *decir* (6–8), *desear* (**37–65**), *dignarse* (8–10), *esperar* (14–17), *fingir* (8–8), *intentar* (**22–38**), *lograr* (**23–40**), *merecer* (5–8), *necesitar* (**32–70**), *parecer* (**44–132**), *pensar* (**26–56**), *preferir* (17–23), *pretender* (**20–32**), *procurar* (**28–44**), *prometer* (15–24), *proponerse* (10–15), *resolver* (6–7), *sentir* (8–9), *temer* (15–20).

The modal and aspect verbs *deber, osar* (6–8), *poder, querer* (**57–627**), *saber* (**51–150**), and *soler* (**40–103**), are discussed under Auxiliaries.

37.34 The subject of the infinitive is different from that of the subject of the main verb.

37.341 With verbs of causation, command, permission, etc. The logical subject of the infinitive may be either a noun or a pronoun. While it is impossible to distinguish in the majority of cases whether the Spaniard of to-day feels this subject to be the direct or the indirect object of the main verb, because of the identity of form for both direct and indirect object, it seems probable that it is considered as a direct object. (See, for further discussion, 2.66). After most of the verbs in this class an object clause in the subjunctive is also found (see 29.341). After *dejar, hacer,* and *mandar* the infinitive predominates; after *impedir* and *permitir* usage is about equally divided; after *aconsejar* and *consentir* the subjunctive is the only form commonly used. UGA 19 *Esta alusión no hizo perder a Luisito su tranquilidad.* ([60]–685)

The commonest verbs in this class are: *dejar* (**52–186**), *hacer* (**60–414**), *impedir* (9–13), *mandar* (18–30), *permitir* (18–34).

37.345 With verbs of sense perception. The use of the infinitive after verbs of sense perception is parallel to that after verbs of causation, etc. The logical subject of the infinitive is generally expressed as the direct object of the main verb. After verbs in this class the present participle is also used, modifying the direct object of the verb. The participial construction is more vividly descriptive, (see 38.22). On the indefinite or passive force of the infinitive in this and the preceding section, see 37.80. TRI 225 *La oyó contestarle.* ([54]–296)

The commonest verbs in this class are: *mirar* (6–7), *oír* (**34–65**), *sentir* (19–32), *ver* (**54–188**).

37.35 The infinitive is used as direct object, without complementary force. It is often in this case modified by an objective complement. ROM 14 *Creía necesario advertir que las canciones populares no eran obras impersonales.* (12–15)

37.41 As subjective complement. BYN 56 *La cuestión es pasar el rato.* (**52–184**)

37.43 In apposition with a noun or pronoun. RIC 269 *Sólo una cosa es necesaria: poseer a Dios.* (**32–74**)

IN ELLIPTICAL CONSTRUCTIONS

37.45 The infinitive, without a preposition, is used in a number of constructions without a verb.

37.451 After adversative conjunctions, following a negative. OCC 199 *No hay ya sino vivir de la mejor manera posible.* (6–6)

37.453 Especially in the phrase *no hacer sino.* SAS 9 *Carlos no hace sino seguir a su prima.* (7–10)

37.455 And *no hacer más que.* ARN 52 *Mi mujer no hacía más que hacerme señales.* (10–18)

37.46 After comparative conjunctions.

37.461 como. IDO 30 *Nada le parecía tan glorioso como encadenar a los adversarios.* (9–10)

37.463 de (only in the idiom *no poder menos de*). SIE 90 *Pasa, como no podía menos de pasar.* (9–11)

37.465 que. After a comparative adjective or adverb. PEL 33 *¿Qué cosa puede haber mejor que mostrarnos agradecidos?* **(28–63)**

37.466 After antes. LIN 106 *Habías matado a tu marido antes que tolerar esas ofensas.* (9–11)

37.468 After otro. IBA 151 *No puedo hacer otra cosa que rezar por la salud de su alma.* (5–8)

37.47 After interrogatives and relatives.

37.48 After pronouns.

37.481 Interrogatives. **qué.** ZAM 99 *No sé qué hacer.* (14–17)

37.482 After a preposition. BEN 34 *Ya sabemos a qué atenernos.* (3–4)

37.483 Relatives, with antecedent expressed. **que.** IMP 15 *Nada nos queda que hacer aquí.* **(32–59)**

37.484 After a preposition.

> **que.** FAL 162 *No encontraba la sonrisa con que detener al hombre miedoso.* (8–10)
> **quien.** SIE 44 *Es mucho más cómodo tener un marido a quien pedírselo.* (4–4)

37.485 Relatives, without expressed antecedent. **que.** JAN 14 *No halló que decirle.* (9–9)

37.486 After a preposition. **que.** RUS 70 *Tiene con que vivir.* (11–14)

37.49 After adverbs.

37.491 Interrogatives.

> **cómo.** DEB 94 *No sé cómo demostrárselo.* (17–17)
> **dónde.** TIG 27 *No sabe dónde encontrar a usted.* (3–3)
> **si.** SJQ 80 *No sé si atribuirlo a eso o a la vulgaridad de mi ser.* (8–11)

37.493 Relatives, with antecedent expressed. **donde.** JES 227 *Se le veía paseando por la calle Real en busca de un establo donde alquilar caballos.* (7–7)

37.5 The infinitive is used as object of a preposition in adjectival and adverbial phrases. But its use has also been extended to a large number of cases in which the adverbial phrase has become a mere complement of another verb. In these cases, the original force of the preposition has often been lost and it has become a sort of sign of the infinitive like English "to." It is often difficult to determine whether a prepositional phrase with the infinitive should be construed as the complement to a verb or verbal locution, as an adjectival modifier of the noun in a verbal locution, or as an adverbial phrase, modifying the verb. In general, the phrase is considered a complement only when it is essential to complete the meaning of another verb; it is classed as modifying a noun only when it may be so used in the absence of a verbal locution. Other uses are considered adverbial. The subject of the infinitive after a preposition is normally identical with that of the main verb, but it may be different from the main subject and it may be indefinite.

37.54 As complement to a verb. LLA 73 *¿ No os atrevéis a mirarme?* ([60]-2036)

The commonest verbs in this class are: *acabar de* (" to finish ") (**21–33**), *acabar por* (**24–34**), *acercarse a* (5–5), *acertar a* (15–21), *acordarse de* (7–9), *acostumbrarse a* (6–10), *acudir a* (6–6), *alcanzar a* (9–13), *alegrarse de* (5–6), *andar a* (6–7), *aprender a* (7–13), *apresurarse a* (6–8), *aspirar a* (6–8), *atreverse a* (**38–76**), *atreverse de* (5–7), *bajar a* (5–5), *bastar para* (15–16), *cansarse de* (6–7), *cesar de* (11–14), *comenzar a* (**31–85**), *concluir de* (6–9), *concluir por* (5–7), *consistir en* (13–19), *contentarse con* (7–13), *contribuir a* (8–11), *correr a* (7–9), *decidirse a* (11–16), *dedicarse a* (5–11), *dejar de* (**42–90**), *disponerse a* (15–21), *echar a* (8–16), *echarse a* (15–21), *empeñarse en* (14–22), *empezar a* (**46–162**), *empezar por* (8–8), *encargarse de* (10–13), *entrar a* (13–19), *gustar de* (6–9), *ir a* (of actual motion) (**54–318**), *irse a* (16–28), *limitarse a* (12–14), *luchar por* (6–9), *llegar a* (of actual motion) (8–9), *negarse a* (13–15), *pasar a* (6–6), *pensar en* (14–19), *ponerse a* (**31–60**), *prepararse a* (6–7), *quedar en* (8–8), *quedarse a* (5–6), *reducirse a* (5–8), *resistirse a* (5–5), *renunciar a* (6–6), *romper a* (7–7), *salir a* (15–21), *servir para* (15–25), *tardar en* (**22–28**) *tender a* (6–9), *tratar de* (**28–60**), *venir a* (of actual motion) (**51–171**).

37.56 As complement, with a different subject.

37.561 The subject is expressed. ABU 199 *Me obligará a decirlo segunda vez.* ([47]-181)

The commonest verbs are: *ayudar a* (13–14), *enseñar a* (7–9), *invitar a* (6–9), *llevar a* (9–12), *obligar a* (**30–57**).

37.565 The subject is indefinite. This construction is found only with the preposition *a;* the infinitive is practically an abstract noun. UGA 34 *Sofía le había dado a entender que compartía su esperanza.* ([22]–33)

The two common expressions are: *dar a* (14–22) and *echar a* (5–6).

37.583 As subjective complement. Only in expressions of the type of *es de notar,* in which the prepositional phrase is adjectival, with indefinite or passive force. IMP 73 *No era de esperar que la siguiese.* (16–19)

37.61 In elliptical constructions.

37.611 After adversative conjunctions, following a negative. CAT 5 *No he venido aquí a tocar crestas, sino a cumplir con los deberes de mi ministerio.* (4–4)

37.616 After comparative conjunctions. ***que.*** JAN 23 *Te preocupas más de tocar el piano que de hablar conmigo.* (5–6)

37.62 In adjectival phrases, modifying a noun or pronoun. The preposition most frequently used is *de,* but other prepositions are found after nouns which have a certain verbal force.

37.63 With *de.* The prepositional phrase is usually of the objective or of the appositive type. JAN 101 *Le inquietaba el deseo de hacer algo.* ([60]–750)

The commonest nouns and pronouns after which this construction occurs are: *ansia(s)* (7–7), *arte* (6–7), *cosa* (9–10), *costumbre* (11–13), *deseo(s)* (**24**–**45**), *el (la, los, las)* (18–25), *esperanza(s)* (6–6), *esto (eso, aquello)* (8–9), *favor* (12–21), *gana(s)* (**20**–**39**), *gusto* (7–9), *honor* (6–11), *hora(s)* (15–19), *manera* (13–25), *medio* (5–5), *miedo* (7–12), *modo* (18–25), *momento* (9–10), *necesidad* (16–20), *ocasión* (7–9), *orden* (7–9), *peligro* (5–5), *pena* (7–7), *placer* (5–6), *posibilidad* (7–7), *propósito* (16–20), *punto* (8–10), *tiempo* (15–19), *valor* (5–5).

37.641 With *a.* JOA 19 *Yo tengo derecho a ponerme esos zapatos.* ([21]–35)

The only noun commonly followed by *a* is *derecho* (15–23).

37.643 With *con.* RUS 19 *¡Cuidado con echar un borrón!* (3–3)

37.645 With *en.* SJQ 87 *Mi empeño en salir era porque el campo está delicioso.* ([7]–10)

The only noun commonly followed by *en* is *empeño* (5–5).

37.647 With *para.* SAS 51 *Me siento con fuerzas para matar a quien quiera quitármela.* ([39]–108)

The nouns most commonly followed by *para* are: *fuerza(s)* (5–6), *motivo* (8–10), *permiso* (5–7).

37.648 With *por.* NER 37 *Recordaba las luchas del pueblo por recoger las buenas onzas de oro.* ([11]–16)

37.65 In adverbial phrases.

37.66 Modifying an adjective. The preposition most frequently found is *de*, but other prepositions occur.

37.67 With *de*. IGN 16 *Soy capaz de ponerme enfermo.*   ([46]–170)

The commonest adjectives followed by *de* are: *capaz* (**40–77**), *deseoso* (7–10), *difícil* (7–8), *digno* (6–8), *fácil* (5–5), *incapaz* (8–16).

37.681 With *a*. MUJ 34 *Es usted propenso a enamorarse.*   ([13]–20)

37.687 With *para*. SEC 47 *Carecemos de los medios necesarios para huir.*   ([21]–36)

The only adjective commonly followed by *para* is *necesario* (5–5).

37.688 With *por*. RIC 21 *Montó de nuevo a caballo, impaciente por llegar a Llanes.*   (3–3)

37.69 Modifying a past participle. The preposition most frequently found is *a*.

37.691 With *a*. ZUN 42 *Se mostró dispuesto a complacerme.*   ([37]–96)

The participles most frequently followed by *a* are: *acostumbrado* (7–7), *decidido* (5–5), *dispuesto* (18–29), *obligado* (15–22).

37.694 With *de*. BRA 160 *Estaba tentado de llamaros.*   ([18]–28)

37.695 With *en*. JES 237 *Parecía muy preocupada en arreglar la banda.*   ([10]–14)

The only participle commonly followed by *en* is *empeñado* (5–6).

37.697 With *para*. ABC 34 *Sólo el señor Azaña estaba capacitado para contestar la pregunta.*   (6–6)

37.7 Modifying a verb. The infinitive with a preposition is used in a wide variety of adverbial phrases to modify a verb. The logical subject of the infinitive is usually identical with the subject of the main verb, but it is often indefinite, so that the infinitive becomes almost a substantive. Uses of the infinitive after a preposition with expressed subject are discussed in 37.861. In the present outline, the functions of the more common prepositions, *a*, *con*, *de*, *en*, *para*, and *por* are discussed first, followed by lists of the other prepositions, simple and compound.

37.71 With *a*.

37.711 Expressing condition. The subject is often indefinite. ROM 97 *A haberlo conocido, de seguro lo hubiera citado.*   (12–19)

37.715 Expressing purpose. Especially after verbs of motion, when the goal is indicated by an expression of place.　MAY 121　*En vano asoman a llamarle.*　　　　　　　　　　　　　　　　　　　　　　　　**(39–78)**

37.716 Expressing unfulfilled state.　RAN 22　*Tengo un asunto urgente a ventilar con un amigo.*　　　　　　　　　　　　　　　　　　**(6–9)**

37.718 As indirect object.　SEC 9　*Dedique usted las venticuatro horas del día a mirarse en los ojos de una mujer.*　　　　　　　　**(7–11)**

37.719 In idiomatic phrases, with the infinitive modified by an adjective, such as *a poco andar, a más correr*, etc.　RUS 75　*La hace acostarse a medio cenar.*　　　　　　　　　　　　　　　　　　　　　　　　**(7–7)**

37.72 With *con*.

37.723 Expressing concession.　PEL 234　*Ninguno de los dantistas castellanos, con haber sido tantos, intentaron la aclimatación del terceto.*　　**(6–7)**

37.725 Expressing condition.　SEC 72　*Con mirarla na má, la alberca rebosa.*　　　　　　　　　　　　　　　　　　　　　　　　**(3–3)**

37.727 Expressing means.　URU 20　*Pero vos con defender al chinito ese lo estás echando a perder.*　　　　　　　　　　　　　　　**(11–15)**

37.728 Especially after impersonal expressions of sufficiency or excess (*bastar, sobrar*).　TIG 12　*A la muger le basta con querer a un hombre para ser feliz.*　　　　　　　　　　　　　　　　　　　　　　**(6–7)**

37.73 With *de*.

37.731 Expressing cause.　SIE 55　*Ya estoy hasta la coronilla de pagarle trampas.*　　　　　　　　　　　　　　　　　　　　　　　**(9–11)**

37.733 Expressing condition.　ALT 12　*De no sorprenderle la muerte, hubiera contraído matrimonio con la infanta.*　　　　　**(16–19)**

37.735 Expressing purpose, with a noun.　ABC 48　*Máquinas de escribir. Venta exclusiva.*　　　　　　　　　　　　　　　　　　**(10–11)**

37.736 In idiomatic phrases of the type of *dar de comer*, originally expressing purpose.　PAL 12　*Le daremos de cenar.*　　　　**(9–14)**

37.737 After *ser*, of the type of *es de notar*, originally purpose.　IBA 370　*Su muerte era de esperar.*　　　　　　　　　　　　　**(16–19)**
　　See also 37.583.

37.739 After verbs followed by *de*, the infinitive having almost substantival force.　PIN 89　*¿Habéis decidido quitarme las tierras? — ¿Quién habla de quitar?*　　　　　　　　　　　　　　　　　　**(8–9)**

37.74 With *en*.

37.743 Expressing the field of reference within which the action or state of the main verb operates.   VIG 59 *Bien hizo en no conformarse con la opinión ajena.*   **(25–44)**

37.75 With *para*.

37.752 Expressing purpose.   SON 19 *El Niño tendía los brazos para alcanzar un pez.*   **(60–930)**

37.753 Especially after expressions of excess.   UGA 10 *Se sentían demasiado jóvenes para advertir el obstáculo.*   **(16–23)**

37.754 The excess may be implied by *muy*.   LIN 98 *La tuya es cuestión muy importante para tratarla a la ligera.*   **(4–6)**

37.755 After expressions of lack.   IBA 160 *Le faltaba poco para llorar.*
                                                                    (10–26)

37.756 After expressions of sufficiency.   IMP 191 *Lo había hecho con la suficiente habilidad para no ofender a Guillermo.*   **(20–45)**

37.757 The sufficiency may be implied.   REY 109 *Tenemos tiempo para hacer las cosas despacio.*   **(11–20)**

37.758 Even after verbs of motion, when the goal or destination is otherwise indicated.   DEB 3 *Me consolaba cuando a ella iba para querellarme.*   **(20–45)**

37.759 Expressing the succeeding stage in a sequence and equivalent to a coordinated clause.   IDO 6 *A una vuelta del camino desaparecieron el mar, la playa, y los cocoteros, para minutos más tarde reaparecer.*   **(24–43)**

37.76 With *por*.

37.761 Expressing cause.   ORT 136 *Baroja es el menos conocido, tal vez por ser el que mayor actividad exige a sus lectores.*   **(42–112)**

37.763 Expressing exchange ("in return for").   ZAM 69 *No sé qué daría por no estar sola.*   **(6–12)**

37.765 Expressing purpose, but conveying also an implication of the reasons which motivate the action or state of the infinitive.   It is especially common with expressions which convey the notion of effort.   ART 12 *Muchos aparentan ser viciosos por no morirse de amargura.* **(33–109)**

37.766 In the idiom *le da por* (*hacerlo*).   ZAM 101 *Le da por reñir.* (3–3)

37.768 Expressing unfulfilled state.   ROD 15 *Las cosas que están por venir.*
                                                                    (4–4)

37.77 With other simple prepositions.

> *hasta.*   JIM 85 *Rozaba su cabezota contra mi corazón, dándome las gracias hasta lastimarme el pecho.*   **(40–76)**
>
> *pa* (in all the uses of *para*).   URU 20 *Es muy linda la mañanita pa ponerle cara fea.*   Colloquial.   **(9–75)**
>
> *sin.*   BEN 35 *Me dejó sin decir palabra.*   **(60–579)**

37.78 With compound prepositions.   PEQ 29 *Era por la noche después de cenar.*   **([45]–159)**

   The commonest of these compound prepositions used with the infinitive are: *a fin de* (12–24), *a fuerza de* (5–7), *a pesar de* (13–18), *a punto de* (16–21), *antes de* (**46–82**), *después de* (with present infinitive) (**32–62**), *despué* *de* (with perfect infinitive) (**22–30**), *en lugar de* (7–8), *en vez de* (17–23), *lejos de* (9–13), *luego de* (6–6).

SEPARATED FROM THE PREPOSITION

37.79 The infinitive normally follows immediately the preposition on which it depends; the subject, object, and modifiers are placed after the infinitive.   RUS 123 *Acaba por encariñarse con ella.*   (*)

37.791 The negative *no*, however, is always placed between the preposition and the infinitive.   PAL 305 *Tuve la flaqueza de no insistir.*
      (50–155)

37.795 Rarely an adverb intervenes.   BYN 32 *No estaba ya sólo nuestro Banco nacional, o por mejor decir, real.*   The use is largely limited to fixed phrases, like that cited or like *a bien morir.*   (8–12)

37.796 Similarly an adverbial phrase may intervene, especially after *para* and *sin*.   JES 37 *Sin al cabo decidirse por ninguno, se había invertido más de un mes.*   (5–6)

37.799 An expressed subject of the infinitive normally follows the infinitive, see 37.98. But rarely, when the subject is a personal pronoun, it is placed between the preposition and the infinitive.   IDO 214 *Los dos habían penetrado, sin ella explicarse cómo, en un callejón.*   (3–4)

THE INFINITIVE WITH PASSIVE OR INDEFINITE FORCE

37.80 In a number of the constructions of the infinitive, both without and with a preposition, the infinitive has passive force. While it is probable that originally the infinitive was active with an indefinite subject, the passive value is now clearly revealed by the frequent use of phrases indicating the agent or means of the action.

37.801 After verbs of causation, etc. without a preposition. SON 50 *Dejó oír su voz cascada.* **(46–80)**

37.802 After verbs of sense perception, without a preposition. PEQ 156 *Yo oía contar muchas veces que un vecino estaba enfermo.* (5–7)

37.804 After *a.* TRI 231 *Cuestión a resolver por Gabrielito en la soledad de su fonda.* (7–8)

37.805 After *de* in the construction *es de (notar).* ROM 212 *Es de desear que la música sea recogida.* (15–19)

37.808 After *sin.* SIE 16 *Están sin desempaquetar unos muñecos japoneses que he traído para el cotillón.* (8–10)

37.809 The simple infinitive is sometimes replaced in these situations by the reflexive infinitive used with passive force. PEL 27 *Es página histórica digna de citarse.* (6–17)

THE INFINITIVE USED INSTEAD OF A FINITE VERB IN MAIN CLAUSES

37.81 The infinitive is frequently used in exclamatory utterance to present the verbal notion, instead of expressing that notion in a finite form. From simple exclamation, expressing various tones of surprise, indignation, and the like, it may pass into an instrument for expressing command. It is found alone and also introduced by a preposition. In both cases it may be used without expressed subject or with subject expressed.

37.82 Without a preposition.

37.821 In exclamations, without expressed subject. PIN 24 *¿ Y qué vais a hacer ? — ¡ Morirnos de hambre!* **(45–155)**

37.823 Often after an interrogative adverb. ORT 107 *¿ A qué vivir ?*
(24–48)

37.826 In exclamations, with subject expressed. SEC 30 *Vamos, tú no estás bueno de la cabeza. ¡ Hacerme yo cómplice!* (11–15)

37.828 In commands. ART 6 *¡ Anda con Dios, hombre! . . . y descansar.* See also 4.492. (10–20)

37.831 After *a,* expressing a command. UNA 91 *¡ Ahora, Tristán, a criar el marqués!* **(20–41)**

37.833 After *a,* with hortatory force, especially in the phrase *¡ a ver!* IMP 13 *Dijimos ayer: « Basta de melancolía. ¡ A vivir! »* **(26–81)**

37.838 After *sin*, instead of finite verb in the negative. BRA 13 *¡ La una, y tu padre sin venir!* (4–4)

37.85 One of the striking features of Spanish syntax is its use of the infinitive with an expressed or implied subject different from that of the main verb to take the place of a subordinate clause with a finite verb. While the older usage of such infinitive-clauses instead of an annunciative clause introduced by *que* has almost disappeared, its use in adjectival and adverbial clauses after a preposition is still common. The infinitive-clause is in this case a substantive, used as object of the preposition, and like other substantives (nouns, adjectives, infinitives, *que*-clauses), it may be modified by the definite article. The subject of the infinitive may be an expressed noun or personal subject pronoun; it may be implied by the context; it may be indefinite, and in this case the construction closely approaches certain adverbial uses of the simple infinitive; finally the infinitive may be impersonal. All of the cases discussed in the following paragraphs are found after a preposition.

37.86 Without the definite article.

37.861 The subject is expressed. PAT 209 *Después de haber marchado tú, doña Laura vino a quejárseme.* (38–79)

37.863 The subject is implied by the context. MGR 18 *Una mujer ha llevado a los Tribunales a otra por haberle robado su marido.* This type of expression, while very common, is likely to lead to ambiguity, since the more frequent practice is to identify the subject of the infinitive and the subject of the main verb. It is especially frequent after *por* and *para*. (40–100)

37.865 The subject is indefinite. RUS 20 *El saldo se convierte en un reloj que marcha sin darle cuerda.* In this construction, the infinitive is almost a substantive, "without winding," instead of "without anyone's winding." It is common in fixed phrases of the type of *a decir verdad, a juzgar por (eso),* etc. (18–30)

37.867 The infinitive is impersonal. ZUN 41 *Además de haber voces combinadas, hay toque de campanas.* (9–10)

37.87 With the definite article, rare except after *a*.

37.871 The subject is expressed. ABU 29 *Del divertirse damas y galanes viene el lujo.* (41–67)

37.873 The subject is implied by the context. IBA 24 *Al hablar de ella, humedecíanse sus ojos.* (15–34)

37.875 The subject is indefinite. UNA 94 *Al decirle que era una niña, se limitó a contestar secamente: « ¡ Sí, nuestro castigo ! »* (4–4)

37.94 Types of phrase. The infinitive-clause after a preposition may form either an adjectival or an adverbial phrase.

37.941 Adjectival phrases with *de*, modifying a noun. STE 247 *Cuando me siento cansada, me da miedo de dejarla también yo.* (9–10)

37.945 Adverbial phrases, modifying a verb. The prepositions most frequently found are:

a (in phrases without the definite article, usually expressing condition). PAL 132 *El café se llamaba Café del León de Oro, a juzgar por la muestra que sobre él se parecía.* ([11]–16)

a (in phrases with the definite article, expressing time). JES 34 *Al detener la música, se escuchó el rumor del agua jugando en el pelón.* ([39]–107)

a los (pocos) días de, (a poco de). PIN 52 *La huelga se declaró a los pocos días de remanecer tú por estos andurriales.* (3–3)

antes de. IGN 56 *Apenas nos tratábamos, antes de morir mi padre.* (12–14)

con (usually concessive). LUG 154 *Una pobre muchacha, maltratada por los años y la miseria, más por ésta, con ser aquéllos muchos, las despedía a voces.* (3–3)

de (usually expressing condition). ARN 49 *De no sobrevenir un estornudo, pa Carnaval tendré las narices que parecerán naturales.* (9–10)

después de. PAL 12 *Poco después de nacer yo, se trasladó mi familia a Avilés.* (5–6)

hasta. ART 14 *Me he estado sobre aquellas rocas hasta ponerse el sol.* (3–3)

para (usually expressing purpose). LIN 63 *Para estar de acuerdo los dos, estudio el odio.* (16–39)

por (usually expressing cause). VIG 103 *El lector cree que por no haberle pasado a él cuanto dice el novelista, no puede pasar.* (**31–51**)

sin. PEL 468 *Sin ser muy severo el gusto de Vallfogono, escribía con relativa sencillez.* (**21–28**)

37.98 Position of the subject of the infinitive.

37.981 The subject of an infinitive normally follows the infinitive. NER 47 *Al iniciársele la osificación del corazón, murió.* ([**42**]–**132**)

37.985 Rarely, when the subject of the infinitive is a personal pronoun, it precedes the infinitive.　DEB 10 *Mi madre murió al yo nacer.*　　(3–4)

PERFECT INFINITIVE

37.99 The perfect infinitive, formed with *haber* and the past participle, is used to express an action or state which is completed at the time of the action or state of the main verb.　It may be used in any construction in which the simple infinitive is used, to express completed action or state.　SIE 13 *¡ Qué contenta estoy de haber vuelto a mi casa!*　　(54–178)

37.993 A special use of the perfect infinitive is its use in a main clause to express a reproof.　ARN 16 *Es lo que yo pensaba hacer, si no me la mutila. — Haberla pegado, so primo.*　　(4–6)

37.995 Structure of the perfect infinitive.　The perfect infinitive is normally considered as a unit, without the intervention of any other element between the auxiliary *haber* and the participle.　FOM 230 *Debió de haber hecho uso de su nombre.*　　([38]–101)

37.996 But a personal object pronoun is regularly attached to the auxiliary *haber*.　OCC 199 *Vivimos sin habernos dado la vida a nosotros mismos.*　　(37–77)

THE PARTICIPLES

38. There are four participles in Spanish: the present active participle ending in *–nte*, the present active participle ending in *–ndo* (the "gerundio"), the perfect active participle, formed with *habiendo* and the past participle, and the past participle, or perfect passive participle.

THE PRESENT PARTICIPLE IN *–ante, –iente*

38.1 The original present participle ending in *–ante, –iente* has almost entirely lost its verbal force and has become a qualifying adjective, a noun, a preposition, etc.

38.19 It is, however, still used at times, modified by an adverbial phrase, in a sense which is so nearly verbal that it may be said to retain something of its value as a participle. FOM 230 *Aquella Remedios, con su nombre oliente a botica, debió de haber hecho uso de su nombre.*
(7–12)

THE PRESENT PARTICIPLE IN *–ando, –iendo*

38.2 The present participle in *–ando, –iendo* is derived from the gerund, a verbal noun, in its use in adverbial constructions. It still retains something of the force of its origin: it is not used as an attributive or predicate adjective; it may be used as object of the preposition *en*. As a participle, it normally expresses an action or state as concurrent with the action or state of the main verb. By itself, it does not indicate any particular modification of the main action. But from the very looseness of the construction it is capable of suggesting almost any adverbial modification which the context requires: cause, condition, manner, means, time, and the like. Aside from its use as a modifier of some element in the sentence, it is also found in absolute constructions.

38.211 Modifying the subject. The participle in *–ando, –iendo*, used to modify an element in the sentence, is always an appositive modifier and, as such, has adverbial force. Modifying the subject, it usually expresses some attendant circumstance or some aspect of the main action. PAT 8 *Teresuca, saltando vivamente, se introdujo en la casa.* (60–2601)

38.213 In the lack of any specific indication, any attempt to analyze the various types of adverbial modification which the participle is capable of expressing must rest on purely subjective grounds and is therefore not attempted here. There is, however, one set of constructions which so clearly seems to indicate means (once expressed by the ablative of the gerund) that it may be recorded. MAY 5 *Acertó a demostrar su gratitud enamorándose de una de sus enfermeras.*   (8–14)

38.215 The subject modified may be the subject of an infinitive. FOM 7 *Oyó traquear el portón, haciéndole comprender absoluta la ausencia del esposo.*   (4–4)

38.216 The participle may be introduced by *como*, to form an imaginative comparison. WAS 143 *Se sonrió como diciendo: « Yo no tengo la culpa. »*   (11–25)

38.217 Introduced by *en*. This construction has become rare in contemporary Spanish. It regularly has temporal value, indicating that the action involved is completed. It has been replaced by *al* + an infinitive. JIM 85 *En llegando bajo la sombría cúpula frondosa, batí palmas, canté.*
                                                                        (5–7)

38.22 Modifying the direct object, as objective complement. This construction is limited to a relatively small number of verbs, expressing such notions as perceiving, finding, leaving, picturing, and the like. UGA 33 *¡ Ya te he visto comprando flores!*   ([**39**]–107)

The commonest verbs which are thus followed by the participle are: *dejar* (5–7), *encontrar* (7–7), *haber* (impersonal; the noun object is logically a subjective complement) (7–7), *tener* (7–10), *ver* (**21–37**).

38.23 Modifying another element of the sentence. In this construction the participle is normally the equivalent of a parenthetical relative clause.

38.231 Modifying a subjective complement. RIC 33 *Es la vida recia y sensual, estallando en carcajadas.*   (4–6)

38.235 Modifying a noun used as object of a preposition. REY 101 *El bote está hundido en la arena con la proa mirando a la costa.* Especially common in descriptive phrases introduced by *con*.   (15–20)

38.25 As an attributive adjective modifying a noun, only two participles are found (*ardiendo* and *hirviendo*). STE 250 *Como el ascua ardiendo de Isaías, habían purificado sus labios.*   (3–3)

38.261 As an adverb. A few present participles (such as *burlando, callando, tirando,* and *volando*) are used frankly as adverbs. JIM 65 *Intenté bajar volando la escalera.*   (10–13)

38.263 *Andando* is used alone as an exclamation. LIN 12 *Te echas un abrigo por encima, y andando.*   (8–10)

38.265 The adverbial force is at times shown by the use of diminutive forms. ARN 14 *Pa como están las cosas, se va tirandillo.*   (4–4)

38.31 The present participle is found in absolute constructions with a noun or pronoun, or without an expressed subject. The absolute construction introduced by *en* is now extremely rare. Like the participle modifying a noun, the participle in an absolute construction normally expresses some attendant circumstance of the main action, but is capable of conveying a wide variety of adverbial modifications.

38.32 With an expressed subject.

38.321 Noun, pronoun or infinitive. URU 48 *Julio viene a verme, estando Olegario en casa.* PIN 119 *Siendo imposible curarle, ¿ qué he hecho ?*

(38–118)

38.323 The subject of the participle may also be the subject of the main verb. TRI 233 *No teniendo él tiempo de bajar, la siseó discretamente.* (3–3)

38.33 Without expressed subject.

38.331 The subject is implied by the context. LIN 66 *Sabes que debo estar en Santander y no pudiendo ir contigo, tú no vas.* (26–56)

38.332 The subject may be identical with an expressed indirect object of the main verb. It is not probable that the participle modifies this indirect object. IDO 15 *Aquella noche le fué imposible dormir, pensando en los actores.* (10–15)

38.335 The subject is indefinite. BEN 37 *Podrá ser malo, pero oyéndolo no lo parece.* (29–68)

38.336 The main verb may be an indefinite reflexive. In this case, the participle is logically a modifier of the indefinite subject of the main verb. BYN 116 *Se pone la mayonesa en una fuente, dándole la forma redonda.* (16–45)

38.338 The participle is impersonal. VIG 61 *No podía ser de otra manera, tratándose de una caricatura.* (15–16)

38.371 Position of the subject. The subject of a present participle used in an absolute construction normally follows the participle. ART 9 *Sentiría que andando el tiempo la tuviesen que enterrar de limosna.*

([40]–116)

38.373 Rarely, the subject precedes the participle. ZAM 26 *Soy más vieja que tú y, el tiempo andando, puedo necesitar de ti.* (5–8)

38.41 The perfect active participle is used to indicate an attendant circumstance which is completed at the time of the action or state of the main verb. It may be used in any construction in which the simple present participle is used. It is now relatively rare. ABC 49 *Habiendo salido cuarenta y uno, pudieron presentarse muy bien cuarenta y dos.*

(7–8)

38.42 The perfect active participle is normally treated as a unit. But a personal object pronoun is regularly attached to the auxiliary *habiendo*. ALT 11 *Habiéndose mezclado en la lucha de las facciones, supo utilizar todas las circunstancias.* (3–4)

THE PAST PARTICIPLE

38.5 The past participle in Spanish is a perfect participle, passive in the case of transitive verbs, active in the case of intransitive verbs. The past participle of a reflexive verb which is intransitive is always active in force and may, when used as an adjective, come to have present force. The past participle is used in constructions which are primarily verbal and also in constructions which are primarily adjectival.

38.51 In verbal constructions. The chief uses of the past participle are found in the formation of the perfect tenses (see 33.) and of the passive voice (see 35.2).

38.53 A special verbal use is the construction in which the participle is used after a preposition with the force of a passive infinitive. It is probable that it involves the omission of the infinitive *ser*. ART 71 *No nací yo para mandada.* (3–5)

38.54 In absolute constructions. The past participle is frequently found in absolute constructions with expressed or implied subject. The participles of transitive and intransitive verbs regularly indicate an action or state which is completed at the time of the main action; the participles of reflexive verbs normally indicate an action or state concurrent with the time of the main action. The particular time relationship between the two actions may be stressed by the use of a preposition or an adverb of time. The absolute construction is the equivalent of an adverbial clause.

38.55 Without preposition or adverb.

38.551 The subject is a noun or pronoun. UGA 60 *Disipado el primer vértigo, Lisandro comprendió que su papel estaba concluido.* (**42–118**)

38.555 The subject is implied. JES 25 *Sentados muy juntos, comenzó Augusto la relación de su caso.*   (12–15)

38.561 Introduced by an adverb of time (*apenas, una vez, ya*). DEB 92 *Una vez bien ordenadas mis ideas, quedéme en grata contemplación del jardín.*   (15–22)

38.565 Introduced by a preposition of time (*después de, hasta*). ZUN 20 *Los está azotando hasta bien entrada la noche.*   (8–9)

38.57 Position of the subject in absolute constructions. The subject regularly follows the past participle in absolute constructions. RIC 17 *Excitada la fantasía con libros de aventura fué poco a poco cultivando el deseo de ver cosas nuevas.*   ([44]–148)
  For the use of the past participle in descriptive absolute constructions, see 25.39.

38.61 In adjectival constructions. The past participle is regularly used as a qualifying adjective in any construction in which a simple adjective is used. It may, on the one hand, retain something of its verbal force, sufficiently to be modified adverbially like a verb; on the other hand, it may lose all verbal force and become a simple adjective.

38.611 As attributive modifier. SON 18 *A lo lejos almenados muros se destacaban negros y sombríos.*   (*)

38.612 As subjective complement. PAL 300 *¡ Así Dios me salve, está muerto!*   (*)

38.613 As objective complement. MUJ 37 *Las doy por oídas.*   (*)
  For further details, see 2.74.

38.615 As appositive modifier. REY 105 *Los hombres y las mujeres, armados de fusiles, miran a la costa.*   (57–1771)

38.616 Introduced by a preposition (especially *después de*). ABU 424 *Sería bueno que después de bien estrellados contra las rocas, nos convirtiéramos tú y yo en dioses.*   (7–9)

38.62 Past participles with active force. The active force of the past participles of intransitive and reflexive verb has already been mentioned. This use extends also to past participles of transitive verbs. In the following paragraphs are listed the most frequent examples of this usage in each of the types.

38.63 Past participles of intransitive verbs. Except in compound tenses, the past participle of intransitive verbs is always active; *llegado* means, not " arrived," but " having arrived," even when it may be translated by English " arrived." ZAM 27 *No quiero verle pálido ni caído.* ([47]–185)

The commonest intransitive participles are: *acaecido* (5–6), *caído* (15–21), *crecido* (5–5), *entrado* (7-7), *llegado* (11–13), *muerto* (**25–47**), *nacido* (10–12), *pasado* (17–18).

38.64 Past participles of reflexive verbs. This is a very large group. Participles of reflexive verbs not only readily become present in force, but also easily lose all verbal force and become simple adjectives. Thus *divertido*, the past participle of *divertirse*, develops from the meaning of " having amused oneself " to that of " amusing oneself," then to " amusing " and finally to " funny." Similarly *atrevido* becomes " daring," *enamorado* becomes " in love," *vestido* becomes " wearing," etc. ORT 85 *Es un guerrero joven, tendido a la larga sobre uno de sus costados.* ([60]–758)

The commonest reflexive participles are: *abierto* (7–11), *aburrido* (5–6), *acostumbrado* (5–5), *aficionado* (10–13), *apoyado* (12–15), *arrepentido* (7–9), *atrevido* (5–7), *callado* (9–15), *cogido* (7–7), *desesperado* (15–21), *dispuesto* (6–8), *divertido* (12–16), *dormido* (16–24), *enamorado* (12–27), *hecho* (in the sense of " turned into " — *hecho una furia*) (10–17), *helado* (7–10), *olvidado* (8–8), *parecido* (5–5), *metido* (6–7), *puesto* (6–6), *sentado* (**24–53**), *tendido* (10–11), *vestido* (6–10).

38.65 Past participles of transitive verbs with active force. The group is a small one. UNA 22 *Todo hombre humano es perezoso y diligente, iracundo y sufrido* (" longsuffering "). ([27]–52)

The only common adjective in this group is *agradecido* (10–11).

V. ADVERBS

39. A word used to qualify the meaning of a verb, indicating the place, time, manner, degree, etc. of its action or state, is called an adverb. Similarly a word used to qualify the meaning of an adjective or adverb, usually indicating its degree, is called an adverb; it is normally the same word as is used to indicate the same quality in a verbal action. A prepositional phrase may be used instead of an adverb and is then called an adverbial phrase.

39.01 The same words are often used in Spanish as adverbs, prepositions, and conjunctions. Thus *bajo* may be an adverb or a preposition; *luego* may be an adverb or a copulative coordinating conjunction or an illative coordinating conjunction. In the present study such words are classified according to their function rather than their traditional form. In general it may be remarked that in modern Spanish prepositions are formed by adding *de* to an adverb (*después de*); subordinating conjunctions are formed by adding *que* to an adverb (*así que*) or to a preposition (*desde que*).

39.1 Formation of adverbs. Historically, adverbs are derived from Latin adverbs, adjectives, prepositions, nouns, etc.

39.11 Adverbs formed with –*mente*. A special group of adverbs is that of adverbs of manner formed with a feminine adjective and the ending –*mente*, originally the ablative of a feminine noun. IBA 372 *¡Qué limpiamente trabajaban!* (60–1440)

39.111 Two coordinated adverbs in –*mente*. With two coordinated adverbs of manner, –*mente* is used only with the second adjective, if the adverbs are connected by a conjunction. VIG 59 *Unamuno ha rectificado su error teórica y prácticamente.* (19–30)

39.115 If the two adverbs of manner are not connected by a conjunction, –*mente* may be repeated with the second adjective. IDO 218 *Hermosamente, divinamente, reconstruían la vida.* For stylistic effect. (3–4)

39.14 Adjectives used as adverbs. Many adverbs, as *alto, fuerte, mucho*, are derived from the neuter of Latin adjectives and are now as clearly adverbial as words derived from adverbs. But any adjective may be used in Spanish as an appositive modifier of the subject or other word in the sentence and agreeing with that noun in gender and number, with adverbial force. This construction is discussed in 25.41.

245

39.15 Nouns and pronouns used as adverbs. In addition to the adverbs which are formed from Latin nouns (*luego*), nouns, usually modified by an adjective, are frequently used to express adverbial notions of time, duration, space, measure, and the like; for discussion, see 3.7. The pronouns which are used as adverbs are largely neuters, of the type of *algo*.

39.16 Prepositional adverbial phrases. One of the most frequent forms of adverbial modification is that consisting of a prepositional phrase. These phrases may have as object of the preposition a noun, a pronoun, an infinitive, a clause, an adjective, or an adverb. We are here concerned only with those phrases formed by a preposition and an adverb, as *por allí*. Another special group consists of phrases formed with an adverb and another adverb used as a post-positive preposition of the type of *aquí dentro*.

39.17 Adverbial clauses. A final type of adverbial modification is found in adverbial clauses in the indicative or the subjunctive. These are discussed in detail in 28.4 and 29.46 and 29.7.

39.2 Types of adverbs.

39.21 Modifying verbs. The number of types of adverbial modification is large. The most common are: place, time, manner, and degree. The relative and interrogative adverbs of place, time, and degree are discussed under relatives (16.) and interrogatives (14.5).

39.22 Modifying adjectives and adverbs. In addition to the adverbs expressing degree (*algo, más, mucho, poco,* etc.), a number of adverbs of manner used with transferred value are also found modifying adjectives and adverbs, as *bien, enteramente, inmensamente, sumamente,* and the like. With *mucho* and *tanto* and with the relative-interrogative *cuanto-cuánto*, only the apocopated forms *muy, tan,* and *cuan* (*cuán*) are now used to modify adjectives and adverbs.

39.25 Distinguishing adverbs. Certain adverbs are used to distinguish a particular word in the sentence, rather than to modify the verb. In this case they usually precede the word distinguished. The chief of these are *aun* (*aún* when stressed), *casi, hasta, siquiera,* and *sólo*. Similarly are used adverbs in –*mente; especialmente, solamente, señaladamente,* etc. and adverbial phrases: *a lo menos, sobre todo,* etc.

39.3 Position of adverbs. While the position of adverbs does not fall within the scope of the present study, certain general principles may be noted. An adverb modifying a verb normally is placed immediately after the verb if it is stressed, before the verb, if it is unstressed. For emotional effects, however, a strongly stressed adverb, especially of place or time, is often placed at the beginning of a sentence. Adverbs which modify adjectives or adverbs normally precede the word modified.

39.4 Comparison of adverbs. In general, adverbs are compared in the same way as adjectives. The most striking difference is that there is no regular form to indicate the superlative of inferiority or superiority.

39.41 Comparison of equality.

39.411 With expressed term of the comparison. *tan ... como.* BRA 169 *Yo no podría decir estas cosas tan bien como tú las dices.* (30–42)

39.42 Without expressed term. *tan* alone. LIN 54 *Yo no puedo consentir que a una hija mía la atropellen tan brutalmente.* (39–150)

39.43 Comparative of superiority. The normal form of the comparative is *más* + adverb. A few adverbs are derived from Latin comparatives. The comparative may be followed by an expressed term or be used without term.

39.431 With expressed term. *más ... que.* NER 63 *Nada hay que evoque más imperiosamente la idea de la libertad que el mar.* This construction was counted under the comparison of adjectives; see 26.31.

39.433 Without expressed term. *más* alone. MAY 13 *Un año más tarde le dijeron que Leandra se casaba con un indiano.* (60–216)

39.437 To express progressive accumulation, the comparative may be modified by *cada vez.* ALT 7 *La institución de los mayorazgos continuó en la misma forma, pero fijándose cada vez más.* (4–7)

39.44 The comparative adverbs which are derived from Latin comparatives do not require *más.*

39.441 *bien — mejor.* ART 16 *Se interpretan mejor sus obras.* (52–138)
For *más bien* in the sense of "rather," see 39.61 s.v.

39.445 *mal — peor.* BEN 33 *Me tratan peor que a un ladrón.* (7–13)

39.448 *mucho — más.* ARN 62 *No sé qué acera me gusta más.* (*)

39.449 *poco — menos.* ROM 20 *Importarían menos.* (32–66)

39.45 Superlative of superiority. The form is identical with the comparative and was in origin undoubtedly a comparative. But there can be no question that by implication the comparative form conveys the notion of the highest degree. The need for such a distinction is indicated by the use of special devices to express the superlative degree.

39.451 *más* alone. ABU 202 *Esta condenada vista se me escapa cuando* *más la necesito.* The only forms frequently found are the special comparatives *más, mejor,* and *menos.*   **(34–69)**

39.456 lo más ... posible. REY 148 *Hagamos nuestros preparativos lo más lentamente posible.*   **(5–7)**

39.46 Absolute superlative. As with adjectives, the absolute superlative of adverbs is superlative only in the sense that it is derived from a Latin superlative; in meaning it is merely a device for expressing a high degree, without implication of comparison.

39.461 Ending in *–ísimo.* CAT 7 ¿ *Tueses ?* — *Bastantísimo.*   **(9–10)**

39.47 Other methods of intensification. The most frequent means of intensifying the degree of an adverb are the use of *muy* and *tan;* see 39.61 *s. v.* A few other devices may be recorded.

39.473 The adverb may be repeated. TIG 21 *Ya estás hablando clarito, clarito.*   **(23–61)**

39.475 Similarly an adverbial phrase. SIE 50 ¿ *De veras, de veras estamos tan mal ?*   **(3–4)**

39.48 Comparative of inferiority. PIN 112 *Menos mal, porque los misterios me preocupan.* All the examples noted were in the idiom *menos mal,* used instead of *tanto mejor.*   **(6–6)**

39.49 Superlative of inferiority. No form was used with sufficient frequency to be included in this study.

39.5 Special uses of adverbs.

39.51 As substantives.

39.511 As true nouns. Certain adverbs, as *sí, no, entonces,* may be used as nouns, with adjectival modifiers. IMP 206 *Los tres sí, sí, sí de Celia, cortantes, como tajos de guillotina.*   **(7–8)**

39.513 After a preposition in adjectival phrases modifying a noun. PEL 17 *En las costumbres de entonces tenía más de camarada que de pedagogo.*   **(43–134)**

39.515 The word modified may be the demonstrative pronoun *el, la, lo,* etc. SIE 18 *Estás enfadado todavía por lo de antes.*   **(19–29)**

39.517 After a preposition in adverbial phrases. LUG 151 *Encaminábanse hacia allá a prima tarde.*   **(*)**
The special combinations of preposition and adverb which are most frequently found are listed in 39.61.

39.52 As adjectives.

39.521 Attributive. DIV 345 *Le permitieron reembolsar al público la casi totalidad de sus depósitos.* (7–7)

39.525 Predicate. UNA 156 *¿No es así, señor conde?* Especially *así, bien, cómo.* (31–84)

39.526 As objective complement. URU 57 *Me la encuentro así.* (8–9)

39.527 Appositive, with the force of a relative clause. RUS 23 *No tengo vergüenza cuando conservo en mi casa un hombre así.* (22–37)

39.55 As prepositions.

39.551 With a personal object pronoun used as indirect object of the verb. ABU 213 *¡Menudo chaparrón nos viene encima!* See also 8.275. (25–34)

39.555 Following the noun involved. JIM 47 *Se lo llevó calle abajo.* See also 41.81. ([22]–39)

39.6 Individual adverbs and adverbial phrases. The exigencies of space make it impossible to illustrate adequately the use of individual adverbs. But it seems desirable to give some picture of the relative frequency of their use in contemporary prose. In the following list there are included the commonest simple adverbs and adverbial phrases in which these adverbs form a part. A few adverbial phrases involving the use of adjectives, nouns, and pronouns have been included, in order to make possible a comparison of the frequencies of varying forms to express the same notion. The adverbial expressions are entered in each case under the first significant word, adverb, noun, etc., not under the preposition which introduces the phrase. Illustrative examples are given only when the same expression is cited with different meanings or uses. For negative adverbs see 40.63.

39.61

abajo	(27–48)	*ahí*	(42–126)
desde abajo	(4–4)	ahí fuera	(3–4)
acá	(12–23)	de ahí	(13–16)
para acá	(7–9)	por ahí	(19–38)
por acá	(3–5)	*ahora*	(58–224)
acaso	(40–142)	ahora mismo	(26–53)
por si acaso	(4–4)	desde ahora	(5–6)
adelante	(32–61)	hasta ahora	(17–31)
en adelante	(5–5)	por ahora	(10–16)
hacia adelante	(5–5)	*algo* — Modifies verb. REY 60 *Me*
adentro	(8–11)	*duele algo la cabeza.* (9–9)
hacia adentro	(3–3)	Modifies adj. or adv. BEN 63 *Soy*
afuera	(7–10)	*algo loco.* (25–41)

Modifies past part. WAS 136 *Algo
sorprendida contestó.* (8–10)

alrededor (5–6)

alto (4–4)

allá (**46–114**)

  allá abajo (4–5)

  allá arriba (6–8)

  allá dentro (3–4)

  allá lejos (6–8)

  de allá (4–6)

  más allá " farther on " (11–13)

  para allá (4–5)

  por allá (7–7)

allí (**50–274**)

  allí mismo (6–6)

  de allí (11–12)

  desde allí (5–5)

  por allí (16–30)

anoche (18–34)

antaño (8–14)

anteayer (5–6)

antemano — de antemano (8–8)

antes " before " (**52–180**)

  " rather " (9–12)

  cuanto antes (6–6)

  de antes (3–3)

aparte (7–11)

apenas (**46–112**)

  apenas si (13–19)

aprisa (3–3)

aquí (**54–450**)

  aquí dentro (3–3)

  aquí mismo (5–7)

  de aquí (**24–34**)

  de aquí en adelante (3–4)

  desde aquí (6–7)

  fuera de aquí (3–3)

  hacia aquí (3–4)

  hasta aquí (7–7)

  por aquí (**20–36**)

arriba (**23–31**)

así — Modifies verb. PIN 28 *Así
me gustan.* (**60–506**)

Modifies past part. JAN 13 *Una*

mujer así enamorada. (3–4)

  así como . . . así (3–5)

atrás (**27–37**)

  hacia atrás (10–10)

aun (stressed, **aún**) (**56–346**)

ayer (**36–71**)

  desde ayer (3–3)

bajo (6–6)

balde — de balde (5–7)

  en balde (3–3)

bastante — Modifies verb. IBA 11
Has trabajado bastante. (**20–38**)

Modifies adj. or adv. LUG 364 *Un
pintor bastante mediano.* (**20–28**)

bien — Modifies verb. PAL 307 *No
me era posible prepararme bien.*
(**54–256**)

Modifies adj. or adv. ALT 469 *Bien
pronto se constituyó.* (**31–45**)

Modifies past part. RUS 23 *Estoy bien considerado.* (**32–74**)

casi — Modifies verb. UGA 59
Hasta tocarle casi la ropa.
(**36–74**)

Modifies adj. or adv. VIG 29 *Ha
leído a casi todo Unamuno.*
(**54–182**)

cerca (**21–28**)

  de cerca (9–12)

cierto (11–13)

  por cierto (14–23)

claro (19–43)

como " about " (5–5)

continuo (4–6)

cosa de " about " (3–3)

cuando — cuando más (3–3)

  cuando menos (4–4)

  de cuando en cuando (14–18)

  de vez en cuando (11–19)

cuasi — Modifies adj. or adv. (4–6)

debajo (6–6)

delante (18–30)

  por delante (8–9)

demasiado — Modifies verb. IBA

150 *Me sofoco demasiado.*
(19–29)
Modifies adj. or adv.   BYN 34
Demasiado jóvenes.   (**28–73**)
dentro   (**20–27**)
  por dentro   (7–11)
despacio   (13–22)
despacito   (3–3)
después   (**54–242**)
detrás   (15–23)
  por detrás   (7–8)
encima   (19–29)
  de encima   (6–6)
  por encima   (3–3)
enfrente (en frente)   (11–12)
entonces   (**51–279**)
  desde entonces   (13–16)
  hasta entonces   (13–14)
  por entonces   (3–3)
exacto   (3–3)
fuera   (**20–30**)
  de fuera   (3–3)
  por fuera   (6–6)
fuerte   (5–5)
gran cosa   (4–4)
gratis   (4–9)
harto — Modifies adj. or adv.
(6–7)
hasta " even "   RUB 25 *Hasta su
  misterio es matemático.*
(**46–165**)
" as many as " PEL 233 *Admite
  hasta treinta maneras.*   (3–4)
hoy   (**48–200**)
  desde hoy   (5–6)
  hasta hoy   (6–7)
  hoy día   (3–3)
  hoy mismo   (10–11)
igual   (5–14)
lejos   (**32–77**)
  de lejos   (9–12)
  desde lejos   (6–9)
ligero   (3–4)
luego   (**52–270**)

desde luego   (19–28)
hasta luego   (11–18)
mal — Modifies   verb.   IMP 13
  Hablo mal.   (**40–115**)
Modifies past part.   DEB 3 *Mal
  empedradas callejuelas.* (**29–45**)
mañana   (**37–95**)
  hasta mañana   (7–18)
  mañana mismo   (6–7)
más — Modifies verb.   PAL 130 *Me
  divertía más.*   (**60–261**)
Modifies adj. or adv., see Comparison, 26.
Modifies a phrase.   RUS 76 *Se
  bebe más a gusto.*   (14–18)
" rather "   ZAM 261 *Siento, más
  que un amor, una pasión.*
(16–25)
  más bien " rather "   (14–26)
  más o menos   (**20–28**)
  más y más   (3–3)
medio — Modifies adj. or adv. ZAM
  111 *Vengo medio loco.* (13–17)
Modifies past part.   JES 33 *Medio
  cortado, sonrió.*   (8–9)
mejor   (**52–138**)
menos   (**29–62**)
  a lo menos   (6–10)
  al menos   (**24–32**)
  por lo menos   (**30–42**)
menudo — a menudo   (17–29)
mismo — lo mismo   (15–20)
mu (for muy)   (4–28)
muchísimo   (7–8)
mucho — Modifies a verb.   ZAM 76
  Les querrás mucho.   (**46–162**)
Verb or adj. implied.   ZAM 77
  Mucho, sí, señorita.   (14–19)
Modifies comparative adj., attributive.   RAN 39 *Una citación
  mucho más conminatoria.* (7–9)
Predicate.   LIN 22 *Era mucho
  más honroso.*   (19–26)
Modifies *más* used as neuter

pron. UGA 50 *Mucho más*
mereces.　　　　(4–4)

Modifies comparative adv. RAN 88
Han progresado mucho más.
　　　　(15–19)

muy — Modifies positive adj. BEN 6
Hay muy poca religión.
　　　　(54–732)

Modifies past part. PAT 25
Ciertos señoritos muy conocidos.
　　　　(38–72)

Modifies noun used as adj. IMP
199 *Muy hombre.*　　(3–4)

Modifies adjectival phrase. VIG
71 *Dos tipos muy del pueblo*
español.　　　　(11–13)

Modifies positive adv. PAT 12
Casarse muy pronto. (49–195)

Modifies adverbial phrase. FAL
23 *Se puso muy frente a ella.*
　　　　(17–25)

poco — Modifies verb. SAS 106 *Poco*
confías en ti mismo. (30–55)

Modifies adj. or adv. ALT 190
Costumbres poco respetuosas.
　　　　(34–51)

a poco　　　　　(4–4)

poco a poco　　　(19–34)

un poco — Modifies verb. STE
249 *Yo seré un poco su padre.*
　　　　(35–64)

Modifies adj. or adv. PAX 332 *Un*
poco raro ¿ no es cierto?
　　　　(28–67)

poquillo — un poquillo　(3–3)

poquito — un poquito　(6–11)

primero　　　　(29–55)

prisa — de prisa　　(3–3)

pronto　　　　(45–138)

de pronto　　　(32–79)

por de pronto　　(3–3)

por lo pronto　　(3–3)

quizá　　　　(20–32)

quizás　　　　(23–68)

recién — Modifies past part.
　　　　(20–32)

recientemente — Modifies past
part.; see 25.24　　(4–4)

repente — de repente　(17–27)

seguida — en seguida　(40–100)

sí　　　　(54–1050)

Intensifying a verb. ART 15 *Él sí*
es loco.　　　　(36–63)

Replacing a verb. MUJ 21 *Me*
parece que sí.　　(28–66)

siempre　　　　(60–462)

para siempre　　(29–48)

siquiera　　　　(23–27)

solamente　　　(20–30)

sólo　　　　(58–322)

tan sólo　　　　(9–11)

tal　　　　(9–12)

tal vez　　　　(34–88)

talmente　　　(3–3)

tan — Modifies adj. BEN 7 *Es tan*
joven.　　　　(60–645)

Modifies past part. LIN 123
Estaba tan enamorado. (29–53)

Modifies adjectival phrase.
ROM 207 *Esos romances tan del*
gusto de los siglos XVI y XVII.
　　　　(5–6)

Modifies adverb. BYN 31 *Se for-*
tifican tan naturalmente.
　　　　(45–114)

Modifies adverbial phrase. RIC
262 *No lo tomes tan a lo trá-*
gico.　　　　(15–19)

tanto — Modifies verb. ABU 415
Tanto me quieres. (43–92)

Verb or adj. implied. RUS 31
¡ Y tanto !　　　(8–13)

Modifies comparative adv. VIG
105 *¡ Tanto peor para él !* (3–3)

en tanto　　　　(6–8)

entre tanto (entretanto)　(18–22)

mientras tanto　　(9–9)

tanto . . . como　　(23–37)

un tanto   (10–13)   *todo*   (8–9)
tarde   (**42–83**)   Agrees attributively with adj.
de tarde en tarde   (3–3)   modified. RUS 139 *Soy toda*
tiempo — de tiempo en tiempo   *tuya.*   (9–15)
                        (5–8)   Agrees in predicate. JAN 7 *La*
tempranito   (3–3)   *sentía temblar toda entera.*
temprano   (**20–23**)   (6–8)
todavía   (**51–183**) *ya*   (**60–1146**)

VI. NEGATION

40. The simple negative in Spanish is *no*. But other words are used to reinforce *no* or to express a negative by themselves. Spanish differs from English in the use of negatives chiefly in the fact that, if a negative is expressed, or clearly implied, in the sentence, all other indefinite words and adverbs and conjunctions will be expressed in their negative forms, instead of in indefinite forms.

40.1 Uses of *no*.

40.11 Modifying verbal forms.

40.12 Finite forms. *No* regularly precedes a finite form of the verb. It may be separated from it only by an object pronoun. IGN 14 *Le dije que no tardaría en volver.* IBA 151 *¿ No se lo dije?* (*)

40.121 With some modal auxiliaries, the negative may be transferred from the infinitive which it modifies to the auxiliary. URU 31 *No debe estar muy lejos.* (26–50)

40.123 Rarely a negative is transferred from an indefinite adjective to the verb. RUB 82 *No son pocos los golpes.* (3–3)

40.13 Modifying an infinitive. OCC 198 *¿ Y ésa es su razón de usté para no jugar?* Note that *no* is placed between a preposition and the infinitive. See 37.791. (60–429)

40.14 Modifying a present participle. RUS 124 *No protegiéndolos con desprecio.* (12–17)

40.15 Modifying a past participle. ABU 33 *Cuentas no liquidadas.* (17–29)

40.155 The past participle is used as a noun. ALT 466 *Los no bautizados.* (3–3)

40.21 Modifying an adjectival expression.

40.211 An adjective. JES 141 *No mucha gente.* (20–38)

40.217 The adjective is used as a pronoun. VIG 40 *En ocasiones — no muchas, por cierto.* (13–19)

40.22 Modifying an adverbial expression.

40.221 An adverb. IDO 109 *No menos tibio y radiante.* (30–49)

40.225 An adverbial phrase. NER 22 *No de otra suerte que el amputado siente que posee.*

40.24 In elliptical expressions. *No* is frequently found in expressions in which it does not modify any expressed word.

40.25 Alone.

40.251 In answers to a question. FAL 168 *¿ No será contraproducente todo eso ? — No.*   (48–516)

40.252 The *no* may be repeated for emphasis. TIG 30 *Deje usted, tengo yo aquí. — No, no.*   (18–36)

40.255 *No* may be added for emphasis after a negative verb. SJQ 39 *De prisa no voy, no.*   (20–48)

40.257 *No* may be used in questions, instead of *¿ no es verdad ?* SEC 38 *Éste es tu marido, ¿ no ?*   (10–24)

40.258 After *que*, in an indirect quotation or exclamation. URU 32 *Me daba vergüenza decirle que no.*   (25–40)

40.259 After the coordinating conjunction *o*. JES 27 *Con justicia o no, soportaba un estigma social.*   (24–38)

40.26 With another expression. When *no* is used in elliptical expressions with another word or phrase, it usually precedes the word with which it is found. But if the word which is used with *no* is one which would normally precede the verb, if it were expressed, it will precede *no* in the elliptical expression.

40.27 *No* precedes.

40.271 In answers to a question. MUJ 39 *¿ Volvieron ya ? — No, todavía.*
                                                                         (15–24)

40.272 After *aunque*. ALT 464 *Nuevamente se reorganizó la Inquisición, aunque no de una manera esencial.*   (4–5)

40.273 After *cuando*. IDO 108 *Esa noche casi todos eran de la misma condición social, cuando no del mismo círculo.*   (5–5)

40.274 After *si*. RET 18 *Igual, si no mayor, significación.*   (3–3)

40.275 After a coordinating conjunction. NER 47 *Era una especie de escultura, pero no trágica.*   (31–58)

40.276 Asyndetic, without connective. UNA 15 *Y por el que hayamos querido ser, no por el que hayamos sido, nos salvaremos.*   (15–24)

40.279 In adversative constructions followed by *sino*.   BYN 33 *Se dedicó al negocio de crear dinero, no con valioso oro, sino en papel.*   **(26–41)**

40.28 *No* follows.

40.281 In answers to a question.   WAS 146 *¿ No lo ha hallado entonces ? — Todavía, no.*   **(34–127)**

40.285 After an interrogative adverb.   MUJ 14 *¿ Por qué no ?*

(Not counted)

40.3 Pleonastic uses of *no*. The use of *no* after comparatives and other expressions implying a negative has almost disappeared in modern Spanish. It represents, of course, a survival of a more primitive paratactic construction.

40.31 After a comparative.   TRI 216 *Le parecía mejor debutar con una comedia de costumbres que no con género trágico.*   **(5–5)**

40.34 After conjunctions.

40.342 Expressing time. Pleonastic *no* is found only after *hasta que* and *mientras*. To the latter the use of *no* gives the force of "until."

> **hasta que.**   PIN 131 *Hasta que no suene el segundo toque, no empezaremos a caminar.*   **(6–6)**
> **mientras.**   IGN 36 *Mientras no se me demuestre lo contrario, lo creo imposible.*   **(7–10)**

OTHER NEGATIVE EXPRESSIONS

40.41 A large number of expressions — adjectives, adverbs, conjunctions, pronouns, etc. — are used in Spanish with negative force. Some of these, such as *nunca*, were negative in origin. Others, such as *nada*, were indefinite in origin, but through frequent use in negative sentences acquired negative force in their own right. Their negative use is, however, somewhat limited. While they are negative when they precede the verb or when they are used alone without a verb, they still regularly are accompanied by *no* when they follow the verb.

40.42 Used before a verb, without *no*.   ORT 85 *Nadie sabe quién es el autor.*   **(60–495)**

40.43 Used after a verb, with *no*.   MAY 66 *No voy a nada malo.* **(60–951)**

40.431 Occasionally, they have negative force, without an expressed *no*.   ORR 99 *Esto parará en nada.* Especially *nada más que* and *nada menos que.*   **(10–18)**

40.44 Alone, without a verb.

40.441 In answers, in conversation.   SEC 77 *¿ Qué ha sucedido ? — Nada.*
(52–250)

40.443 In elliptical constructions after a coordinating conjunction. BEN 12 *Leo las noticias y nada más.*   (20–40)

40.444 Coordinated, without conjunction.   MGR 43 *Mi prima es vocal; mi tercera, nada.*   (10–10)

40.447 After *como.*   RET 37 *En Colombia se reveló el humorista Luis Carlos López, que ha traducido, como nadie, la vida de provincia.*   (9–10)

40.5 After an implied negative. The negative, rather than the indefinite forms, are used after expressions which imply a negative.

40.51 In a subordinate clause, after a negative main clause. ORT 120 *Nadie pretenderá que aquello a que me refiero sea en nada parecido a mi entender.*
(11–16)

40.53 In questions.

40.531 In a direct question.   BRA 22 *¿ Hay nada más práctico que la ilusión ?*
(26–34)

40.533 In a subordinate clause in a direct question.   FOM 237 *¿ Creen ustedes que mamá rinda cuentas a nadie ?*   (3–7)

40.55 After a comparative.

40.551 Comparative adjective or adverb.   SON 50 *Dejó oír su voz cascada, más amable y misteriosa que nunca.*   (30–47)

40.553 After *antes.*   WAS 23 *Una caterva de perros salió antes que nadie a recibir a los viajeros.*   (5–5)

40.56 After a superlative.   PAL 134 *Jugábamos del modo más divertido que jugó nadie en el mundo.*   (3–3)

40.57 After *sin.*   WAS 7 *Contestó sin mostrar alegría ninguna.*   (52–132)

40.575 After *sin que.*   RIC 20 *Saludaban a aquel joven caballero sin que nadie pudiese sospechar el motivo.*   (13–15)

40.581 After verbs implying a negative, such as *negar, prohibir, quitar.* ZUN 16 *Prohibió a sus amigos que bajo ningún pretexto le tributasen alabanzas.*   (8–8)

40.59 After other words implying a negative, such as *apenas, difícil,* ("not easy"), *mal, poco* ("not many"), etc.   PAL 20 *Era enorme. Imposible imaginar nada más interesante.*   ([15]–23)

40.6 Common negative expressions, other than *no*. In the following lists of the most frequently used negative adjectives, adverbs, conjunctions, and pronouns there are included not only those words which may be used as negatives either with or without *no*, but also a number of words and expressions which are regularly found only with *no*, but with special force. Words or expressions which may be used as negatives without *no* are indicated by an asterisk.

40.61 Negative adjectives. *alguno.* With negative force only when it follows a noun. RAN 14 *No se ha operado evolución alguna.* **(25–40)** **ni un.* MAY 14 *¡ Y ni un deseo noble, ni una pasión firme!* **(21–39)** **ni un solo.* SEC 26 *Sabe que no te has ausentado ni un solo día del cortijo.* (4–4) **ningún otro.* ROD 211 *La triste idea me hiere más que en ninguna otra ocasión.* (5–6) **ninguno (ningún).* Before the noun. RUB 16 *Sin ser esclavo de ningún Próspero, engorda y se multiplica.* **(52–104)**. Less frequently after the noun. UNA 91 *No llevó alegría ninguna el niño.* (12–17)

40.63 Negative adverbs. *aun.* Precedes the verb. BEN 41 *Aun no pido limosna.* **(22–32)**. Less frequently after the verb. ART 11 *No te había saludado aún.* (14–20). *casi.* With a negative in the sense of "hardly." SEC 83 *Con esto del porrazo casi no puedo hablar.* (18–21). *del todo.* With a negative in the sense of "not at all." RUS 24 *Ya sabe usted que no ando mal del todo.* (7–8). **en (mi) vida.* SIE 88 *Salga usted de esta casa y no vuelva usted en su vida.* (4–4). **en toda la noche.* ZAM 109 *Llevo suficiente dinero para que el banquero no cese de bendecirme en toda la noche.* (3–5). **jamás.* ORR 96 *Jamás se lo hubiera figurado así.* **(33–84)**. *manera —* de ninguna manera.* MAY 68 *No me estorbas — ¡ de ninguna manera!* (3–3). *más.* With a negative in the sense of "not again," "never again." SAS 61 *Partiré mañana mismo para no volver más.* **(32–61)**. For *no . . . más que* "only," see 40.64. *modo — *de ningún modo.* ZAM 85 *Lo que es eso, de ningún modo.* (5–5). **nada.* Modifying a verb. JOA 42 *Ya sabes que no me importa nada.* (11–18). Modifying an adjective or adverb. PAT 24 *No me es nada simpático.* (10–12). **ni.* With the force of "not even." Modifying a verb. SAS 55 *No quieres ni oírme.* (9–15). Modifying an adjective. ZAM 45 *Ni media palabra más.* (16–32). Intensifying a noun. TRI 46 *¡ En todo ello no hay ni sombra de pecado.* **(34–89)**. **ni aun.* PEL 234 *Ni aun los mismos traductores de Dante le emplean nunca.* (5–7). **ni siquiera.* ROM 13 *Ni siquiera canta para el pueblo.* **(22–41)**. **nunca.* IBA 364 *No volverían nunca.* **(60–279)**. **nunca más.* IMP 18 *Algunos nunca más se volvieron a ver.* (7–8). *parte — *a ninguna parte.* SIE 61 *No conduce a ninguna parte.* (3–3). **por ninguna parte.* SAS 113 *No la encuentro por ninguna parte.* (4–4). **siquiera.* CAT 5 *Sin despedirse siquiera se puso la teja y salió.* (15–18). *todavía.* With a negative in the sense of "not yet." Precedes the verb. SON 112 *Todavía no baja al locutorio.* (7–11). More frequently after the verb. FOM 92 *No te levantes to-*

davía. (11–21). **ya.** With *no* in the sense of " no longer." Precedes the verb. FAL 22 *Ya no se le puede llamar el príncipe.* (**45–135**). Less frequently after the verb. NER 69 *No queda ya ni el recuerdo.* (**29–43**). **ya más.** JES 237 *No puedo estar ya más aquí.* (3–3).

40.64 **no ... más que ...**, **no ... sino ...**, and other expressions for " only." From its original meaning of " not more than," the combination *no ... más que* has developed that of " only." The *no* of the expression may be reinforced or replaced by another negative word or even by an expression implying a negative. In elliptical expressions without a verb, *no ... más que* is usually replaced by *nada más que.* A special usage is that of both *no más* and *nada más* after the word modified. In addition to these forms with *más*, the construction with *no ... sino* is common. Related to these constructions is the use of *nada menos que* after a verb in the sense of " actually."

40.641 Constructions with **no ... más que.**

no ... más que. REY 116 *No hay más que arroz y queso.* (**48–173**). The *más* may be an adjective modifying a noun. PIN 151 *La desesperación de no tener más tierra que la de la fosa.* (14–15). **nada ... más que.** SEC 78 *No han quedado aquí nada más que las personas de absoluta confianza.* (4–5). **nadie ... más que.** BEN 32 *Son las que nos sacan las faltas a las demás, para que las señoras no atiendan a nadie más que a ellas.* (4–4). **nunca ... más que.** MUJ 31 *Nunca te di más que una orden.* (4–4). **sin ... más que.** LUG 147 *La triste sota quedó desamparada sin más amigos fieles que un perro gordo y un real.* (9–13). **Interrogative adverb or pronoun + más que.** SIE 51 *¿ Para quién vivo más que para ti?* (4–5). Before a prepositional phrase, *más que* precedes the preposition, instead of following it, showing that all sense of real comparison has disappeared. URU 39 *No sirvo más que pa' trabajar como un burro.* (10–15).

40.643 **nada más que** in elliptical expressions without a verb. In conversational style. MAY 11 — *¿ Qué pides? — le dijo. — Que te acuerdes mucho de mí. — ¿ Nada más que eso?* (5–5). After a coordinating conjunction. RUS 142 *Le pido el consentimiento y nada más que el consentimiento.* (4–7). Without connective. ART 33 *En primer lugar, Rojas solamente es mi amigo, nada más que mi amigo.* (8–10). In colloquial style replaced by **na más que** in any of these situations. ARN 90 *La culpa la tié el Jurao y na más que el Jurao.* (3–3).

40.645 **no más** and **nada más** used after the word modified.

no más. RUB 85 *El título no más del poema toca un bombo infamante.* In American writers *no más* in this usage has become almost the equivalent of *mismo.* (11–29). **nada más.** After a noun or pronoun. RUS 19 *Yo ya no soy más que un número. Acaso un cero nada más; pero un número.* (12–24). After a verb. IMP 196 *Me admiro, nada más, de tu ilusión.*

(4–5). In colloquial style replaced by **na más.** SJQ 135 *Se araña na más de mirarlo.* (3–3).

40.647 nada menos que. Used after an affirmative verb. OCC 263 *Le falta nada menos que el latido esencial de la Enciclopedia.* (7–10)

40.649 no . . . sino. PAT 220 *El tren no para sino seis minutos.* (**28–89**). **no . . . más sino.** A combination of *no . . . más que* and *no . . . sino.* BEN 67 *No quisiera más sino que vieran ustedes mi cuerpo.* Before a clause introduced by *que* this construction avoids the conflict of two *que's.* (3–3).

40.65 Negative pronouns. ***nada.** UGA 9 *Nada rima mejor con nuestro espíritu.* (**57–327**). ***nada de** + a noun. BRA 31 *No se asusten ustedes; nada de alarmas.* (15–20). ***nada de** + neuter adjective or pronoun. ROD 85 *Nada de lo que obra afuera la mueve.* (9–12). ***nada más.** IGN 37 *Con eso tenemos para vivir con algún desahogo, pero nada más.* Especially common in elliptical expressions. (**22–49**). ***nadie.** WAS 18 *Ninguno lo saludó porque nadie lo conocía.* (**50–218**). ***naide.** ART 6 *No me gusta faltar a naide.* (4–5). ***ningún otro.** RET 22 *No ha habido ningún otro en América.* (6–6). ***ninguno.** PAX 336 *Todas las jóvenes se excusaron; ninguna se atrevía a salir.* (**35–55**). With the meaning of "nobody." FAL 224 *Ninguno perdió el momento.* (6–8). ***ninguno de** + noun or pronoun. IGN 86 *No se puede ofender ninguno de ustedes dos.* (19–29). **otra cosa.** With a negative in the sense of "nothing else." BRA 142 *¿No piensa usted en otra cosa?* (16–25).

40.651 Negative pronouns used as nouns. The only form now in common use is *la nada.* LLA 54 *Ese tu amigo de la niñez, recogido de la nada, me vengará.* (6–6)

40.66 Negative preposition. The only negative preposition is *sin.* RAN 23 *Yo estaré sin falta en el café.* (**60–1137**)

40.68 Negative conjunctions.
***ni.** MAY 10 *No tenía creencias formales ni costumbres religiosas.* (**54–362**). ***ni . . . ni . . .** BEN 60 *No has hecho bien ni por mí ni por tus hijas.* (**44–98**). ***ni tampoco.** OCC 264 *Feijoo no la puede aceptar. Ni tampoco la otra solución.* (8–12). ***ni . . . tampoco** (divided). ROM 20 *Ni es la primera tampoco.* (3–3). **sino** "but." Before nouns, pronouns, etc. UNA 17 *La realidad en la vida de don Quijote no fueron los molinos de viento, sino los gigantes.* (**50–201**). Before verbs. FOM 15 *María no respondió sino continuaba desvistiéndose.* (9–11). **sino** "except." FOM 92 *No cabalgó nunca sino en caballitos de palo.* (12–14). **sino que.** "but." Before a verb, in a main clause. ABC 21 *No desenvuelve, sino que contraría y agrava los preceptos de la ley.* (**22–42**). *sino que,* after *no parece,* forming the equivalent of an affirmative. SAS 134 *No parece sino que*

tener plata fuese una virtud. (3–3). For *sino* as the second element in phrases meaning " not only . . . but also," see 40.685. ***tampoco.** UNA 87 *Yo — dijo ésta — tampoco me opongo.* (**46–130**).

40.685 *no sólo (no solamente) . . . sino* meaning " not only . . . but also." The expressions for " not only . . . but also " have become stabilized in modern Spanish, the common form being *no sólo . . . sino.* The few variations are listed below. *no sólo . . . sino.* ALT 7 *No sólo por los triunfos políticos, sino por otras dos circunstancias.* (9–18). *no sólo . . . sino que.* TRI 53 *No sólo no me estorba usted, sino que su presencia es para mí el mayor embeleso del mundo.* (9–14). *no sólo . . . sino también.* ROD 206 *Ha de someter a crítica severa no sólo la realidad de la nueva aptitud, sino también las ventajas que pueda aportar.* (3–3). *no solamente . . . sino también.* PEL 227 *No fué solamente un innovador del metro, sino también de la estrofa.* (4–4).

40.7 Expressions used to reinforce a negative. In popular speech there is a strong tendency to reinforce negative expressions by the addition of some word indicating insignificant value, such as *jota, pito, punto, pizca,* etc. They are often followed by *de.* Naturally the number of examples in literary texts is relatively small. CAT 22 *Don Gabriel no le hacía pizca de caso.* (7–7)

VII. PREPOSITIONS

41. A word or phrase which is used to indicate the relationship between a substantive and another element of the sentence is called a preposition. The substantive may be a noun, pronoun, infinitive, clause, adjective used as a noun, or phrase, used as a substantive. The phrase formed by the preposition and the substantive may be adjectival or adverbial. An adjectival phrase may modify a noun as attributive, as predicate, or as appositive. It may itself become a noun. An adverbial phrase may modify a verb, an adjective, or an adverb.

41.1 In addition to the simple prepositions, Spanish, like other languages, uses many compound expressions, which are called compound prepositions, to connect substantives with other words. The compound prepositions fall into several main groups: those consisting of an adverb and a preposition (*antes de*); those consisting of a preposition, a noun, and another preposition (*en lugar de*); those consisting of a noun and a preposition (*frente a*); those consisting of an adjective and a preposition (*junto a*). The words for "except" form a special group of simple prepositions, which were in origin adjectives used in an absolute construction.

41.2 Special uses of prepositions.

41.21 Two prepositions used before a single noun. This construction is relatively rare in Spanish. ORT 118 *Juzgo de o sobre algo.*   (5–5)

41.22 A preposition introduces two or more coordinated substantives. When a preposition is followed by two substantives, the question of the repetition or omission of the preposition with the second substantive is largely one of style. The repetition of the preposition tends to stress the distinction between the two substantives, while the omission of the preposition tends to identify the two substantives as a unit. But these tendencies are never rigorously observed. The figures show a somewhat greater tendency toward repetition with nouns than with infinitives; this is natural in view of the abstract character of infinitives which makes them merge more easily into a unity.

41.23 Simple prepositions.

41.231 Repeated, before nouns. SEC 48 *Gozarán de la luz y del sol.*
(60–882)

41.233 Not repeated, before nouns. JIM 77 *Con sus hilos de oro y plata.* (57–570)

41.235 Repeated, before infinitives. JAN 303 *Yo se lo avisaré para que Ud. no se moleste en venir y en esperar.* (45–100)

41.237 Not repeated, before infinitives. REY 99 *Está un poco lejos para ir y volver.* (46–132)

41.24 Compound prepositions.

41.243 Not repeated, before nouns. TRI 50 *Debajo de unas sedas y batistas.* (8–10)

41.247 Not repeated, before infinitives. ABC 28 *Con objeto de acelerar la labor legislativa y llegar a las vacaciones.* (3–4)

41.249 The last element only is repeated. This is the normal construction. IBA 151 *Disparando tiros en contra de la religión, de la reina, y de todo lo antiguo.* (36–86)

41.25 A noun used in apposition with a noun or pronoun which is dependent on a preposition. In this situation, the preposition is not normally repeated. IBA 32 *¿ Ve usted a Coleta, ese borrachón que nos oye ?* (*)

41.253 Occasionally, however, the preposition is repeated. VIG 115 *Ramiro se enamoró de ella, de Gertrudis.* (6–12)

41.31 Attraction of the preposition in clauses introduced by a substantive relative. When the relative pronoun *que* is the object of a preposition in the combinations *el que* and *lo que,* the preposition is normally anticipated and placed before *el* or *lo.* This usage has been made more natural because of the confusion between substantive relatives and interrogatives in indirect questions (see 14.38). SAS 124 *¡ Parece que supieran a lo que van!* See also 15.32; 15.42. (20–26)

41.32 If the substantive relative thus introduced by a preposition is followed by *ser* and a noun used as subjective complement, the preposition is repeated before the subjective complement. This construction is found not only with *el que* but also with *quien.* TIG 53 *Con quien aquel hombre pasaba la noche era con la capitana.* This usage is found also with indirect objects; see 35.45. (6–9)

41.4 A preposition introduces a clause. A characteristic of Spanish is its use of prepositions before clauses to form adjectival and adverbial phrases.

41.41 The clause is introduced by the conjunction *que*. JIM 68 *Me doy cuenta de que los que alborotan son los pájaros.* For further discussion see 28.29; 29.39. **(60–384)**

41.42 The clause is an indirect question.

41.421 Introduced by an interrogative pronoun. PEQ 84 *No puedo ya hacer memoria de quién me lo dió.* (5–5)

41.423 Introduced by an interrogative adverb. The commonest adverb is *si*. TRI 50 *Había perdido la noción de si le tocaría jugar a ella.* (14–18)

41.43 The clause is introduced by a relative adverb. *como.* SON 185 *Cuán diferente de como lo habíamos visto la primera vez.* (8–8). *cuando.* UNA 157 *¿ Es que no me acuerdo de cuando trajo a los dos médicos?* (5–7)

41.5 The preposition omitted. In the telegraphic style of modern life, the preposition is often omitted in telegrams, advertisements, dates of letters, newspaper headlines, etc. MGR 47 *Disponibles: 51 razas gallinas; 20 razas conejos.* (4–10)

41.6 The commonest prepositions, simple and compound.

a (*) — « *a* embebida. » *A* is regularly absorbed in pronunciation in a preceding final *–a* or a following initial *a–*. This pronunciation is sometimes reflected in written discourse. IMP 203 *Iría salir.* (12–14). *a cambio de* (3–3), *a cargo de* (4–5), *a casa de* (10–17), *a causa de* (12–13), *a costa de* (8–8), *a falta de* (4–4), *a favor de* (4–5), *a fin de* (13–25), *a fines de* (4–8), *a fuer de* (3–3), *a fuerza de* (10–13), *a la manera de* (5–5), *a la orilla de* (3–9), *a lo largo de* (10–15), *a manera de* (3–4), *a más de* (6–6), *a menos de* (3–3), *a merced de* (3–3), *a modo de* (6–8), *a nombre de* (3–3), *a orillas de* (4–4), *a partir de* (5–7), *a pesar de* (**37–90**), *a poco de* (5–6), *a principios de* (5–8), *a propósito de* (10–12), *a punto de* (16–20), *a raíz de* (3–3), *a través de* (18–34), *acerca de* (11–21), *además de* (14–23), *al alcance de* (4–4), *al borde de* (4–4), *al cabo de* (3–4), *al calor de* (3–3), *al compás de* (8–8), *al fin de* (4–4), *al final de* (4–4), *al fondo de* (3–3), *al frente de* (4–4), *al lado de* (**28–53**), *al modo de* (4–6), *al pie de* (13–19), *al servicio de* (3–3), *al son de* (6–8), *al través de* (9–18), *alrededor de* (10–16), *ante* (**47–200**), *antes de* (**52–130**), *aparte* (3–3), *aparte de* (12–16), *arriba de* (4–4), *bajo* (**48–236**), *camino de* (5–10), *cerca de* — Place. DEB 84 *Cerca de la ventana.* (**35–57**) — Numerical approximation. RET 139 *Cerca de 40.000 pesos.* (8–10). *con* (*), *con arreglo a* (4–4), *con motivo de* (5–7), *con referencia a* (3–3), *con respecto a* (4–5), *con rumbo a* (3–3), *conforme a* (4–5), *contra* (**46–168**), *cuando,* " at the time of " (4–4), *de* (*), *de acuerdo con* (6–8), *de casa de* (3–3), *de fines de* (6–6), *de parte de* (5–5), *de vuelta de* (3–3), *debajo de* (18–38), *debido a* (5–5), *delante de* (32–66), *dentro de* (46–148), *desde* (60–444), *después de* (58–280), *detrás de* (26–44), *donde* (for *en casa de*) (3–7), *durante* (46–152), *e* (for *de*) (6–15), *en* (*), *en atención a* (3–3), *en beneficio de* (3–3), *en brazos de* (6–6), *en busca de* (16–19), *en calidad de* (6–6), *en casa de* (22–36), *en caso de* (3–3), *en compañía de* (12–13), *en contra de* (8–8), *en cuanto a* (21–31), *en derredor de* (3–3), *en dirección a* (3–3), *en dirección de* (3–3), *en favor de* (7–8), *en forma de* (8–9), *en honor de* (5–6), *en lugar de* (14–19), *en manos de* (15–16), *en medio de* (28–51), *en nombre de* (3–3), *en obsequio de* (3–4), *en orden a* (3–3), *en pos de* (3–7), *en presencia de* (13–17), *en prueba de* (3–3), *en punto a* (4–9), *en representación de* (3–3), *en señal de* (3–3), *en tiempo de* (6–18), *en tiempos de* (3–3), *en torno a* (10–17), *en torno de* (10–14), *en unión de* (6–6), *en uso de* (3–4), *en virtud de* (5–6), *en vísperas de* (3–4), *en vista de* (7–9), *encima de* (10–14), *enfrente de* (8–8), *entre* (60–684), *excepto* (5–5), *frente a* (32–59), *fuera de* (49–100), *gracias a* (20–36), *hacia* (48–198), *hasta* (57–471), *incluso* (4–4), *juntamente con* (3–3), *junto a* (36–113), *junto con* (7–11), *lejos de* (29–43), *lo que es* " as for," (followed by subject pronouns) (7–9), *luego de* (9–11), *más allá de* (13–18), *mediante* (5–16), *menos* "except" (18–21), *merced a* (8–12), *mientras* (9–9), *no obstante* (8–11), *pa* (for *para*) (11–147), *para* (*), *por* (*), *por causa de* (3–3), *pór culpa de* (3–5), *por falta de* (7–10), *por medio de* (11–14), *por obra de* (5–6), *por parte de* (5–5), *por razón de* (3–3), *referente a* (3–4), *respecto a* (8–12), *respecto de* (5–9), *salvo* (4–5), *según* (48–112), *sin* (60–1137), *sobre* (60–927), *tocante a* (3–5), *tras* (30–71), *tras de* (7–7).

41.71 Combinations of two prepositions, simple or compound. Combinations of two prepositions are common. Each preposition normally retains its independent force, except in the combination *para con*, which has acquired the meaning of "toward" in speaking of mental or emotional attitudes. CAT 35 *Pasó por encima de la señora, que se había desmayado.* ([43]–135)

The commonest combinations are: *de a* (13–14), *de entre* (10–12), *de por* (5–5), *para con* (6–7), *por de* (3–3), *por debajo de* (5–6), *por delante de* (5–8), *por encima de* (20–25), *por entre* (15–20).

41.81 Adverbs used after a noun with the value of prepositions. A number of adverbs are used after a noun to form phrases which have the force of prepositional phrases. IDO 4 *Por la misma falda del monte, cuesta arriba.* ([21]–36)

The commonest adverbs are: *abajo* (4–9), *adelante* (4–5), *arriba* (10–16).

41.815 The noun which is followed by the adverb may be introduced by a preposition (*de* or *por*). In this case both preposition and adverb

retain their independent values, as in the case of the use of two prepositions. PEQ 90 *Se va por el claustro adelante dando grandes trancos.* (4–4)

41.817 Adverbs used in connection with a personal object pronoun may
be the equivalent of prepositions. MUJ 14 *Le echa todas las flores encima.*
See also 8.275.

VIII. CONJUNCTIONS

42. Words and expressions which are used to connect two or more elements of the sentence are called conjunctions. If the elements connected are of equal rank, the connectives are called coordinating conjunctions. If one of the elements is subordinate to the other element, the conjunctions are called subordinating conjunctions.

COORDINATING CONJUNCTIONS

42.1 There are a few words which are primarily used as coordinating conjunctions: *y, o, pero, ni, sino, también,* etc. There are other words which are used both as adverbs and as conjunctions: *entonces, luego,* etc. Finally there are words which are used both as subordinating and as coordinating conjunctions: *de modo que, porque,* etc. In each case, the classification of each word depends upon its function in a given sentence and not upon its historical or traditional form. At times, conjunctions are found in pairs, one preceding each of the elements connected. Such pairs are called correlatives. The various conjunctions may be classified, according to the types of connection established between the two coordinated elements, as copulative, adversative, alternative, illative, causal, and explanatory.

42.21 Copulative conjunctions. Copulative conjunctions are used to connect two elements of the same rank when the second element is represented as added to the first element or as subsequent to the first element in time.

42.211 Simple forms. The normal copulative is *y (e)*. Those stressing addition are *además, asimismo, también,* etc. Those stressing temporal sequence are *al fin, después, en fin, entonces, luego,* and the like.

The commonest simple copulatives are: *además* (**50–152**), *al fin* (**30–51**), *asimismo* (7–8), *después* (**22–60**), *e* (before *i–, hi–*) (**44–170**), *en fin* (10–21), *entonces* (**22–52**), etc. (12–37), *inclusive* (3–3), *incluso* (3–3), *luego* (**42–118**), *por fin* (12–28), *también* (**60–450**), *y* (*) — In a series, repeated before each element. SJQ 77 *Las pulgas, y los mosquitos, y las moscas, y los perros, y las lagartijas, y las vacas.* In a series, repeated only before the last element. TIG 8 *Flor, fruto, y sombra.* — Before exclamations. MUG 20 *¡ Y yo sin verlo!* (**24–162**). — Before exclamatory questions. ROD 208 *¿ Y nosotros ?* (**29–222**); *y además* (17–37), *y aun* (5–8), *y después* (5–8), *y encima* (3–3), *y entonces* (4–4), *y luego* (**26–70**), *y también* (6–9).

For the use of relative pronouns with the force of copulative conjunctions, see 15.27.

42.213 Correlative forms. FOM 11 *Era una mujer elegante, tanto de temperamento como de imaginación.*

The commonest correlative copulatives are: *entre . . . y . . .* (9–12), *lo mismo . . . que . . .* (10–17), *primero . . . después (luego,* etc.) *. . .* (15–22), *tanto . . . como . . .* (14–25), *ya . . . ya . . .* (9–19).

42.22 Adversative conjunctions. Adversative conjunctions are used to connect two elements of the same rank when the second element is contrasted with the first element. The commonest word is *pero.* Only simple forms are found. REY 11 *Sí, pero yo soy distinto.*

The commonest adversatives are: *aunque* (3–4), *empero* (placed after the element connected). ORT 104 *El vino les ha dado, empero, una momentánea intuición del máximo secreto.* (3–3), *en cambio* (**33–58**), — (Placed after the element connected) (5–6), *mas* (**26–70**), *no obstante* (8–11), *pero* (**60–1676**), *sin embargo* (**45–168**), *solo que* (11–16), *y sin embargo* (5–6).

42.23 Alternative conjunctions. Alternative conjunctions, sometimes called disjunctive conjunctions, are used to connect two elements of the same rank when the second element is represented as an alternative for the first element. The commonest word is *o (u).* Both simple and correlative forms are used.

42.231 Simple forms. ALT 7 *Varón o hembra.*

The only common simple alternatives are: *o* (**60–990**), *o bien* (7–8), *u* (before *o–, ho–*) (17–23).

42.233 Correlative forms. RUS 145 *O estás loco o habría que cortarte la lengua.*

The only common correlatives are: *o . . . o . . .* (11–15), *sea . . . o sea . . .* (3–3), *ya . . . ya . . .* (3–3).

42.24 Illative conjunctions. Illative conjunctions are used to connect two elements of the same rank when the second element is represented as the result or outcome of the first element. The English equivalents are "and so," "therefore," "so then," and the like. All of the expressions used as illatives are in origin adverbs or subordinating conjunctions. Only simple forms are found. MGR 18 *Así, para algunas mujeres el marido es su salvador.*

The commonest illatives are: *así* (7–15), *así es que* (3–4), *así pues* (3–3), *así que* (5–8), *conque (con que)* (**21–42**), *de manera que* (6–16), *de modo que* (5–10), *de suerte que* (4–5), *entonces* (**26–91**), — Placed after element connected, (5–6), *luego* (16–36), *por consiguiente* (5–8), *por ende* (3–4), *por eso* (**25–58**), *por esto* (5–10), *por lo tanto* (7–12), *pues* (**45–282**), — Placed after the element connected, (18–49), *pues bien* (10–12), *pues entonces* (9–10), *y así* (8–9).

42.25 Causal conjunctions. Causal conjunctions are used to connect two elements of the sentence when the second element is represented as the cause of the first element. There is, in modern Spanish, no word corresponding to English " for." But a few subordinating conjunctions and one adverb are used to express the same type of coordination as does " for." BRA 166 *Porque yo soy ahora joven como antes.*

The only common causal coordinators are: *como que* (**23–41**), *porque* (**28–80**), *pues* (**14–48**), *que* (**38–96**).

42.26 Explanatory conjunctions. Explanatory conjunctions are used to connect two elements of the sentence when the second element is presented as an explanation, interpretation, or illustration of the first element. DIV 170 *Imponer una paz de reconciliación, es decir, la ruina de los vencedores.*

The commonest explanatory forms are: *es decir* (**30–74**), *esto es* (8–13), *mejor dicho* (7–8), *o* (10–18), *o bien* (6–13), *o mejor* (3–3), *o sea,* (13–21), *por ejemplo* (12–26).

The negative coordinating conjunctions are discussed in 40.68.

SUBORDINATING CONJUNCTIONS

42.3 Subordinating conjunctions are of two types: annunciative, used to introduce subordinate substantive clauses, and adverbial, used to introduce adverbial modifiers of the verb. The first type is discussed under the uses of *que* (42.41). The second type consists of words of several classes. Some are in origin relative adverbs (*como, cuando, que*); others are formed by a preposition and an annunciative *que* (*desde que, para que*); still others are made up of an adverb or adverbial phrase modified by the relative adverb *que* (*a tiempo que, siempre que*). The uses of the adverbial conjunctions with the indicative and with the subjunctive have been discussed in detail in 28.4, 29.46, and 29.7. We are here concerned only with their use in elliptical constructions without an expressed verb.

42.31 Adverbial conjunctions used without a verb. It is common in Spanish as in other languages, to use subordinating adverbial conjunctions in abridged forms of expression in which the verb is implied from the context and not expressed. This is true in particular of conjunctions of concession, manner, and time.

42.32 Causal conjunctions. *porque.* LUG 365 *A éste le van a aprobar porque sí.* (3–3)

42.33 Concessive conjunctions. *aunque.* With an adjective or past participle. TRI 125 *Mi hija, aunque bien armada por fuera, es por dentro algo delgada.* (10–16). With a present participle. RAN 81 *Antoñino lo* *reconoció así, aunque aduciendo un motivo justificante.* (3–3). With an adverbial expression. UNA 154 *La pobre le ofendió a usted gravemente, aunque sin intención ofensiva.* (12–17). With a noun. TIG 7 *Aunque viuda, paréceme mujer que nunca probara varón.* (6–6). **si bien.** ROD 91 *Esto, si bien caso estupendo y peregrino, no sale fuera de lo humano.* (3–3). **ya que.** ART 78 *Ya que no otra cosa, debo tener lo que un delincuente cualquiera, valor.* All cases noted are followed by a negative. (4–4)

42.34 Conditional conjunctions. si. ALT 190 *Si común a todos los pueblos, aparece en Navarra notablemente favorecido por las leyes.* (5–5). **si no.** ART 41 *He sido, si no usted mismo, un reflejo de usted.* (5–7)

42.35 Conjunctions of manner. The most frequent conjunction in this group is *como*, but there are also included a variety of other expressions which are used to indicate a comparison. **así como.** PAX 8 *¿ Algo así como el cuervo de San Antonio abad?* (13–18). **al igual que.** ALT 187 *No faltaban tampoco, al igual que en la época anterior, las luchas entre concejos.* (3–3). **como.** see 42.351. **cual.** ROM 10 *Grimm veía, cual restos venerables de esa poesía primitiva, los romances recogidos en el siglo XVI.* (4–15). **igual que.** MAY 7 *Anduvieron juntos, igual que las alas de un pájaro.* (5–18). **lo mismo que.** JIM 100 *Y Platero, lo mismo que un niño pobre, corre tímido.* (16–25)

42.351 como. In origin, *como* was a relative adverb of manner. But its use has been greatly extended so that it is now found as a true subordinating conjunction in a variety of meanings, and also as a correlative of quality or of quantity after *tal*, *tan*, and *tanto*. Because expressions of manner often involved a comparison, it was easy to omit the verb in the clause introduced by *como*, provided it was identical with the main verb of the sentence. And hence *como* has become a sort of particle of comparison, equivalent to English " as " or " like ", which serves to introduce a noun or pronoun in a sort of loose apposition. In addition to these uses to express a real comparison, *como* is also used as an equivalent of *como si*, to introduce imaginative comparisons; this use is especially common with adjectival and adverbial expressions.

42.353 In real comparisons. A verb is not repeated. BRA 14 *Tú desearías, como yo, vivir en una buena casa.* A form of *ser* is understood and also *tal*. LLA 11 *Era como esas flores pálidas que doblan cuando las mira la luna.* A form of *ser* is understood and also *tan*. RUS 136 *Tendremos una azotea con flores, grande como esta mesa.* Introducing an appositive of the subject. ZAM 130 *Aquélla aparece en mi memoria como algo azul.* Introducing an appositive of the object, with *a*. TIG 22 *Como a mi otra mitá le considero.* Without *a*. ZUN 15 *Considerando como verdaderos criminales a todos los músicos del orbe.* (Total: **60–1392**)

42.355 In imaginative comparisons. With an adjective or past participle. JAN 7 *Irene lo siguió como fascinada.* With a present participle. BRA 112 *(Como soñando.)* With an adverbial expression. LLA 79 *¡ Dime todo, como a un confesor.* With a subjective complement. TIG 44 *Vas a ser mujer de quien es como mi padre.*   (Total: **50–219**)

42.36 Temporal conjunctions. *a la vez que.* ORR 180 *Sandoval les miró con curiosidad a la vez que con disimulo.* (3–4). *antes que.* IMP 199 *Por lo menos la plegaria a Afrodita la rezaría Guillermo antes que él.* (11–13). *cuando.* ZAM 106 *Buena y limpia, como hecha de luz, era yo cuando niña.* (13–14)

USES OF que

42.4 The most widely used of all subordinating conjunctions is *que*. It is the chief conjunction used to introduce substantive clauses; it is found with a variety of adverbial functions; and it is used in a number of elliptical expressions without a verb. It is even sometimes used as a coordinating conjunction. In addition to these purely conjunctive uses, *que* is also a relative pronoun and a relative adverb; see 15. and 16.6.

42.41 Annunciative uses, introducing a substantive clause.

42.411 Subject clauses. IGN 77 *Me gusta que cada cual conserve su rango.* For details, see 28.2 and 29.31. Even after a relative pronoun. FAL 14 *El extranjero tropezó con un hombre que se veía que era cruel.* (3–3)

42.413 Object clauses. STE 19 *Anúnciele usted que sus sobrinas acaban de llegar.* For details, see 28.2, 29.34, 29.51. Even after a relative pronoun. FAL 17 *Recordando a la que todos sabían que se había ahogado ayer.* (6–10)

42.415 Clauses used as subjective complement. SAS 12 *La verdad es que el baile no está muy animado.* For details, see 28.27, 29.371, 29.55.

42.42 Clauses used as object of a preposition.

42.421 Forming adjectival phrases. IGN 36 *Las cinco mil que pides, hazte cuenta de que no existen.* For details, see 28.291, 29.391, and 29.571.

42.423 Forming adverbial phrases. TIG 50 *En eso se distingue el verdadero cariño: en que es libre.* For details, see 28.295, 29.41, and 29.575.

42.47 Annunciative *que* used pleonastically before an indirect question introduced by an interrogative adverb or pronoun. This construction is due to a fusion of the normal usage of indirect discourse and of indirect questions. ZUN 31 *No; digo que ¿ cómo es que está allí?*   (**20–33**)

42.48 Annunciative *que* **used in elliptical expressions without a verb.**

42.481 Followed by *sí* or *no*. MUJ 21 *Me parece que sí.* **(35–92)**

42.483 Even when there is no main verb. BRA 22 *¿ Que no ?* (3–9)

42.485 Followed by other expressions. SIE 87 *Diga usted que a las dos, si le parece.* **(26–55)**

42.51 Annunciative *que* **omitted.** The omission of *que* is relatively infrequent. It is most common in relative clauses when the verb which requires *que* is felt as parenthetical.

42.511 In subject clauses. BRA 98 *Llama al criado que se supone está en la pieza inmediata.* (3–3)

42.513 In object clauses after verbs of declaring, perceiving, etc. JOA 86 *Tengo un presentimiento que creo se va a cumplir.* (3–5)

42.515 After verbs of wish, command, request, etc. JES 36 *La anciana rogó a Augusto le excusara.* This is the one group in which omission is common outside of relative clauses. (5–7)

42.517 After verbs of emotion. ORR 99 *Mi aventura fué cosa que espero no habrá de repetirse.* (3–3)

42.54 Annunciative *que* **replaced by** *como.* In conversational style, sometimes even in literary style, *que* is replaced by *como.* Originally this form must have been the interrogative adverb *cómo,* but it has lost all force of manner and has become a practical equivalent of *que,* just as English " how " has become the equivalent of " that." It is most frequently found in contemporary usage after verbs of declaring, perceiving, etc. CAT 12 *Ya ves como no mando ni en los animales domésticos(!)* (17–32)

42.6 Annunciative *que* **in main clauses.** The use of *que* in main clauses is a development of its use when a verb is implied from a preceding sentence. From these it spreads into uses where the implication of a preceding verb is slight or wholly lacking.

42.61 In statements.

42.611 Beginning a sentence. FAL 212 *Que se va a recalentar el motor.* **(31–160)**

42.613 After an asseverative expression (*claro, por cierto,* etc.) JAN 8 *Sin duda que era curiosa la turbación de esa muchacha.* **(39–86)**

42.615 Especially after *sí* and *no.* IGN 42 *¡ Caramba, eso sí que es difícil!* **(24–65)**

42.617 After adverbial conjunctions. ABU 17 *En fin, que en tomates y berenjenas no hay quien nos tosa.* (10–20)

42.62 In exclamations.

42.621 Beginning a sentence. IGN 81 *¿ Ha oído usted ? ¡ Que se marcha al Japón!* (15–40)

42.623 After an exclamatory expression. TIG 11 *¡ Vamos, que es usted lince!* **(28–64)**

42.63 In questions. BRA 102 *¿ Que no tiene posición ?* **(23–55)**

42.64 In commands. UNA 99 *Que entre la luz.* For details, see 29.16–29.18.

42.65 In wishes. STE 254 *Que Dios nos bendiga a todos.* (19–31) See also 29.153.

42.71 As a subordinating adverbial conjunction. The uses of *que* in this function are discussed in 28.42, 28.46, 28.48, 29.465, 29.73, 29.79.

42.74 As a coordinating conjunction. This is a function in which the use of *que* has become rare.

42.753 Adversative. *Que* is found with adversative force only after a negative, and the contrast lies rather in the context than in *que* itself. LLA 44 *No es cuento, que es historia.* (3–3)

42.76 Alternative. Found only in fixed phrases. RAN 97 *Los grandes podrían, bien que mal, arreglárselas sin escultores.* (7–8)

42.77 As a correlative, introducing the term of a comparison of superiority or inferiority. BEN 33 *Me tratan peor que a un ladrón.* For details, see 26.31.

42.771 The comparison may be implied by a word other than a comparative.

> *antes.* VIG 39 *Hace de ella una crónica antes que una novela.* **(21–28)**
> *contrario.* OCC 198 *Al contrario que usté, yo digo que gano el tiempo.* (3–3)
> *más,* in the sense of " rather." UNA 10 *Cervantes más buscó la ejemplaridad que hoy llamaríamos estética que no la moral.* (15–16).
> *más bien.* ORT 107 *Más bien que vivir esta aspereza presente, recordemos la egregia existencia de un vago pretérito.* (5–6)
> *otro.* MAY 70 *Iban sin otro punto de claridad que aquel encendido en el trono de la Virgen.* **(23–34)**

42.773 After *contrario, distinto, diferente,* etc. the term of the comparison is expressed more frequently by a preposition.

a.　RET 18 *Esta definición marca un proceso distinto al orden de su aparición.* (3–4)

de.　FAL 165 *El alma tendrá que ser muy distinta de la ambicionada.* (6–6)

42.78 As a correlative to expressions expressing or implying equality.
igual.　RAN 87 *La lucha entre Vigo y Pontevedra continúa hoy igual que en el año 1835.* (20–38)

el mismo (lo mismo).　JAN 115 *Creyó respirar la misma atmósfera hostil que en casa de su madre.* (39–80)

42.781 After *mismo* the preposition *de* is sometimes used.　SIE 46 *No es la misma de siempre.* (5–5)

42.79 As a correlative to demonstratives of quality or quantity and expressing result. *tal.*　PAX 17 *Hablaba el guía con tal fuego, con tal mímica, que le entendí.* (20–43). *tan.*　JOA 79 *Eres tan tonta que ni lo ves.* (49–142). *tanto.*　JAN 113 ¿ *Era tanta su fatalidad que en su casa lo rechazaban por el amor de una mujer?* (29–40).

USES OF si

42.8 In origin, *si* was a subordinating adverbial conjunction expressing condition. But its use was early extended to indirect questions in the meaning of "whether," when the element of uncertainty was strong. Hence it has become a sort of annunciative, comparable in its use in indirect or in direct questions and in exclamations to the use of *que* in statements, questions, and exclamations. Its use in conditional sentences is treated at length in 31. The present section is devoted to its annunciative uses.

42.81 Annunciative in indirect questions.

42.811 The question is object or subject of a verb.　RIC 267 *A ver si está cargada.* (51–168)

42.813 The question is in apposition with a noun or pronoun.　TIG 14 ¿ *Qué entienden si usted lo hace por bien?* (3–3)

42.815 The question is object of a preposition.　MAY 58 *Disputan sobre si han de venderse primero los anillos o el dedal.* (9–13)

42.82 The question may be introduced by a pleonastic *que.*　UNA 151 *Te pregunté a mi vez que si podías creerlo.* (10–18)

42.83 The verb of the question may be expressed by an infinitive. sᴊǫ 80 *No sé si atribuirlo a eso o a la vulgaridad de mi ser.* (8–11)

42.84 The verb of the question may be implied. sᴀs 70 *Nos vamos a ir prontito. Quién sabe si esta misma semana.* (6–9)

42.85 Annunciative in main clauses.

42.86 In direct questions. ɪᴅᴏ 215 *Si le habrán dicho algo malo de mí, se preguntaba una vez.* (4–6)

42.87 In exclamations.

42.871 Beginning the sentence. ᴀʀᴛ 13 *¡ Si pensará que es doña Precisa!* (34–**156**)

42.873 Introduced by *que*. ɴᴇʀ 25 *¡ Que si estoy seguro! ¡ Qué ocurren-cia!* (3–6)

42.875 After an exclamatory expression. sᴊǫ 131 *¡ Hombre, si el compa-ñero no ha dicho nada todavía!* (21–**52**)

42.88 In wishes. ɪʙᴀ 149 *¡ Si viese usted lo que me cuesta conquistar ciertas almas!* See also 29.153. (21–**34**)

IX. INTERJECTIONS

43. An exclamatory word which is used to express a complete thought or emotion is called an interjection. They are the most primitive form of the sentence. A few words are exclusively interjections, but many other words, — verbs, adverbs, nouns, adjectives, etc. — may also be used as interjections.

43.1 Words used exclusively as interjections. In this group are included expressions which are primarily revelation of emotions. While each of them has a general field within which it is used, it is impossible to give an adequate translation for each of them. An attempt has been made however to indicate the general notion conveyed.

ah — Surprise **(40–321)**, *adiós* — Farewell **(24–95)**, Greeting (4–4), *ay* — Pain **(34–253)**, *ay de (mí)* — Self commiseration (4–4), *bah* — Scorn (16–37), *caramba* — Surprise (11–33), *ea* — Encouragement (11–18), *ché* — To attract a person's attention (especially in Argentina and Uruguay) (5–12), *eh* — Interrogation **(28–155)**, *chist* — To enjoin silence (5–6), *he ahí* — To point out a person or thing (7–8), *he aquí* — To point out a person or thing (18–30), *hola* — Greeting **(23–55)**, *hum* Dissatisfaction (3–5), *oh* — Surprise **(29–144)**, *ja, ja* — Laughter (17–82), *ojalá* — Wish (10–13), *quiá* — Incredulity (5–11), *uf* — Disgust or exhaustion (6–8).

43.2 Verbal forms used as interjections. These forms are without exception imperatives or subjunctives of command. *anda* (9–23), *atiza* (3–3), *calla* (3–5), *mira* (6–21), *vamos* **(29–122)**, *vaya* **(25–59)**, *vaya que* (+ verb) (5–9), *vaya un* (+ noun) (7–12), *viva* (12–35).

43.3 Nouns, adjectives, and adverbs used as interjections. *alto* (4–4), *amén* (5–5), *bien* (15–35), *bravo* (3–4), *bueno* **(33–189)**, *claro* (16–67), *cuidado* (5–5), *eso* (3–4), *hombre* (15–74), *largo* (3–3), *nada* (5–9), *pero* **(46–280)**, *pues* **(38–302)**, *ya* (3–6).

43.4 Oaths. Spanish has none of the Puritan feeling of the impropriety of using holy names in polite speech. They have a violence comparable to English " oh dear," " gee," and the like. *Ave María Purísima* (4–4), *Dios* (4–9), *Dios mío* (9–44), *Jesús* (15–46), *por Dios* **(25–60)**, *válgame Dios* (5–7), *Virgen santa* (3–3).

X. STYLISTIC PHENOMENA

44. Since language is a medium of communication, it tends constantly to fall into patterns which will serve as readily recognizable instruments. The task of syntax is to identify and classify these normal patterns of speech. But the individual speaker is forever adjusting language to the emotional or social needs of the moment. He is constantly selecting, from a variety of possible patterns, the particular instrument which serves his purpose. If he be an artist, he does this consciously, striving for beauty; but the man in the street, no less than the artist, is unconsciously moulding the common instrument for his wholly personal use. To discover the significance and the values of these personal, individual aspects of the use of language is the problem of stylistics.

44.1 The present study does not pretend to enter into that field. But there are a number of phenomena, which illustrate the types of alternative which the individual faces as he seeks to express himself which may at least be mentioned. Some of these have been included in the body of the study, because there was the possibility that variations in usage might correspond to actual differences in function. Such, for example, is the section on the repetition and non-repetition of prepositions (41.23). A few more are listed below.

44.2 Asymmetry. In strict logic, a given construction would demand a balanced symmetry in following coordinated constructions. But speech is not logical, because it is a human expression, and language is filled with asymmetrical usages.

44.21 Articles are used and omitted. RUB 17 *La otra Annie, la de los ósculos y las caricias y oraciones por el adorado.*

44.22 Nouns or pronouns and clauses are paired. URU 67 *Entonces me acordé de vos y que te quiero como si fueses m'hija.* BEN 16 *Sí, gracias a Dios y a que hay que ponerse bien con Él.*

44.23 Nouns and infinitives are paired. PEL 235 *Claro es que esto le obligó a grandísimas amplificaciones y a poner mucho y malo de su propia cosecha poética.*

44.24 Infinitives and clauses are paired. TIG 19 *Venía de Traspeñas a que la colocara de ama de cría y a echar al hijo al torno del Hospicio.*

277

44.25 *le* and *lo* alternate. SAS 130 *Bueno, hijo, mi carácter, que no le escogí yo, que no lo compré en una tienda.*

44.26 *−ra* and *−se* subjunctives alternate. IDO 9 *Comparable en aquel segundo a un rostro enigmático, que de un lado sonriera y del lado opuesto llorase.*

44.3 A single word is used in two functions.

44.31 A relative pronoun. OCC 192 *Las inglesas, más civilizadas, no conceden al traje sino un valor estricto del convencionalismo social, del que no se puede prescindir ni tampoco se debe exagerar.*

44.32 A verb. JOA 26 *Me dice que no es nada, que tenga un poco de paciencia.*

44.4 A single preposition is used where two different prepositions are required by the verbal meanings. SJQ 35 *En invierno, voy y vengo a Madrid.*

44.5 A relative clause is continued in a coordinated clause as a main verb. ZUN 37 *Era un fenómeno que tenía seis cabezas y le salían los pies por la boca del estómago.*

44.6 Ellipsis. The most frequent of all the stylistic phenomena which characterize spoken discourse is ellipsis, the omission of some element of the sentence, often a verb, which is readily understood from the context. Examples of ellipsis have been cited in the study of the various substantives, but its use is by no means limited to them. In the proper background of conversation, with the natural accompaniment of facial expression, of gesture, of intonation, any word becomes capable of expressing any thought or feeling. The printed page conveys only the symbols of the sounds; only through imagination can the reader reconstruct the scene in all its living details. And that would take us outside the field to which this study is dedicated.